For Reference

Not to be taken from this room

Investment and Securities Dictionary

To Linda Thomsett, my best friend

Investment and Securities Dictionary

Compiled by
Michael C. Thomsett

McFarland & Company, Inc., Publishers
Jefferson, North Carolina, and London

Also by Michael C. Thomsett:

Builders Guide to Accounting
Builders Office Manual
Fundamentals of Bookkeeping and Accounting
Contractors Year-Round Tax Guide
Computers: The Builder's New Tool
Homeowner's Money Management

Library of Congress Cataloguing-in-Publication Data

Thomsett, Michael C.
Investment and securities dictionary.

1. Investments — Dictionaries.   2. Securities —
Dictionaries.   I. Title.
HG4513.T48   1986   332.6′03′21   85-43594

ISBN 0-89950-225-3 (acid-free natural paper)

Manufactured in the United States of America.

McFarland & Company, Inc., Publishers
   Box 611, Jefferson, North Carolina 28640

Table of Contents

Introduction: What This Book Will Do for You

The Investment and Securities Dictionary is a comprehensive summary of terms used in the markets of stock exchanges, syndications, broker-dealers, investment managers, sponsors and financial planners.

The more than 2,000 entries include technical words and phrases, industry agencies and associations, and regulatory bodies. References are included to those laws and regulations affecting investors and investment professionals in their everyday lives.

Major sections of the book include:

Glossary of Terms. The body of the book, fully cross-referenced for complete and thorough research, with many illustrations.

Abbreviations List. A summary of abbreviations used in the industry, including agencies and organizations, laws, and jargon of the investment community.

Guide to Prospectus and Offering Documents. A summary of the major sections of prospectuses and circulars, including the primary purpose and subject matter of each.

Bond Classification List. A complete alphabetical listing of every type of bond, all of which may be cross-referenced to the Glossary of Terms.

Whether you are an active professional in investing, a financial planner, or involved in a related service industry, this book summarizes the terminology of the business. If you are a part-time enthusiast or an investor, *The Investment and Securities Dictionary* will help you to converse and correspond with professionals with whom you deal. It provides you with a wide range of information and allows you to quickly gain insights into specific areas of interest, with the complete cross-referencing feature.

This book will become one of your most valuable references whenever you need clarification of a term, or when you need to increase your understanding of a new or complex investment subject.

Glossary of Terms

A

A-B deal   a structure of real estate partnerships under which two classes of investors are sought. One group acts strictly as creditors, loaning funds to the partnership. The other group purchases units of limited partnership interest in the same way as a standard real estate program.

An advantage of the A-B deal is that no outside financing is needed for leveraging. A-B creditor investors do not share equity in properties, and are not equity participants. See **leverage**.

ABC agreement   an arrangement under which a seat on the New York Stock Exchange (NYSE) may be purchased with funds borrowed or advanced by another party. There are three primary options: (a) the existing seat is kept by the individual in the agreement, and another purchased for the outside party; (b) the seat is sold and proceeds remitted to a lender; and (c) the seat is transferred to an individual employed by the lender. See **New York Stock Exchange (NYSE)**.

abandonment   a method for disposing of a capital asset no longer useful, useable or valuable. An abandonment may be treated in the same way as a sale, in which case capital gain or loss rates would apply. In other instances, abandoned property is not considered a capital sale or exchange, and ordinary gain or loss rates would apply. Assets damaged or obsolete may be abandoned, and the term may also be applied to inventory no longer useable. See **capital gain; capital loss**.

accelerated cost recovery system (ACRS)   a system replacing an older method for depreciation of capital assets, originated as part of the Economic Recovery Tax Act of 1981 (ERTA). ACRS provides for the recovery of asset costs over a defined period of time (class life). All assets fit into one of several class lives and rates are set. Elections may be made to apply straight-line depreciation to assets in a single class life, whereas ACRS rates are accelerated, reverting to straight-line in the latter portion of the life of the asset. The result of ACRS is more rapid depreciation of assets and the elimination of previously mandated salvage values. See **class life; depreciation; Economic Recovery Tax Act of 1981 (ERTA)**.

accelerated depreciation   a method of writing off the basis of a capital asset which achieves deductions more rapidly than straight-line depreciation would allow. Acceleration is built into the ACRS rates of the Economic Recovery Tax Act of 1981 (ERTA).

The degree of acceleration is identified as a percentage. For example, a 200% DB (declining balance) would allow depreciation of each year's beginning balance remaining in the asset at twice the rate (200%) that would be allowed under

1

accelerated depreciation
$5,000 asset

Year	Straight Line	150% DB	175% DB	200% DB
1	$1,000	$1,500	$1,750	$2,000
2	1,000	1,050	1,138	1,200
3	1,000	735	739	720
4	1,000	515	481	432
5	1,000	360	312	259

straight-line rules. 175% DB would indicate a rate of depreciation one and three-quarters faster than that allowed under straight-line. See **depreciation; Economic Recovery Tax Act of 1981 (ERTA); straight-line depreciation.**

acceleration clause   a provision allowing a lender to call a mortgage principal balance immediately or on an accelerated basis, if a certain event occurs. The clause may indicate the lender's acceleration rights if payments are delinquent, for example. See **mortgage.**

acceptance ratio   a comparison between the volume of bonds sold during a week, and the volume of new issue bonds offered. Also referred to as "placement ratio," this comparison is an indicator of investor attitude. A high ratio – above 90% – indicates a high ratio of acceptance. See **bond.**

accounting rate of return   a test applied to real estate investments which identifies net cash returns after taxes, in a given tax rate or bracket. The method does not reflect the timing of returns and so cannot be called a true investor rate. Its major strength as a means to compare investment performance is the wide acceptance of the calculation as a means for qualification and success of a program, and its wide application by analysts of real estate programs. See **real estate.**

accounts payable   a liability reflected under the "current" section of a balance sheet, which may include the total of amounts due within one year for the purchase of inventory or other direct costs, general overhead expenses, and other amounts owed. Excluded are liabilities for payroll, notes, and taxes payable. See **balance sheet.**

accredited investor   an investor exempted from the limitation of total investors allowed to participate in a private placement. Generally, no more than 35 persons may purchase units. However, with the meeting of certain suitability standards, it is assumed the investor is sophisticated enough not to need the protection of regulation.

Those suitability standards are: (a) institutional investors; (b) individuals with net worth of $1 million or more; (c) individuals earning $200,000 or more per year;

or (d) individuals who purchase $150,000 or more of an offering when that purchase does not exceed 20 percent or more of their total net worth. See **limited partnership; Securities Act of 1933; Securities and Exchange Commission (SEC).**

accretion   the process of adjusting in equal installments the difference between cost and redemption value of a bond. This difference, the original issue discount, is treated as interest income in the year of adjustment. See **bond; original issue discount (OID).**

accrual   (1) an entry on the books of an organization recognizing an item of income, cost or expense before cash has exchanged hands, set up to reflect an impact on profits and losses in the period during which the income was earned or the cost/expense incurred.

(2) an accounting basis which recognizes income, costs and expenses in the applicable period, as opposed to the cash method, under which no entries are made until a cash transaction has occurred.

(3) the designation of an amount of interest payable on a bond, by the buyer to the seller, to reimburse the seller for interest accrued during the holding period up to the day before settlement. See **and interest; cash basis.**

---

accrual of bond interest

```
$1,000 bond
6% coupon rate
last interest payment date, March 15
transaction settlement date, May 28

number of days to accrue interest: 68
```

formula:

$$\frac{\text{accrual days}}{\text{one year}} \times \text{interest rate} \times \text{bond value} = \text{accrued interest}$$

$$\frac{68}{360} \times 6\% \times \$1000 = \$11.33$$

---

accumulated earnings tax   a penalty assessed against corporations deemed to have earned net profits in excess of their reasonable needs. It is intended to cause the payment of appropriate dividends to shareholders, as opposed to the retention of those earnings. See **corporation; dividend; earned surplus; net income.**

accumulation   (1) applied to discounted bonds, the appreciation in value from purchase date until (a) maturity or (b) the call date, if a callable bond.

(2) a technical term generally referring to the activity of buying and holding securities. See **appreciation; buy; callable bond; discount; maturity date; security.**

accrual examples

a) Income Accrual:

1. Income is earned
2. Payment is received

   net result

	Cash		Accounts Receivable		Income	
	DR	CR	DR	CR	DR	CR
1.			$1,000			$1,000
2.	$1,000			$1,000		
net result	$1,000		$ -0-			$1,000

b) Expense Accrual:

1. Expense is incurred
2. Payment is made

   net result

	Cash		Accounts Payable		General Expense	
	DR	CR	DR	CR	DR	CR
1.				$ 500	$ 500	
2.		$ 500	$ 500			
net result		$ 500		$ -0-	$ 500	

accumulation area a term used in technical analysis to identify "support" areas in an issue; when a series of low points are established over a period of time (floor), the accumulation area, or support level may indicate investor willingness to purchase that issue at that price. See **floor; support level; technical analysis.**

accumulation unit indication of the level of equity held in an annuity. A purchaser of fixed and variable annuities deposits sums with an insurer which are referred to as accumulation units and are the property of the annuitant. These units may be surrendered (returned to the annuitant) before the selected date of annuitization, or converted (exchanged) for one of several annuity options at a pre-selected date. See **annuity; fixed annuity; variable annuity.**

acid test ratio a ratio used to measure liquidity of an organization, involving the comparison between current assets without inventories, to total current liabilities. An acid test ratio of "1 to 1" is considered acceptable in most industries. Below that is unfavorable. See **balance sheet ratios.**

acid test ratio

$$\frac{CA - I}{CL} = X/Y$$

```
CA = current assets
 I = inventory
CL = current liabilities
 X = asset factor of ratio
 Y = liability factor of ratio
```

active bond a type of bond for which a high volume of trading is expected, to the extent that it will be freely handled as are stock issues. See **floor; free security.**

active box broker-dealer industry slang indicating the place where securities are held for one of several reasons: (a) awaiting instructions from their owner; (b) being held for financing, if owned by the broker-dealer; or (c) held in pledge against customer margin loans. See **broker-dealer; margin account.**

active market (1) description of a high level of transactions in a single security.
(2) description of a grouping of securities characterized by a high volume of trading activity. See **security; volume.**

actual cash value (ACV) a contract's value upon maturity or redemption. See **cash value; maturity date; redemption.**

accumulation area

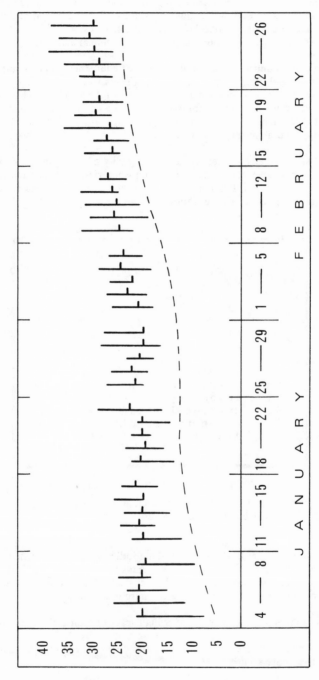

----- accumulation area

actuarial assumptions projections of future values or events, especially those of individual mortality, compensation, appreciation of assets, and earning power; such projections are used to estimate future pension and retirement values and annuity and life mortality valuations in variable annuity products. See **fixed annuity; pension plan; profit sharing plan; variable annuity.**

ad valorem "value added"; an assessment based on the value of products, descriptive of a fixed percentage tax. See **tax basis.**

add-on minimum tax a feature of federal tax law, by which certain tax preference income is subject to tax above and beyond regular tax rates. This tax was created and amended by the Tax Reform Acts of 1969 and 1976 to minimize the advantages of tax-advantaged investments (tax shelters). See **minimum tax; tax preference; Tax Reform Act of 1969; Tax Reform Act of 1976; tax shelter.**

adjustable rate mortgage (ARM) a real estate mortgage with a rate of interest that is modified periodically based upon the relative change in a predetermined, independent interest rate index. See **fixed-rate mortgage; flexible-rate mortgage; mortgage; real estate.**

adjusted basis (1) the net value of a capital asset for tax purposes, consisting of the original purchase price; increased by the value of capital improvements; decreased by depreciation claimed or allowable.
(2) for investors, the net purchase price of a security after broker commissions; or investment amount adjusted by the operations and financing of a partnership. See **capital gain; commission; depreciation; partnership.**

Sales Price		$ 84,600
Purchase Price	$ 57,000	
Plus: Capital Improvements	15,000	
Less: Accumulated Depreciation	(45,800)	
Adjusted Basis		$ 26,200
Net Capital Gain		$ 58,400

adjusted basis

adjusted gross income the amount of income reported by an individual for federal income purposes, consisting of total income and loss from all sources, less allowable adjustments. These adjustments include moving expenses, employee business expenses, IRA deductions, payments to a Keogh retirement plan, penalty on early withdrawal of savings, alimony paid, deduction for a working couple when both work, and disability income exclusion. See **Federal Income Tax Act of 1913; individual retirement account (IRA); Keogh plan.**

adjustment bond a bond normally issued when the issuing company would otherwise become bankrupt. It is exchanged with other outstanding bonds on the condition that interest will accrue and be payable only if earned. Bondholders of outstanding issues must authorize the exchange. See **income bond.**

advance-decline index a comparison between daily or weekly numbers of traded issues which have risen in price to those that have declined. This index is used as a gauge of current market sentiment and trends. For example, one theory holds that three consecutive days in which advances lead declines by 1,000 issues or more is a very bullish signal.

The index may be expressed numerically (advances led declines 3 to 1) or as a factor (1200 advances and 400 declines is an index of "3").

Advance-decline analysis is based on the premise that general market sentiment is reflected in the relative numbers of issues trading at higher and lower prices than the previous period. See **bear; bull; issue; technical analysis.**

advance refunding a practice to fully ensure against default of municipal securities, also known as prerefunding. Proceeds of the issue are invested in U.S. Government securities, which are placed into an escrow account. The maturity dates of the government securities are coordinated with those of the municipals. They can be used only for redemption of the municipals. See **prerefunding; redemption.**

advance ruling a decision as to the tax status of proposed investments, particularly partnerships, that is requested from the Internal Revenue Service before the offering is sold. See **limited partnership.**

advertising a communication intended for public distribution concerned with the offering or sale of services or products or recruiting activities.

The NASD has specified that advertisements by securities dealers may not be false or misleading. A broker-dealer is responsible for all advertisements that will be used by members of that firm. A general securities principal of the broker-dealer must approve each advertisement and retain a copy for three years. Additional restrictions apply to ads other than tombstone ads. See **general securities principal; National Association of Securities Dealers (NASD); rules of fair practice; tombstone ad.**

advisor's client account an account opened for a client by an investment advisor. When such an account is opened, the advisor is required to obtain information necessary to ensure proper suitability of the client for the activities anticipated, and proper supervision by the broker-dealer. See **broker-dealer; investment advisor; new account form; suitability.**

affidavit of domicile an executor's statement required at the time of death, so that securities may be transferred. The affidavit attests to the domicile state at the time of death and, together with a state's tax waiver, is required before transfer may be completed. See **estate planning.**

affiliated member a corporation contracted with stock exchanges other than New York, who have agreed to abide by exchange rules. This agreement, signed with the Stock Clearing Corporation, enables the corporations to make payments and deliveries within the rules of the NYSE. See **clearing member; control person; Stock Clearing Corporation (SCC).**

affiliated person an individual in a position to materially affect the management decisions of an organization. Included are officers, directors, members of immediate families, or anyone holding or controlling 10 percent or more of the company's stock. See **control person; control stock.**

aftermarket   a term used to describe the trading in a security following its initial public offering. See **freeriding; hot issue; offering; over-the-counter (OTC); secondary market; security; stabilization; withholding.**

aftertax   a rate of return applied to bonds which are purchased at a discount. The rate is used to compare yields net of taxation, and assumes a maximum tax and capital gains rate that would be paid by a corporate holder. See **bond; discount.**

agency arrangement   (1) acting as an agent for the account of someone else, by agreement.

(2) A type of bond exempted from registration under terms of the Securities Act of 1933.

(3) In the cattle feeding industry, an agreement under which a feed operator manages a herd and contracts directly with investors. See **agent; cattle feeding; Federal Intermediate Credit Bank (FICB); Securities Act of 1933; Tennessee Valley Authority (TVA).**

agency bond   a category of bonds issued and backed by the credit of the United States, yet yielding rates competitive with or higher than Treasury obligations. See **Bank for Cooperatives (CO-OP); Export-Import Bank; Federal Home Loan Bank (FHLB); Federal Intermediate Credit Bank (FICB); Federal Land Bank (FLB); Government National Mortgage Association (GNMA); Inter-American Development Bank (IADB); Tennessee Valley Authority (TVA); World Bank.**

agent   (1) One who acts in behalf of another, having been given the power to represent, including the buying, selling and commitment for the account of the principal.

(2) Under the laws of state securities trading, one who acts in behalf of a broker-dealer or an issuer for securities transactions in that state. See **agency arrangement.**

aggregate exercise price (AEP)   (1) descriptive of the total amount that may be exercised under the terms of stock option contracts. When more than one option is bought or sold, it is the aggregate total exercise potential of those options which makes up the AEP.

(2) the strike price multiplied by the face value of underlying securities, in cases of Treasury bills and notes the Ginnie-Mae options. As in the case of bond premiums, the option value (strike price) also represents a percentage of face value. See **call; option; put; strike price; Treasury bill; Treasury note.**

aggregate indebtedness   Used in the broker-dealer industry, the total of amounts payable to customers. Generally, this debt would consist of amounts due to customer credit balances. Computing of aggregate indebtedness is required by the Securities and Exchange Commission. See **broker-dealer; net capital requirement; SEC Rule 15c3-1; Securities and Exchange Commission (SEC).**

aggrieved party   (1) one who files a complaint against an NASD member or member agent as defined by the rules of fair practice.

(2) one requesting stock exchange, NASD or MSRB arbitration to settle disputes with a member or member agent. See **arbitration; member organization; Municipal Securities Rulemaking Board (MSRB); National Association of Securities Dealers (NASD); rules of fair practice.**

allied member (1) a term for individuals who are partners, officers, employees or directors of a member firm, but who are not exchange members.

(2) employees who are also voting stockholders in a member organization who also act as members of the board of directors; own five percent or more of the voting stock; or are identified in the organization as principal executive officers. See **board of directors; member organization; National Association of Securities Dealers (NASD).**

alligator spread reference to an option spread transaction in which the broker commissions are greater than the profits to the client would be. See **broker; commission; option; spread.**

all or none (AON) (1) a condition attached to a buy or sell order. It specifies that a transaction is to be completed in total or not at all. Thus, the total size of a transaction is conditional. An AON condition may be expanded to restrict the time of execution by indicating FOK, fill or kill. If immediate execution of the entire order is not possible, then the entire order is cancelled and no partial order may be filled.

(2) In an underwriting, the AON condition may be attached to the subscription offering. Failing subscription of all shares, the issuer may cancel the entire offering. See **buy; fill or kill (FOK); offering; round lot; sell order.**

alternate energy classification of investment program in non-traditional energy sources, including all areas except oil and gas: solar, thermal, wind energy. See **private placement; program; public offering; tax shelter.**

alternative minimum tax a tax effective since 1979 designed to ensure a liability in most circumstances. See **add-on minimum tax; tax basis; tax preference.**

alternative order a two-part order in which the successful execution of one part automatically cancels the other part. It is a combination of a limit order (to transact below current value) and a stop order (to transact above current value) on the same issue. These are also called either-or orders. See **buy; limit order; sell order; stop order.**

American Commodity Exchange (ACE) 711 NE Third Street, Gresham OR 97030; a regional commodity exchange for the Pacific Northwest region. See **commodity; exchange; regional exchanges.**

American depository receipt (ADR) a receipt for shares held in a deposit in a foreign branch of an American bank, when those shares are in a foreign corporation. ADR's are negotiable and are used by foreign corporations to sell shares in the United States. See **beneficial owner.**

American Municipal Bond Assurance Corporation (AMBAC) an insuring organization covering municipal bonds to the extent of both principal and interest. Premiums for coverage are paid by the bond issuer. See **guaranteed payment; municipal bond.**

American Stock Exchange (AMEX) 86 Trinity Place, New York NY 10006; the second largest U.S. stock exchange. Until 1921, AMEX was the New York Curb Exchange. The organization deals in markets for the issues of organizations that do not meet the criteria for membership of the New York Stock Exchange, where listing requirements and minimum size of an organization are more demanding. See **curb exchange.**

American Stock Exchange Clearing Corporation (ASECC) a subsidiary of AMEX formed to help member organizations with trading activities. Apart from its rulemaking, this organization has subcontracted its duties to the Securities Industry Automation Corporation (SIAC). See **member organization; Securities Industry Automation Corporation (SIAC).**

American Stock Exchange Market Value Index an index prepared each trading day of all AMEX issues grouped geographically and by industry. See **common stock; index.**

American Stock Exchange Price Change Index an index prepared each trading hour of all AMEX common stock issues, reflecting unweighted prices movements. See **common stock; index.**

AMEX Options Switching System (AMOS) an automated system for directing option orders to trade locations and, upon execution, reporting back to the member who placed the order. See **execution; option.**

AMEX Rule 411 A dictate of the American Stock Exchange similar to the NYSE "know your customer" rule. See **American Stock Exchange (AMEX); know your customer.**

amortization (1) an accounting term referring to the recognition of expense over a period of use or application. For example, an insurance premium paid for a three-year period would be amortized over 36 months, in equal installments.
(2) a general term in accounting covering the practices under which an asset is deducted as a business expense. This includes depreciation and depletion. Example: "Depreciation is used to amortize the cost of a fixed asset over the term of that asset's class life."
(3) the method of expensing organization costs of business or intangible assets. Generally, costs to organize are amortized over a sixty-month period. The costs of improvements are amortized in a method similar to straight-line depreciation, with the distinction that the reduction of improvements is referred to on a balance sheet as "accumulated amortization." Under an alternate method, the accumulation is not shown separately but the gross value of the asset is reduced.
(4) a term used in reference to the payments on a loan in which interest is charged only on the new outstanding principal balance, commonly used in mortgages on real estate over long terms.
(5) the process of recognizing for tax purposes the premium paid on purchase of a bond. If a bond is purchased "at a premium," a higher amount is paid than the bond's redemption value. This premium is amortized over the period of time between purchase and the redemption date. See **deferred asset; depletion; depreciation; interest; premium; prepaid assets; prepaid expenses; prepaid interest; redemption.**

and interest in the transaction of a bond, a reference to the payment on interest from the previous interest payment date to the date immediately before settlement. The buyer pays the seller for the interest earned during this holding period. See **accrual; bond; interest.**

annual audit (1) an accounting term referring either to an internal examination and closing of the company's books, or an external and independent examination by

amortization of expense

Insurance premium paid for three years, $180.00.

Amortization:

Description	Month	Asset: Prepaid Insurance		Insurance Expense	
		Dr.	Cr.	Dr.	Cr.
Premium Paid	January	1800.00			
Amortization	January		50.00	50.00	
"	February		50.00	50.00	
"	March		50.00	50.00	
Sub-total		1650.00		150.00	

another firm, usually a certified public accountant.

(2) An external examination by certified public accountants of a broker-dealer's books and records, which is required by SEC Rule 17a-5. See **broker-dealer; Securities and Exchange Commission (SEC).**

annual meeting   a meeting held for the stockholders of a corporation, which may be formal or informal, depending upon the scope of ownership and whether or not the stock is held publicly. This meeting's purpose is to discuss the year's results, the major decisions and recommendations of the board of directors, and election of board members. See **board of directors; corporation; stockholder.**

annual percentage rate (APR)   the actual percentage of interest that will be paid, based upon the compounding method used. Disclosure is required on all loans, under the federal Truth in Lending Act. See **compound interest; interest.**

Annual Percentage Rate (APR)

	14% Interest	Balance
Beginning balance		$1,000.00
January	$ 11.67	1,011.67
February	11.80	1,023.47
March	11.94	1,035.41
April	12.08	1,047.49
May	12.22	1,059.71
June	12.36	1,072.07
July	12.51	1,084.58
August	12.65	1,097.23
September	12.80	1,110.03
October	12.95	1,122.98
November	13.10	1,136.08
December	13.25	1,149.33
	APR	14.933%

annual report   (1) a formal report issued by corporations to its stockholders. In addition to the financial reports and notes of an independent certified public accountant, the report commonly contains product expansion and progress reports; comments from the president and chairman on the company's financial and industry status; and reports on corporate projects underway.

(2) Form 10K filed with the Securities and Exchange Commission every year, as required by law for all registered corporations. See **balance sheet; corporation; financial statement; Form 10K; income statement; net income; retained earnings; Securities and Exchange Commission (SEC); stockholder.**

annuitant   one who receives the benefits promised in an annuity contract, usually also the beneficial owner. See **accumulation unit; beneficial owner, fixed annuity; variable annuity.**

annuity a contract between an individual and a life insurance company, in which the annuitant deposits a lump sum (single-payment annuity) with the company, or makes periodic payments into the contract (flexible annuity). In return, the company provides on-going life insurance coverage and, upon annuitization (a preselected date when annuity benefits begin), payments are made to the annuitant.

The method of payments may call for guaranteed monthly benefits for life; for a period of time; or for the lives of two people (joint and survivor annuity). A variable annuity is treated as a security and falls within the jurisdiction of the Securities and Exchange Commission. See **accumulation unit; fixed annuity; variable annuity.**

annuity trust as applied to the use of charitable trusts, a device providing for payments of a fixed amount to a charitable beneficiary. This allows current tax deductions and avoidance of estate taxes. See **estate planning; estate tax; trust.**

annuity unit a term used by insurance companies to compute the valuation of accumulation units in an annuity contract upon annuitization (the beginning of annuity benefit payments). See **accumulation unit; fixed annuity; variable annuity.**

annuity wraps a type of product under which insurance companies offered benefits to individuals associated with savings and loans or mutual funds. Rather than depositing cash, the individual pledged mutual fund shares or certificates held by the savings institution, receiving in exchange an annuity contract.

In 1980, the Internal Revenue Service ruled against deferral of taxes on earnings in annuity wraps, arguing that the owner of the certificate of deposit in a savings and loan continued to own that certificate and, accordingly, would be taxed on its earnings. A similar 1981 ruling applied the same conclusion to annuity wraps with mutual funds. See **mutual fund; savings and loan association; tax deferral; wraparound annuity.**

appreciation (1) to investors, a desirable increase in value of a holding, such as the growth of fund shares or shares of stock.

(2) generally, an increase in value of any asset. This growth may be due to rarity, inflation, shortages, investor demand and other factors. See **collectibles; growth stock; inflation; value.**

approved person an individual in a control position of a member organization who is not an employee (an employee in a control position is referred to as an "affiliated person").

Approved persons may be on the board of directors or a consultant acting in a control position. Such a person is approved by the board of governors of an exchange and is bound by its rules and constitution. See **affiliated person; board of directors; board of governors; control person; control stock; member organization.**

arbitrage (1) the buy and sell of the same security in different markets but at approximately the same time. The purpose of arbitrage is to profit from differences in price on two exchanges.

(2) the buy and sell of different securities that are related in some way, to profit from the difference in prices. This form of arbitrage may apply to potential mergers or conversion of one issue's shares into the shares of the other. See **buy; conversion arbitrage; long; merger; position; security; short sale.**

arbitrage bond   a type of bond issued with the intention that proceeds are to be used to buy other bonds paying higher rates. See **advance refunding; municipal bond; prerefunding.**

arbitrager   a person or entity practicing arbitrage, applied more often to broker-dealers and individuals in their employ than to individuals alone. See **long; position; short sale.**

arbitration   (1) in the securities industry, a means for deciding disputes between two parties. This process results in a decision which is binding upon both parties. The NASD, the MSRB, and the exchanges all have procedures for arbitration.

(2) In a general application, any remedy to disputes settled as an alternative to litigation. Many contracts in the securities industry between principals and agents, broker-dealers and representatives, and other non-employee relationships contain clauses in which both parties agree to settle disputes through binding arbitration. See **aggrieved party; member organization; Municipal Securities Rulemaking Board (MSRB); National Association of Securities Dealers (NASD).**

arrearage   dividends that are unpaid to the preferred stockholders of a corporation, when their shares are "cumulative" preferred. See **cumulative preferred; dividend; preferred stock.**

as agent   a role that is filled by a person or organization acting as a broker or broker-dealer in a transaction. The "as agent" (or sub-agent) designation involves no financial risk for the transaction, but one acting in the capacity will receive a fee or a commission for services rendered. See **as principal; broker-dealer.**

Asian CD   a certificate of deposit issued in an Asian city, usually denominated in United States dollars. See **certificate of deposit (CD).**

Asian Development Bank bond   a bond issued by the Asian Development Bank. This organization has more than 40 nations as members, with the purpose of furthering economic and cooperative growth in Asia. The U.S. holds one-third of the organization's capital stock.

The bank's bonds receive the highest ratings and are taxed fully. See **bond.**

asked price   stock market term indicating the lowest price that will be taken by the holder of a security. If a seller is willing to sell a unit of shares at an indicated price, that price is being "asked" by that seller. Also called a quotation, the asked price is compared to the bid, which is the highest price offered by a potential buyer. The term "bid and ask" refers to the bidding between buy and sell offers. See **bid; buy; offering price; quotation; sell order.**

as principal   description of the role a broker-dealer plays when it is dealing for its own account. In buying from a market maker and selling to customers, the transaction is a mark-up. In the opposite transaction, buying from customers and selling to a market maker, it is referred to as a mark-down. See **as agent; broker-dealer; mark down; mark up; market maker.**

assessable unit   a type of direct participation program interest in which the total amount to be invested is made in stages. The investor is required to make an initial deposit and subsequent additional contributions in future months or years. See **direct participation program; staged payment.**

assessed valuation (1) as used in reference to municipal securities, the value assigned to property. When bonds are to be retired primarily from property tax revenues, as is usually the case for local municipalities, assessed valuation is a crucial factor for comparisons. It must be realized, though, that this may be arbitrary as a valuation method. The assessed valuation basis applied by different municipalities varies greatly.

(2) Generally, a reference to an estimated value for some purpose, such as financing a secured debt, which may be applied to a wide number of properties. See **municipal bond.**

asset depreciation range (ADR) Under rules for depreciation of capital assets prior to passage of the Economic Recovery Tax Act of 1981 (ERTA), a wide number of possible "useful lives" could be assigned to property. The ADR was a guideline which set minimum and maximum depreciation periods for a large number of assets in specific utilizations. ERTA replaced the old depreciation method with ACRS, simplifying the depreciation with class lives in replacement of the old useful life concept. See **accelerated cost recovery system (ACRS); capitalization; class life; depreciation; Economic Recovery Tax Act of 1981 (ERTA).**

asset ratios ratios applied to components of a balance sheet, primarily involving comparison between two separate asset balances, or between an asset and a liability or capital account. There are three primary asset ratios: the current ratio, the working capital to funded debt ratio (working capital is the net of current assets minus current liabilities), and the acid test (quick assets) ratio. See **acid test ratio; balance sheet ratios; current ratio; funded debt ratio; quick asset ratio; ratios; working capital ratio.**

assets the properties and items with a value to them that are owned by a person or business. The primary sub-classifications of assets are (a) current: cash and other assets that will convert to cash within one year; (b) long-term: equipment, machinery, real estate and other capital assets, net of depreciation; (c) prepaid and deferred: expenditures for future costs or expenses, such as insurance, interest or rent, that are set up as assets to be amortized over an applicable period; and (d) intangibles: assets with a determinable value, but may not be salable, including goodwill, contractual provisions like covenants not to compete, and the value assigned to patents or copyrights. See **balance sheet; current assets; deferred asset; intangible asset; long-term assets; prepaid assets; value.**

assignment (1) moving of title to the economic interests in a contract or asset from one investor or registration to another. In the case of limited partnerships, the existing limited partner may assign interests by aggreement with someone else, or may transfer interests by requesting the general partner to amend the agreement and accept the substitute partner.

(2) a form normally included on the reverse of a certificate for a security, to be used for assigning ownership from one registration to another. The same effect may be achieved with a written assignment letter.

(3) a notice sent by the Options Clearing Corporation to an option writer when the option(s) written has been chosen to fulfill an offsetting buy. The exercise of that option will result in assignment to a seller, who, upon exercise is said to have had his

Current Ratio:

$$\frac{\text{Current Assets}}{\text{Current Liabilities}} = \text{a to b}$$

Working Capital to Funded Debt:

$$\frac{\text{(Current Assets} - \text{Current Liabilities)}}{\text{Funded Debt}} = \underline{\quad\quad}\%$$

Quick Assets Ratio:

$$\frac{\text{(Current Assets} - \text{Inventory)}}{\text{Current Liabilities}} = \text{a to b}$$

asset ratios

---

or her option "assigned." See **bond power; exercise; option; stock power; transfer.**

associate member an organization or person who has the right to transact business through an exchange member, but otherwise has no access to the floor; or, a firm who uses the services of the Stock Clearing Corporation (SCC) but is not a member of the exchange. See **American Stock Exchange (AMEX); Stock Clearing Corporation (SCC).**

associate specialist one who assists a regular specialist. The associate is a trainee who may act as an agent while under the supervision of either the regular or a relief specialist. See **relief specialist; specialist.**

associated person a person acting for or with a broker-dealer as a partner, director, officer, salesperson, manager, trader or employee. See **broker-dealer.**

Association of Member Firm Option Department (AMFOD) an organization structured to defining and improving option markets, and a division of the Securities Industry Association (SIA). See **member organization; option; Securities Industry Association (SIA).**

association taxed as a corporation a company with characteristics of a corporation rather than a partnership or a trust. This organization will not pass through to the investor the tax benefits of ownership, but retains liabilities and write-offs at the organizational level. See **corporation; partnership; trust.**

assumable mortgage a mortgage that the owner can assign to a buyer upon sale of a property. See **mortgage; real estate.**

assumed bond a bond which has been taken over by an acquiring company in the case of a merger, or which is held by a reorganized corporation or entity. See **joint bond; merger.**

at risk monies invested via cash payment or signing of notes for which the investor is liable. In order to claim a deduction for tax benefits associated with an investment, the amount of basis upon which those deductions are based must be "at risk." See **nonrecourse loan; recourse loan; tax-advantaged investment; tax basis.**

at risk limitations rules setting upward limits on the amount of deduction that will be allowed in an investment. See **nonrecourse loan; recourse loan.**

at the close a type of order specifying the trade must occur at the close of business of a trading day, or as close as possible to the close. An "at the close" order is to be executed within the last 30 seconds of the day, but there is no guarantee that it will be placed. This is a form of an "at the market" order specifying the time to be placed. See **execution; order ticket.**

at the market (1) an order to obtain the best possible prevailing price for a buy or sell transaction.
(2) an indicated guideline price of property that should or would be paid under normal circumstances, used in reference to arms-length transactions. See **buy; order ticket; sell order.**

at the money the point at which an option's strike price matches the current market value of the underlying issue. Movements away from the "at the money" point increase the chance for exercise (for sellers) or loss on the investment (buyers). For calls, positive movement in the stock enriches the value of the options. For puts, negative stock movements enrich the value of the options. Thus, "at the money" is used as a measurement of an option's relative time value. See **call; execution; option; premium; put; strike price.**

at the opening (OPG) a limit order specifying that a trade is to be executed on and as a part of the initial day's trade in a particular issue. If this is not possible, the "at the opening" order is cancelled automatically. This form of order may not be placed as an "at the market" order by regulation, as no market will have been established until the initial day's transaction has been completed. See **buy; limit order; market order; sell order.**

auction marketplace general term applied to the system of buying and selling on an open exchange. Buyers compete with one another for the best possible price, and sellers compete with one another, and any exchange member may participate. As part of the marketplace, the specialist transacts for his or her own account, equalizing supply and demand distortions. See **buy; sell order; specialist; trade.**

authorized shares the highest number of shares which may be issued by a corporation. The number of issued shares may be equal to or less than the authorized total, either common or preferred class shares. An increase in the total authorized

```
                    at the money


A call option with a
strike price of $55:


70

65                          in the money

60

55 ————at the money————————————

50

45                          out of the money

40
```

shares must be approved by shareholders, and requires an amendment to the charter of the corporation, as well as approval from the state agency overseeing corporate matters. See **corporation; outstanding stock; stock.**

automatic exercise   action that is taken by the Options Clearing Corporation (OCC) when expiring options that are in the money are expiring. It is assumed that an option seller would (a) cover, or buy in the money option, or (b) allow to expire as worthless an out-of-the money option. Automatic exercise is an action taken to protect option writers who have overlooked the obvious actions that should be taken. Any option that is three-quarters of a point or more in the money will be automatically exercised. Investors may avoid automatic exercise easily, by taking actions on a trading day at or before expiration date, as the OCC will not take this action until after the close of trading. See **assignment; expiration date; in the money; option; Options Clearing Corporation (OCC); secondary market.**

automatic reinvestment   a benefit allowed to investors in mutual funds. Dividends or capital gain distributions may be reinvested in additional shares of the fund, rather than taken by the investor in cash. The investor, unless using this feature as part of a qualified retirement or other tax-deferred plan, will be taxed on automatically reinvested funds in the year they are credited. See **capital gain; dividend; mutual fund.**

automatic withdrawal   a benefit allowed to investors in mutual funds. The same amount will be distributed to the investor each month (or quarter), from dividends and capital gain distributions. If the current earnings are not sufficient to meet the specified withdrawal amount, the fund will liquidate shares. See **mutual fund; redemption; voluntary accumulation program.**

automatic reinvestment

Assuming 2% dividend per quarter:

Dividend Date	Amount of Dividend	Balance of Account
Balance January 1		$10,000.00
March 31	$ 200.00	10,200.00
June 30	204.00	10,404.00
September 30	208.08	10,612.08
December 31	212.24	10,824.32
Total Dividends	$ 824.32	

```
                -return with reinvestment   8.24%
                -return with cash
                     withdrawal ($800.00)    8.00%
```

average down a technique used to offset declines in stock prices. As the price falls, a number of shares are purchased in addition to the original purchase. This has the effect of averaging the overall basis in the issue. See **issue; market value.**

Shares	Purchase Date	Price Per Share	Average Price
100	June 8	$ 55	$ 55
100	July 8	54	54 1/2
100	August 8	50	53
100	September 8	49	52
100	October 8	47	51
100	November 8	45	50

averaging down

average inventory to sales ratio a traditional method for computing the turn-over of inventory. This is not a dependable analysis, however, as it compares two unlike results. Inventory reflects cost or market while sales represent a marked-up result. The degree of mark-up may vary between types of products, making the ratio less valid than one comparing average inventory to cost of goods sold. See **inventory ratios; ratios; real turnover; sales.**

$$\frac{\text{average inventory*}}{\text{total sales}} = \text{number of inventory turns}$$

* (1) overall average:

$$\frac{\text{beginning inventory plus}}{\text{ending inventory}}{2}$$

(2) detailed average:

$$\frac{\text{inventory balance each}}{\text{month during the period}}{\text{number of months}}$$
in the period

average inventory to sales ratio

average up (1) a strategy in which an investor buys lots of shares as the market value increases. This has the effect of increasing the average price basis, used by investors who believe the stock will continue to increase in value, or by one who believes an established amount should be invested periodically, regardless of the stock's movements.

(2) a seller's strategy, under which shares of an issue are sold while the market value increases, which has the effect of increasing proportionate gains as long as the increases continue. See **issue; market value.**

Shares	Purchase Date	Price Per Share	Average Price
100	March 15	$ 18	$ 18
100	April 15	21	19 1/2
100	May 15	21	20
100	June 15	22	20 1/2
100	July 15	23	21

averaging up

averages popular measures of the stock market, involving the continued analysis of a select grouping of issues. Most popular and well-known is the Dow Jones Industrial Averages, a selection of 30 corporations. See **Dow Jones Industrial Averages (DJIA); Dow Jones Transportation Averages; Dow Jones Utility Averages; Standard and Poor's Corporation.**

avoidance the planned and legal reduction or elimination of tax liabilities. Avoidance is any action of planning to minimize tax liabilities, including the timing of business and personal expenses and the deferral of income. Any illegal means of reducing taxes is referred to as evasion.

Examples of avoidance for investors include a timely sale of holdings to create a capital loss in the current year; selling for long-term gains offset by short-term losses; opening of qualified retirement plans (IRA or Keogh); and writing of options that do not expire until the following year (cash is credited in the current year but is not taxed until exercise, purchase in the secondary market, or expiration). See **evasion; tax preference.**

B

baby bond any bond issued in a denomination below the normal $1,000, most commonly in the amount of $100. See **bond; face value.**

back-dating the practice of allowing a mutual fund purchaser to pre-date a letter of intent so that previous investments, added to a current one, will discount the total load charge on the transaction. See **letter of intent; load; mutual fund; sales charge.**

back office departments of a broker-dealer not involved directly in sales activities. While the term is applied broadly to describe any number of functions, it is most frequently used in reference to the purchase and sales and cashiering departments. See **broker-dealer; cashiering; purchase and sales department (P-S).**

backing away an action that is illegal under the rules of fair practice of the NASD, in which a market maker does not honor a firm quote on a minimum of 100 shares or 10 bonds. See **firm quote; market maker; National Association of Securities Dealers (NASD).**

backspread a technique or practice which is contrary to accepted strategies. See **reverse strategy.**

balanced company a mutual fund which invests in a combination of common and preferred stocks and bonds, also called "balanced fund." See **bond; common stock; investment company; mutual fund; preferred stock.**

balance order matching of a day's sales and purchases to determine the net shares or units of securities to be delivered or received. See **issue; trade.**

balance sheet a basic financial statement which presents the total, by classifications, of assets, liabilities and net worth. The term is applied to corporations, partnerships, trusts and individuals. It is called a balance sheet for two reasons: the state-

Balance Sheet

Current Assets	$ 630,000
Long-Term Assets	845,000
Prepaid Assets	18,000
Deferred Charges	4,000
Intangible Assets	11,000
Total Assets	$ 1,508,000
Current Liabilities	$ 302,000
Long-Term Liabilities	410,000
Deferred Credits	82,000
Total Liabilities	$ 794,000
Net Worth	$ 714,000
Total Liabilities and Net Worth	$ 1,508,000

ment shows the balance in each account classification as of a specific date; and the total of all assets balances with the total of liabilities plus net worth. See **assets; financial statement; liabilities; net worth.**

balance sheet ratios a ratio used for analysis of financial condition, involving the comparison between components of a balance sheet. Common balance sheet ratios include the current ratio, the quick asset ratio, owners' investment versus creditors' interest, and working capital to funded debt ratio. See **acid test ratio; asset ratios; current ratio; quick asset ratio; ratios; working capital ratio.**

balloon effect a condition seen in which a serial bond is redeemed, at least partially, over a period of years, with a final redemption (balloon) at a final date. The practice gives investors an added measure of protection, as part of their principal is no longer at risk as partial redemption is made. The balloon effect can be applied to the rate of interest to be paid, with an increase in the rate earned in the later part of the term. See **interest; principal; redemption; serial bond.**

balloon payment a condition attached to a financing plan calling for a lump-sum payment which retires all or part of the principal balance on a pre-determined date. Loan payments are amortized over a term, with a balloon due on a date earlier

balloon effect

	Redemption	Balance
Original Issue		$500,000
5th year	$ 50,000	450,000
8th year	50,000	400,000
11th year	50,000	350,000
14th year	50,000	300,000
17th year	50,000	250,000
20th year	250,000	-0-

$10,000 loan at 14%
Balloon due after 10th year

Based on 25-year term, balloon of $9,039:		Based on 15-year term, balloon of $5,723:	
Year	Year-end Balance	Year	Year-end Balance
1	$ 9,953	1	$ 9,789
2	9,898	2	9,546
3	9,835	3	9,267
4	9,763	4	8,946
5	9,680	5	8,577
6	9,585	6	8,153
7	9,476	7	7,666
8	9,350	8	7,106
9	9,205	9	6,463
10	9,039	10	5,723

balloon payment

than that term, having the same effect as early retirement. See **amortization; mortgage.**

bank an organization providing services for the transaction and management of money and other assets. Banks may be typified by five characteristics: charter (federal or state banks); operations (savings or commercial); ownership (a stock or mutual form); membership (there are Federal Reserve System member and non-member banks); and insurance (whether or not the organization holds federal deposit insurance). See **commercial bank; Federal Deposit Insurance Corporation (FDIC); Federal Reserve Board (FRB); mutual savings bank; savings bank.**

bank float   funds available to banks while funds backing demands are being transferred between institutions. See **commercial bank; savings bank.**

Bank for Cooperatives (CO-OP)   an agency sponsored by the Farm Credit Administration which offers financing to farmers and agricultural cooperatives. See **Farm Credit Administration (FCA).**

bank holding company   a company which owns 25 percent or more of the voting stock in a bank or in several banks. Such companies are regulated by the board of governors of the Federal Reserve. See **board of governors; Federal Reserve Board (FRB); holding company.**

bank quality   a bond assigned one of the four highest ratings by the popular ratings services (BBB or higher by Standard and Poor's and Baa or higher by Moody's), also known as "investment grade." Commercial banks are allowed to purchase bank quality bonds for their own accounts. See **commercial bank; investment grade; Moody's Investors Service; ratings systems; Standard and Poor's Corporation.**

banker's acceptance   a bill of exchange which becomes a money market instrument payable within six months in most cases. The purpose of BA's is to provide temporary financing for manufacturers or exporters between origin and sale of goods. See **discount; money market instrument; time draft.**

Barron's Confidence Index   an index which follows the trend in investor sentiment regarding bonds. The theory is: investor sentiment becomes more favorable as lower-grade bond yields fall. The index is published weekly by *Barron's*. See **bond; high-grade security; yield.**

base rent   the amount of rent a tenant pays apart from assessments for extras such as property taxes, utilities or ground fees, used in analysis of real estate direct participation programs. See **real estate; tenant.**

basis   (1) investor basis is the combination of cash paid in and notes signed or other property pledged. For tax deduction purposes, the investor will be limited to a ceiling on deductions based upon recourse financing and true basis.

Original Cost	$ 80,000
Plus: Acquisition Costs	2,380
Plus: Capital Improvements	22,600
Less: Depreciation	(41,800)
Basis in Property	$ 63,180

basis in property

(2) basis in property consists of original cost plus acquisition costs and capital improvements, less depreciation. See **adjusted basis; capitalization; depreciation; nonrecourse loan; partnership; recourse loan.**

basis point .01% (one one-hundredth of one percent), used as a measure for financing, securities sold at discount, and fixed-income securities. See **bond; yield to maturity.**

basis price (1) identification of adjusted cost of property to be used in figuring the amount of gain or loss for tax purposes.
(2) On odd-lot orders, a price set between the bid and offer. It is applied when three conditions are met: the stock is not traded during the day; the bid and offer spread is two points or more; and execution is requested by a customer. See **bid; odd lot; offering price; spread.**

BD form a report that is filed by broker-dealers with the Securities and Exchange Commission (SEC), reporting on firm principals, financial data and status of net capital requirements and compliance. See **broker-dealer; financial statement; net capital requirement; principal; Securities and Exchange Commission (SEC).**

bear (1) a person described as a "bear" is one who believes values in securities markets either will fall or are falling. A bearish person may believe the condition will prevail for a few weeks or months, or over an extended period of years.
(2) Description of a market which is experiencing falling prices of securities or a general attitude or projection that prices are in a falling pattern. See **bear; market value.**

bear raid an illegal act involving the manipulation of a security's value. The security is sold short at lower prices than previous trades. The volume is sufficient to cause deterioration in the price to a level that the short position may be closed at a profit. The Securities Exchange Act of 1934 prevents the depressing of stock prices. Short sales must now be made at prices above a previous trade. See **manipulation; Securities Exchange Act of 1934; short sale.**

bear spread a spread strategy used by option traders, in which a profit is realized when the market value of the stock declines. One option is bought at a strike price higher than the other, which is sold. Expiration date is generally the same. Since the premium will be greater on the lower call, the spread creates a profit. Upside risk is limited by the coverage provided in the purchased call. See **bull spread; call; credit spread; debit spread; long; option spread; put; short; strike price; time value.**

bearer bond a form of bond for which the owner's name is not registered. The issuing corporation will pay interest to an individual upon submission of a coupon but no owner is named on the security itself. See **coupon bond; registered bond.**

beneficial owner the individual who owns securities regardless of their form of registration. Many securities are held in street name, by a custodian or trustee, or are registered to a bank which manages or administers the account. See **custodian; street name; trustee.**

beneficiary the individual(s) who will receive assets and their earnings, as named in an insurance policy, trust or annuity. See **annuity; trust.**

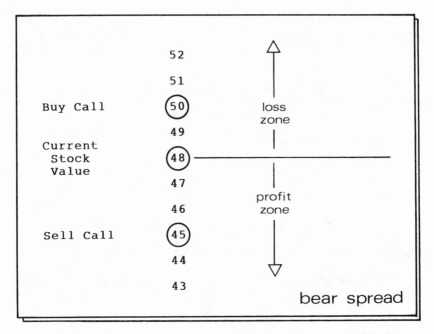

best efforts descriptive of an agreement entered between a corporation or sponsor and an underwriter. The underwriter acts in agency for the issuer, promising to apply "best efforts" in placing a security or offering with investors. However, no guarantee is given that the placement will succeed. See **all or none (AON); offering; underwriter.**

BETA a term used to rate the relative volatility of an issue as compared to the market in general. A rating of "1" would imply a stock has moved historically in the same general direction as the whole market. The lowest rating is "0," meaning no movement (or reaction) to other conditions; the highest rating is a "2," for extremely volatile stocks (based on historical movements). See **index; standard deviation; volatility.**

bid a quotation offered as the highest price someone is willing to pay for an issue. This is the opposite of "asked," which is the lowest price the issue is offered for sale. See **asked price; buyer; offering price; quotation.**

bid wanted (BW) a signal that a holder of a security wishes a potential buyer to offer a bid, as opposed to asking a price first. See **buyer; offering price; quotation.**

big board slang expression for the New York Stock Exchange. See **New York Stock Exchange (NYSE).**

blanket bond also referred to as a fidelity bond, this provides insurance against check forging or other fraudulent activities related to trading of securities. It is required of all NYSE member organizations and covers all principals: officers, partners and employees. See **fidelity bond; member organization.**

blanket certification form   a form completed by foreign broker-dealers and filed with the NASD, in regard to participation in a hot issue security. It is a statement agreeing to comply with NASD regulations concerning hot issues. See **broker-dealer; hot issue.**

blind pool   a feature of direct participation offerings in which funds are raised but no specific investment properties are identified. Rather, the objectives of the offering and the range of activities are specified, and investors depend upon the judgement and experience of the general partners to select viable properties. See **offering; private placement; public offering.**

blind trust   a trust established by an individual who, due to a position held, must avoid conflicts of interest. All rights to manage assets are surrendered to a fiduciary. See **conflict of interest; fiduciary; trust.**

block   a grouping of shares of a single security that is bought or sold as one transaction. The term applies to large numbers of shares, with the most common identification being for 10,000 or more shares. See **bond; stock.**

block positioner   a broker-dealer who purchases a large number of stock shares or bond units in its own account so that smaller lots may be sold to the broker-dealer's customers. See **broker-dealer; Regulation T.**

blotter   a securities transaction record required to be kept by a broker-dealer of all customer activities. It is generally maintained singularly for each security with a master listing for all transactions kept by day. See **broker-dealer.**

blue chip   term applied to a well-known corporation with a history of financial strength, in terms of consistent net profits and dividend payments. See **corporation; dividend; profit.**

blue list   a Standard and Poor's Corporation publication put out each business day, and concerned with municipal bonds currently available to investors. See **coupon rate; issuer; municipal bond; par value; secondary market; Standard and Poor's Corporation.**

blue room   one of the NYSE trading rooms. See **New York Stock Exchange (NYSE).**

blue-sky laws   state securities laws and registration requirements. The term refers to the concept of lacking real substance. A "blue-sky" is worth nothing as there is no tangible value to it. These laws do not pertain generally to subsequent issues of securities already listed on an exchange or to securities already subjected to blue-sky review. See **broker-dealer; issue; Uniform Securities Agent State Law Examination (USASLE).**

board broker   an options exchange member who keeps the public book, ensuring that a fair and organized market is maintained for those options which are in his charge. The broker earns a floor broker's fee for executed orders but may not trade for his own account. He works within the market maker system, not the specialist system. See **Chicago Board Options Exchange (CBOE); limit order; market maker; public book; specialist.**

board of arbitration (1) generally, any board appointed to settle a dispute in the securities industry, between members and allied members or nonmembers of an exchange or agency.

(2) A board appointed by the board of governors of the NASD to hear and settle disputes. See **allied member; arbitration; board of governors; code of arbitration; National Association of Securities Dealers (NASD).**

board of directors (1) a board elected by the stockholders of a corporation to represent the stockholders and direct senior management. The board is led by a chairman and decides appointments of officers, dividend declarations, and decisions of corporate interest, within that organization's charter.

(2) A board governing the New York Stock Exchange, consisting of twenty members elected for a term of two years. This board makes policy decisions for the exchange. See **control person; corporation; dividend; New York Stock Exchange (NYSE); stockholder.**

board of governors the board elected to govern the NASD or the Federal Reserve System. See **Federal Reserve Board (FRB); National Association of Securities Dealers (NASD).**

board room an area where postings of latest transactions in issues were posted, replaced today by electronic ticker tape or quotation machines. See **quotation; ticker tape.**

boiler room sale reference to high pressure sales activities on the part of brokers, promoting securities transactions to customers in speculative issues. See **broker; speculation.**

bona fide arbitrage a form of arbitrage which combines a high chance for profits, built into the structure of the arbitrage, with minimum levels of risk. See **arbitrage; risk arbitrage; special arbitrage account.**

board of governors
Federal Reserve

bond (1) a debt obligation of a corporation or a government. Bonds are issued for a period of more than one year (normally more than five years). A debt issued for a shorter term is called a "note." The bond is issued in denominations of $1,000 and $5,000 most commonly. A promissory note, bond issuers (borrowers) pay interest to the investor until the bond is redeemed. Bonds may be secured by revenues, general strength of the issuer, faith and credit, or mortgages.

(2) Assets placed on deposit in pledge of money or other obligations owed.

(3) A firm obligation in any form, as a pledge of performance or payment per an agreement at some time in the future. See **bearer bond; collateral trust bond; corporate bond; debenture; debt security; equipment trust bond; general mortgage bond; income bond; mortgage bond; municipal bond; receiver's certificate; registered bond; tax-exempt security; United States government securities.**

bond and preferred stock company an investment company designed specifically to invest in issues offering low risk and acceptance income. Some are structured to invest only in tax-exempt securities such as municipal bonds. See **income company; investment company; preferred stock.**

bond anticipation note (BAN) a municipal note issued for short-term financing, which will be repaid from the proceeds of a bond issue that is upcoming. See **debt security; municipal note; short-term debt.**

bond broker exchange member who executes bond transactions. See **broker; market maker.**

bond fund a type of mutual fund investing only in bonds. Some specialize in tax-exempt issues only, and are referred to as tax-exempt bond funds. This fund is an alternative to direct bond ownership, allowing the investor to diversify holdings among several issues at the same time. See **closed-end; investment company; mutual fund; open-end management company; unit investment trust.**

bond interest distribution an adjustment between buyer and seller on settlement date when a bond is transacted with accrued interest and on an "and interest" basis. See **and interest.**

bond power a form of assigning ownership of a bond when it is inconvenient for the current owner to endorse the reverse of the bond certificate itself. The owner transfers or assigns ownership through the use of a bond power, just as though the bond were signed. The bond power is attached to the bond certificate upon transfer. See **assignment; registered bond.**

bond ratio a formula for determining the relative strength of capitalization. Total outstanding bonds are divided by the total of bonds and net equity. In some versions of the equation, only bonds that are more than one year outstanding are included. See **capitalization; corporation; leverage; ratios.**

book (1) a record kept by the specialist of a stock's buy and sell activity, kept in order received for each price.
(2) an approved underwriting's indications of interest.
(3) the accounting action of making an entry to the books of account, i.e. to "book" an entry. See **buy; indication of interest; sell order; specialist; underwriter.**

book value equity value of a corporation computed as total assets less intangible assets, minus liabilities and par value of preferred classes of stock. When combined with other factors, book value may indicate underpriced stock issues or relative strength of the issue in comparison between book value and market value. See **equity; net tangible assets per share; tangible value.**

bond ratio

$$\text{Bond Ratio} = \frac{\text{Bonds}}{\text{Bonds} + \text{Equity}}$$

$$= \frac{\$8.5 \text{ million}}{\$8.5 \text{ million} + \$25.5 \text{ Million}}$$

$$= 25\%$$

book value

```
                    BALANCE SHEET

Current Assets           $   835,000
Long-Term Assets           2,806,000
Intangible Assets          1,250,000
     Total Assets                       $4,891,000


Current Liabilities      $   410,000
Long-Term Liabilities      1,573,000
     Total Liabilities                  $1,983,000

Shareholders' Equity:
     Preferred Stock     $   800,000
     Common Stock          1,000,000
     Retained Earnings     1,108,000
     Total Equity                       $2,908,000

Total Liabilities and Equity            $4,891,000
```

```
                    BOOK VALUE

Total Assets             $  4,891,000
Less: Intangible Assets  (  1,250,000)
Less: Liabilities        (  1,983,000)
Less: Preferred Stock    (  1,000,000)

Book Value               $     658,000
```

book value per share   the net equity per share of stock, determined by dividing total common equity less intangibles, by the number of outstanding common shares. See **balance sheet ratios; stockholders' equity.**

Boston Stock Exchange (BSE)   One Boston Place, Boston MA 02108; the regional exchange serving the New England area and trading in the securities of area firms as well as in many NYSE-listed issues. See **regional exchanges.**

bottom out   condition of a single security or of the entire market when prices have declined as far as they will, and investor interest begins to reverse the trend. See **chartist; technical analysis.**

box   general term referring to the safekeeping of customer securities. Brokerages are required to maintain separate "box" or files for their customers' accounts, as part of the cashiering function. See **active box; cashiering; customer; hypothecation; rehypothecation; segregated account.**

book value per share

Tangible Assets	$1,864,300
Intangible Assets	500,000
Total Assets	$2,364,300
Liabilities	$1,432,000
Common Stockholders' Equity (100,000 shares)	932,300
Total	$2,364,300

$$\frac{(932,300 - 500,000)}{100,000} = \$4.323 \text{ book value per share}$$

bottom out

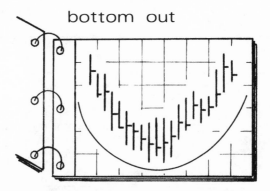

box spread   an option strategy in which a riskless transaction is set up through the use of arbitrage. Two separate spreads are entered at the same time with a built-in profit, so that regardless of what market movements occur, the trader will benefit. See **arbitrage; bear spread; bull spread; call; credit spread; debit spread; option; put; riskless transaction.**

branch office   a remote office of a securities broker-dealer which is supervised by that broker-dealer's headquarters. Subject to the rules and policies of the headquarters office, a branch is most frequently a separate Office of Supervisory Jurisdiction (OSJ) of the broker-dealer. It is headed by a designated branch manager, an individual with a general securities principal license. One OSJ may consist of more than one office location, although it is more common that a single office is active. See **broker-dealer; Office of Supervisory Jurisdiction (OSJ).**

branch office audit   the audit of an Office of Supervisory Jurisdiction. This audit may be conducted by the state securities agencies or the SEC, but the term is most commonly used in reference to a broker-dealer's audit of its own offices. Once per year, the broker-dealer sends a compliance officer or a registered principal to the

box spread

		Proceeds (Cost)
$51		
50	Sell put Oct 50 Buy call Oct 50	$ 250 (125)
49		
48 ◁─── Current Market Value of Stock		
47		
46		
45	Buy put Oct 45 Sell call Oct 45	(75) 350
Total proceeds (before commissions)		$ 400

---

branch office, where customer files, blotters, advertising materials, and other important papers and records are examined. The audit procedure is mandated by securities rules and regulations. See **broker-dealer; Securities and Exchange Commission (SEC).**

branch office manager   the individual appointed by the broker-dealer to supervise the members of a branch office (or OSJ). Usual qualifications include current possession of a general securities principal license. See **broker-dealer; general securities principal; Office of Supervisory Jurisdiction (OSJ).**

branch office manager license   the Series 12 NASD license, which qualifies individuals for office supervision in the view of the NASD. This is not to be confused with a branch manager's license or function. The Series 12 is for office management of an NASD-type operation. See **Office of Supervisory Jurisdiction (OSJ); supervision.**

breadth of the market   (1) related to the market as a whole, a measure of the percentage of total issues traded in a period, usually one day or as part of an analysis over several days in spotting a trend. Expressed as a percentage, the numerator is the

breadth index

Advances	1,014	
Declines	512	
Unchanged	446	1,014 - 512
Total issues	1,972	$\dfrac{1,014 - 512}{1,972} = 25.46\%$

number of issues traded and the denominator is the total number of issues available for trading.

(2) in analysis of relative advance and decline trends for a single day or period, or as part of an analysis of the market trend, the "breadth index" is an expression of the net advances or declines in one day. See **index; issues.**

break-away gap a term used in technical analysis, referring to an actual gap on the chart of a security. This gap is caused when price movement from one day to the next is so drastic that the range seen in one day is far removed from that of a subsequent day. See **technical analysis.**

break-away gap

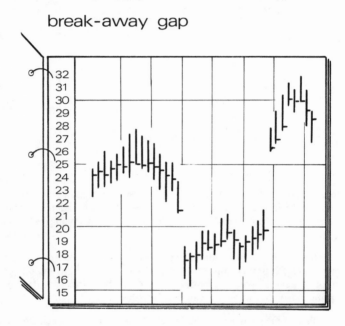

breakeven interest the computed rate of interest that must be earned on an investment to break even, after allowing for the effects of inflation and taxes.

An assumed rate of inflation is applied to reduce the balance of principal, and the tax rate is applied to reduce earnings. When the combined effect is computed, it is found that some earnings rates will result in net losses, depending upon the factors assumed for inflation and taxes.

The computation of breakeven interest is not difficult. Divide the inverse of the assumed tax rate into the assumed inflation rate. Example: in the 28% bracket, the inverse is 72 (100 less 28). If applying an inflation rate of eight percent, breakeven interest is computed as:

$$\frac{8}{(100-28)} \qquad \frac{8}{72} \quad = \quad 11.11\%$$

See **inflation: interest; tax bracket.**

break-even point (1) a closing price at which a transaction breaks even, with no profit for the investor. This should be calculated net of commission costs.

(2) a point of analysis in options trading which identifies the point above or

tax rate	rate of inflation assumed			
	8%	10%	12%	14%
28%	11.11%	13.89%	16.67%	19.44%
33%	11.94	14.93	17.91	20.90
38%	12.90	16.13	19.35	22.58
42%	13.79	17.24	20.69	24.14
45%	14.55	18.18	21.82	25.45
50%	16.00	20.00	24.00	28.00

breakeven interest

break-even point

Bought 500 shares at 16	$8,000.00
Plus: Commission	178.65
Total Cost	$8,178.65
Sold 500 shares at 16 3/4	$8,375.00
Less: Commission	(195.34)
Net Proceeds	$8,179.66

Break-even point for 500 shares purchased at 16 is 16 3/4 at the rate of commission charged.

below which a profit or loss begins to accumulate. Because the value of options decreases with time, the time value of an option will diminish to a break-even point. See **alligator spread; commission; time value.**

breaking the syndicate the ending of an underwriting agreement. Upon break, the individual underwriters are no longer held to agreed prices, and may dispose of securities for an offering. See **syndicate; underwriter.**

breakout a term used in technical analysis describing the action of a security when the chart pattern shows a sudden increase or decrease in price trends. A breakout establishes new highs or lows and a reestablished support or resistance level. See **resistance level; support level; technical analysis.**

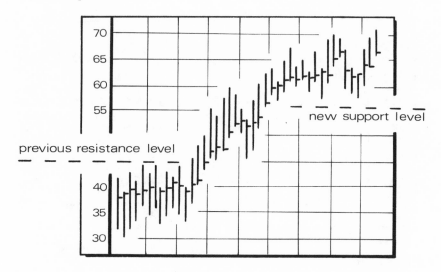

70
65
60
55

new support level

previous resistance level

40
35
30

breakout pattern

breakpoint   the point at which mutual fund commissions are lowered due to the size of a transaction. Most funds allow several breakpoints. The practice of "selling to breakpoint" involves placing a customer in shares of a mutual fund within $1,000 of the breakpoint, considered an unethical practice. See **broker; commission; mutual fund.**

broad tape   reference to one of several news services utilized by brokerages, considered "broad" because more data is included than the summary and coded data communicated on the quote boards. See **brokerage house.**

broker   a person or firm receiving a commission to act in behalf of sellers and buyers, to complete and coordinate the terms of a securities transaction. See **as agent; as principal; agent; commission; member organization.**

broker-dealer   an organization involved in the buying and selling of securities, combining the features of a broker (in the business of transacting securities for another party and earning a commission) and a dealer (in the business of making a market in a security and offering given buy and sell prices to others). See **commission; market maker; securities.**

broker loan rate   the interest rate charged by lending institutions to securities brokers for loans offering securities as collateral. See **collateral; interest; prime rate.**

brokerage house   an organization consisting of commissioned brokers and engaged in the business of buying and selling securities for customers. The term refers commonly to stock and bond firms, although many brokerages today also offer public and private syndications. See **bond; commission; stock; syndicate.**

broker's broker   an individual who buys and sells for his own account. See **dealer.**

broker's collateral loan   a call loan (may be cancelled with one-day notice by lender or borrower) made by a commercial bank to a broker for the short term. It is secured by securities held in the firm's own account or in customer margin accounts. See **call loan; commercial bank; rehypothecation; short-term debt; specialist.**

bucket shop   a description applied to organizations executing customer orders at some point later than acceptance of the order. It is hoped that the "shop" will be able to obtain a more favorable price in the security, although confirmation to the customer will be at the price originally quoted. The practice is outlawed by the Securities Exchange Act of 1934. See **Securities Exchange Act of 1934.**

bulk   a system required by the Securities and Exchange Commission to identify correct ownership of securities left with a broker. While the broker may hold a single certificate for several customers, the bulk system is a method of identifying which customer owns shares or units. See SEC **Rule 15c3-3; segregated account.**

bull   (1) a person who believes the market will rise or continue to rise in value, either generally or in regard to a specific issue or industry group, or type of security.

(2) A type of securities market in which prices and values continue to climb or are in a growth pattern.

(3) A general condition, trend or sentiment of optimism, associated with growth markets and indicative of economic and political influences favorable to growth conditions. See **bear.**

bull spread   a strategy of options trading which anticipates an underlying issue will rise in value. It involves the simultaneous purchase and sale of two options, either calls or puts, on the same security. A bull spread strategy using calls will include the sale of a call with a higher strike price and the purchase of a call with a lower strike price. The opposite combination would be used for puts.

The term applies to situations where an in-the-money option will rise in value more quickly than one subsequently transacted out of the money. The factor of depleting time value helps to make the strategy successful when taking short positions in out-of-the-money options. See **bear spread; call; credit spread; debit spread; long; option spread; put; short; strike price; time value.**

bunching   a technique used by brokerage firms combining several odd lot trades into a single, round-lot transaction. This saves paperwork and commissions are lowered as a result. See **odd lot differential; round lot.**

business conduct committee   a sub-organization of the NASD whose purpose is to hear complaints and make decisions according to the code of procedure. See **board of governors; code of procedure; District Business Conduct Committee (DBCC); National Association of Securities Dealers (NASD).**

business cycle   (1) the period of time required by a manufacturer or producer to produce finished goods.

(2) description of movement in the Gross National Product, between a previous and a new top or base line.

(3) a general term used in business to describe seasonal or annual periods identified and separated by differences in volume, profits or other activities. See **Gross National Product (GNP).**

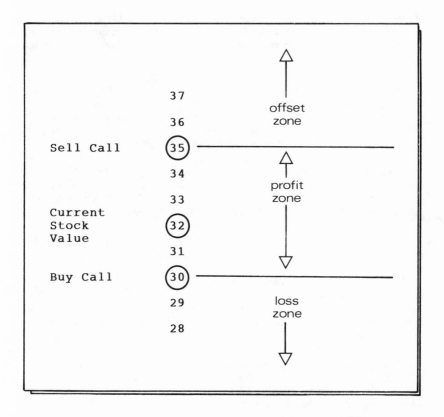

bull spread

business day   (1) in the securities industry, a day on which the stock exchanges are open for business.

(2) according to the New York Stock Exchange, a day on which New York banks transact business.

(3) a general business term identifying a working day or terms of a deadline. See **regular way.**

butterfly spread   an option technique which includes the features of a built-in small profit and little or no risk. It involves selling two calls at a middle strike price and buying one higher and one lower call. The opposite may be applied to puts (buying two in the middle range and selling a high and a low put). The butterfly spread is a combination of a bear spread and a bull spread. See **bear spread; bull spread; call; exercise price; hedge; option; short; strike price.**

buy   the act of completing a transaction in which an individual or organization takes title to a security, contract, note or option for the exchange of cash or other assets, or using margin power. See **marketable securities.**

buy in   the procedure a broker must follow when another broker fails to deliver securities as promised. The broker must "buy in" to the issue to honor a customer's

butterfly spread

		Proceeds (Cost)
61		
(60)	Buy one call, May 60	$ (100)
59		
(58) ◀——— Current Market Value		
57		
56		
(55)	Sell two calls, May 55	850
54		
53		
52		
51		
(50)	Buy one call, May 50	(650)
49		
	Net Proceeds	$ 100

order. The defaulting broker may be held liable for losses resulting from price movement resulting in a buy in. See **default; sell-out procedures.**

buy minus an order to purchase securities at a price lower than a previous price identified by the investor at a certain time. See **limit order; market order.**

buy stop order a form of market order further qualified to buy only at or above a specified price. Upon reaching or passing the identified price, the security is to be purchased at the best available price. See **market order.**

buy the book an order to buy all shares available from the specialist at the offering price, and in some cases, to buy shares from other members who will sell at the same offering price. See **specialist's book.**

buyer the purchaser of a security, contract, option or note who, by completing a transaction, takes title to the investment. See **marketable securities.**

buyer's option a contract which includes a provision for delivery of securities by a certain and specified date. See **cash contract; regular way; seller's option; when issued/distributed.**

buying climax an unexpected and dramatic increase in demand for a security, and resulting rise in price which may include chart break-away gaps. A buying climax may be the result of rumors or news, or only an indication of over-buying in a security. See **break-away gap; technical analysis.**

buying power the maximum amount a customer would be allowed to transact on margin as computed under the terms of Regulation T. See **initial margin; Reg T excess; Regulation T.**

by-laws rules and guidelines established for the operations of an organization. See **board of governors; corporation.**

C

CA an abbreviation for "callable," used in reference to bonds. See **callable bond.**

cabinet crowd slang expression referring to exchange members who engage in trading of inactive bond issues. See **active bond; inactive bond.**

cage designation for the location where the cashiering function of a brokerage business is located. The cage area is restricted to employees not engaged directly in cashiering activities. See **cashiering.**

calendar a schedule of upcoming offerings such as new bond issues or stock offerings. See **offering.**

calendar spread an option strategy in which an investor buys and sells options on an issue which have different expiration dates. If the exercise prices are identical, the strategy is a horizontal calendar spread. If strike prices are not identical, the strategy is a diagonal spread.
The strategy involves selling a short-term option and buying a long-term option on the same stock. The strategy may be applied both to calls and to puts. A spread identified as "bullish" is one in which the investor will profit if the stock's value increases. A "bearish" spread is one producing profits if the market for that stock declines.
Calendar spreads may be used as part of a combination strategy. That consists of a call calendar spread and a put calendar spread, involved at the same time. See **call; combination; diagonal spread; horizontal spread; option; put.**

call (1) an option which has a finite life and gives the owner (buyer) the right to buy a specified number of shares (100 per listed option contract) at a specified price and within the space of time up until expiration date. Upon expiration, the call option becomes worthless. It may be used strictly in speculative trading. An individual buys a call in the hope that the stock will increase in value. If it does so, the value of the call increases accordingly. Calls may be sold in two ways: a naked call (uncovered) produces premium to the seller but assumes an unspecified level of risk. A covered call is one that is sold by someone who owns 100 shares of the underlying stock, and is willing to give up those shares in the event the call is exercised.
(2) the right retained by the issuer of a callable security, to redeem that security at its own discretion, prior to maturity. See **callable bond; callable preferred stock; option.**

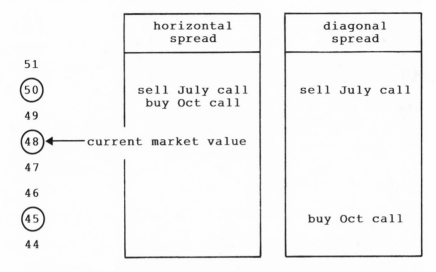

calendar spread

call feature   a characteristic of a security, referring to the issuer's right to call prior to maturity. For preferred stock, the feature provides for retirement by the corporation and payment to the investor of an amount based upon par value or current market value. For a bond, the issue may be redeemed prior to maturity. See **callable bond; callable preferred stock.**

call loan   a loan used to finance the margin trading activities of customers, which is secured by held securities or other collateral. It is designated a "call" loan as it may be called by either party and at any time. See **broker's collateral loan; margin; rehypothecation.**

call money   rate of interest that is paid on a call loan. See **broker's collateral loan; call loan.**

call premium   (1) the amount paid by the buyer and received by the seller of a call option contract. The premium varies based upon the distance between the strike price of the option and the current market value of the stock. Call premium consists of two components: intrinsic value and time value. Intrinsic value is the number of points above strike price the underlying stock has as its market value. Time value is the difference, value which will evaporate as the expiration date draws near.
(2) the payment to holders of callable bonds or preferred stock, when those securities are called in the early years outstanding, which is paid in consideration of the investor's inconvenience. See **convertible security; expiration; intrinsic value; option; strike price; time value.**

call price   the amount that will be paid by a corporation upon exercising its option to call a security. The call price is based upon par value (for bonds) or value per share (preferred stock). See **callable bond; callable preferred stock.**

Holding Period	Percentage	Premium per 100 shares
at issue	100.0%	$ 15.00
one year	87.5	13.13
two years	75.0	11.25
three years	62.5	9.38
four years	50.0	7.50
five years	37.5	5.63
six years	25.0	3.75
seven years	12.5	1.88
eight years	0	-0-

call premium amortization

call protection   the cushion of time between issue date and the first date a corporation may exercise a call provision on that security. The term may be applied generally to any security that does not contain a call provision at all. See **cushion.**

callable bond   a bond containing a call provision, under which the issuing corporation may redeem all or part of an issue upon certain dates before maturity. See **bond.**

callable preferred stock   a type of preferred stock which may, at the corporation's option, be converted to common stock at a pre-determined conversion exchange value. This stock is issued with a call premium feature which amortizes over the first several years. The premium is to be paid to the holder of the stock if it is converted. By the tenth year, this call premium normally will have amortized to nothing. See **call premium; convertible security; preferred stock.**

called away   (1) a term applied when an option is exercised by a buyer and the seller's short position is cancelled. The buyer has the right to call away shares or to force a buy-and-sell transaction by the seller to honor an option. The seller must deliver shares in the event, also called a short call.
(2) reference of the action taken by a corporation redeeming callable securities under a call provision. See **bond; option; preferred stock.**

cancellation   (1) to revoke or void an order prior to execution.
(2) to void an order after execution, with the permission and consent of the buyer/seller on the other side of that transaction. See **buy; sell order.**

cap   a ceiling on either the amount of monthly payment or the interest rate, or upon both, in an adjustable rate mortgage (ARM) contract. See **adjustable rate mortgage (ARM).**

cap rate   a method of computing historical return on past investments or pro-forma estimated return on currently offered investments. Used commonly in the public and private syndication markets, especially real estate, capitalization rate is a standard measure of relative return assumption. It takes into consideration income and expenses.

$$\text{cap rate}$$

$$\frac{(\text{annual gross income} - \text{vacancies}) - \text{operating expenses}}{\text{purchase price}} = \text{cap rate}$$

$$\frac{(\$80,000 - \$8,000) - \$16,000}{\$500,000} = 11.29\%$$

To compute, operating expenses are deducted from gross income (after allowing for a vacancy factor), and the sum divided by the purchase price. See **real estate.**

capital a broad term referring to the net value of equity of a corporation, partnership, individual, trust, or other entity. Capital is the amount of ownership, represented by the difference between assets and liabilities, generally. An organization may, however, be "capitalized" by a combination of equity and debt. In that sense, total capitalization consists of shareholders' equity and funded debt (long-term notes and bonds outstanding). See **assets; balance sheet; liabilities; shareholders' equity.**

capital activity ratio a test of the number of "turns" experienced in a period of time of tangible net worth. The average tangible net worth is divided into net sales for the period to arrive at the turnover. It is a ratio useful in trend analysis over a number of periods, and can help determine the yield value and utilization of cash flow in an organization. See **combined ratios; ratios.**

capital appreciation (1) a term applied to growth in market value of an investment.
(2) an investment objective which indicates an interest in safety of the principal amount against the effects of inflation and taxes. See **investment objective.**

capital expenditure money spent or committed for the acquisition of depreciable, depletable or amortizable assets. A capital expenditure may not be written off as a current business expense, but must be written off over a period of time. To set up an acquired asset and subject it to write-offs like depreciation, it is said that the asset is "capitalized." Generally, any asset that will have applicable utilization beyond the current year and also has a material cost must be capitalized. See **balance sheet; depreciation; fixed assets; long-term assets.**

capital gain the net gain from a transaction of a capital asset, including property, securities, futures contracts and options. A long-term capital gain is one realized on an asset held for more than six months, and is

$$\frac{\text{net sales}}{\text{average tangible net worth}} = \text{capital activity ratio}$$

net sales	$1,105,000
tangible net worth:	
beginning of period	450,000
end of period	520,000
average	485,000

$$-\frac{1,105,000}{485,000} = 2.28 \text{ turns}$$

capital activity ratio

taxed at a favorable rate. A short-term gain is one on assets held six months or less, and is taxed fully. See **assets; long-term capital gain; profit; short-term capital gain.**

capital loss the net loss from a transaction of a capital asset. Short-term losses may be deducted in full for federal tax purposes, up to the annual limit. Long-term losses may be deducted only partially. See **assets; long-term capital loss; losses; short-term capital loss.**

capital market a broad descriptive term for the institutions and instruments comprising the intermediate and long-term funding and transactions of businesses and individuals. The comparable short-term market is called the "money market."

The capital market includes the investments and issues of U.S. and foreign businesses, borrowers and individual investors, and is made up of six classifications of investment instruments: U.S. Government securities with maturities greater than one year; federal agency debts with maturities longer than one year; corporate bonds with maturities longer than one year; state and local bonds and other debts with maturities longer than one year; mortgages; and corporate stock (both common and preferred). See **investment; money market.**

capital preservation an investment objective emphasizing the safety of the principal amount and recovery of that amount after inflation and taxes have been considered. See **investment objective; principal.**

capital stock the equity capital of a corporation, including all classes of stock, both common and preferred. See **common stock; preferred stock; shareholders' equity.**

capital gains and losses

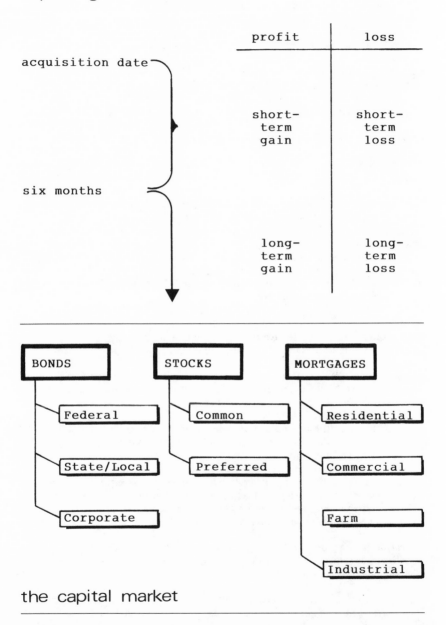

the capital market

capital surplus   the amount of capital of a corporation paid by shareholders above the par value of shares, or of Treasury stock (reacquired shares) subsequently resold and to the extent it exceeds the current par value. See **paid-in capital; par value.**

capitalization   the total investment funds of a corporation, including all classes of stock, capital surplus, retained earnings, Treasury stock, and funded debt (bonds and debentures). See **common stock; debenture; funded debt; long-term debt; preferred stock; total capitalization.**

capitalization ratios   ratios which compare or measure the relationships between funded debt and equity capital, the primary purpose of which is to determine the relative sources of capitalization: from lenders and from shareholders. See **balance sheet ratios; funded debt ratio; ownership ratios.**

carried interest   a term used in the syndication markets, particularly oil and gas programs, referring to that portion of interest in a program in which the sponsor retains equity but may not be responsible for its cost. See **oil and gas; sponsor.**

carry-over   a provision under tax laws allowing taxpayers (corporations and individuals) to apply current losses exceeding set limits or current profits, against future periods.
   A capital loss carry-over is applied against future capital gains to a future annual limit. Net operating losses are applied against future profits. And tax credits (such as the Investment Tax Credit) are carried over and applied against future tax liabilities.
   Losses and credits not applicable to annual limitations may, by some instances, also be carried back and applied against prior periods, involving a refiguring of the prior period's tax liability and application for a refund of taxes already paid. See **capital loss; tax loss carry-forward.**

carrying cost   a term describing interest expense that is payable on a liability. It is used in situations where investors purchase on margin, and is commonly used to describe option traders' margin status. See **interest; option; position.**

cash basis   (1) one of two primary accounting methods in common use, the other being accrual-basis accounting. Under the cash basis, the reporting of income, costs and expenses occurs only when cash is exchanged, regardless of the period in which earned or incurred. The principal advantage of cash accounting is its simplicity. Few journal entries are needed to close the books. The principal disadvantage is in its inaccuracy. Substantial income or deductions are not reflected on the cash basis on financial statements.
   (2) an option available to investors in Series EE bonds, whereby taxes are deferred until redemption. Under the cash basis, the difference between a discounted purchase and redemption value is taxed in one installment. The alternate method calls for taxation of a proportionate amount of the discount over the holding period. See **accrual; Series EE bond; tax basis.**

cash contract   an alternate term for "buyer's option," in which payment for a securities trade is due on the day of the trade itself. See **buyer's option; regular way; seller's option; when issued/distributed.**

cash delivery   a term applied to settlement of a trade under a cash contract, where payment is made on the same day as the security transaction. See **delayed delivery; regular way.**

cash flow   an accounting term describing the positive or negative effect on cash generated from operations. It is computed as the total net income plus depreciation accruals, and adjusted for other sources and applications of funds. Available cash

Cash Flow

Cash-basis net income	$ 835,000
Plus: non-cash expenses:	
Depreciation	42,000
Amortization	16,000
Plus: other sources of funds:	
Loan proceeds	55,000
Sale of assets	12,000
Less: Applications of funds:	
Repayment of loan principal	(12,000)
Dividends paid	(92,000)
Purchase of assets	(110,000)
Cash Flow	$ 746,000

---

may be used to purchase fixed assets, reduce accounts or taxes payable, or declare and pay dividends. Net profits may be used to reduce liabilities or allow an increase in receivables or inventory. In addition to net profits, cash flow may come from loan proceeds, increases in receivables, or the sale of assets. See **amortization; depletion; depreciation; dividend; net income.**

cash management bill   a very short-term debt security issued by the U.S. Government to provide cash balances for a few days only. See **debt security; short-term debt.**

cash-on-cash   a simple method of computing return on investment, in which the distributions are divided by the amount of the original investment. Not considered is the time involved to yield the return, nor the timing of periodic investments. It is the most common method of calculating non-annual yield, while it does not reflect a true return when investments held for differing periods are subjected to this calculation and then compared. See **return; yield.**

$$\frac{distributions}{invested\ cash} = cash\text{-}on\text{-}cash\ return$$

cash-on-cash

cash on delivery also called "delivery versus payment," a reference to the payment for a security trade upon receipt of a certificate or other document showing a transfer of ownership. See **buy; delivery versus payment (DVP).**

cash ratio a ratio which measures a company's immediately available liquid assets against the current liabilities, the purpose of which is to judge that company's ability to meet immediate and payable demands. It is computed by dividing the total of cash and marketable securities, by the total of current liabilities. See **acid test ratio; quick asset ratio.**

cash ratio

$$\frac{(cash + marketable\ securities)}{current\ liabilities} = cash\ ratio$$

cash sale (1) reference to any security sale made under a "cash on delivery" arrangement, in which payment is made on the same day as the transaction.

(2) an accounting term describing a sale paid in cash, as opposed to one made on credit. In cash of a cash sale, the asset account (cash) is increased and offset by an increase in the revenue account (sales). Under a credit sale, a different asset account (accounts receivable) is increased, to be offset later when cash is received. See **cash on delivery; regular way.**

cash value (1) the current value of an option if it were to be exercised. The amount by which a call option is in the money, for example, is the current cash value of that option contract.

(2) the net value of a security or group of securities in a portfolio if liquidated. An investor may have "paper" profits or losses which will not be realized unless liquidated. In this case, the net value of those holdings is the current cash value.

(3) an accounting term applied in several ways. Cash value of an asset is the amount to be realized in an outright sale, regardless of the book (net of depreciation value). The term may also be applied to current valuation of inventories or to accounts receivable that have been factored or discounted. See **intrinsic value; option; value.**

cashiering a department of a broker-dealer which handles security certificates, cash and other negotiable instruments; the transfer of borrowed funds, and receipt and payment of collateral loans and other cash transactions of the organization. See **back office; broker-dealer.**

cattle breeding a classification of investments in both public and private syndication markets, which emphasizes a cattle herd's expansion, often through artificial insemination methods. This is considered a high-risk type of syndication which offers significant tax deferral achieved through depreciation deductions and investment tax credits, and potential capital gains upon sale. See **investment program; tax-advantaged investment.**

cattle feeding   a form of investment program found in both public and private syndications, which assumes that the eventual value of livestock will exceed the cost of feed. This form of investment carries high risks and offers short-term tax deferral for investors. See **investment program; tax-advantaged investment.**

cemetery spread   a slang expression used to describe a spread strategist's consequences when an option or index takes a direction other than anticipated. See **bear spread; bull spread.**

central bank   one of the Federal Reserve member banks in one of twelve district cities (Atlanta, Georgia; Boston, Massachusetts; Cleveland, Ohio; Chicago, Illinois; Dallas, Texas; Kansas City, Missouri; Minneapolis, Minnesota; New York, New York; Philadelphia, Pennsylvania; Richmond, Virginia; San Francisco, California; or St. Louis, Missouri). See **Federal Reserve Bank.**

Central Certificate Service (CCS)   now called the Depository Trust Company. See **Depository Trust Company (DTC).**

central registration depository (CRD)   a system which has automated and tracks the registration records of broker-dealer representatives for the states in which they transact business. The CRD system enables broker-dealers to file the same information in several states at once, and upon the same anniversary date for annual renewals, making the annual registration process much simpler than under previous systems, requiring individual registration in each state. See **broker-dealer; registered representative.**

certificate   a document proving ownership of a security, which is engraved and watermarked to discourage forging. A certificate includes the name and exact registration of the security's owner. Upon transfer, the certificate is endorsed and transferred to a new owner. Certificates are not used for registration of options, treasury securities and many agency bonds, replaced by computerized entry of ownership in the issuer's record-keeping system. Even for securities requiring certificates, investors may avoid taking possession of the document by registering in "street name." See **issue; negotiable instrument; street name.**

certificate of beneficial interest   a term describing shares or units of ownership in organizations investing primarily in the debts of other organizations. A beneficial interest is held in the debt (such as a mortgage or bond). The term is used in place of "common stock." See **debt security; equity security.**

certificate of deposit (CD)   shortened version of a certificate of time deposit, a CD is issued to investors from commercial banks, in amounts of $100,000 or more. CD's pay fixed interest and may be sold in the secondary market before maturity. See **debt security; Regulation Q; time deposit.**

certificate of incorporation   the document issued by a state corporate division or secretary of state, identifying a corporation as an approved and legal company in that state. See **corporation.**

certificate of indebtedness   a Treasury issue issued between $1,000 and $500 million, and with maturities up to one year. These are similar to T-bills with the exception that they pay a fixed rate of interest. See **bearer bond; bond; coupon; Treasury bill; yield to maturity.**

certificate of limited partnership   a notification which is made public, announcing the formation and purpose of a new limited partnership. This is required under provisions of the Uniform Limited Partnership Act. See **limited partnership; Uniform Limited Partnership Act (ULPA).**

Certified Financial Planner (CFP)   a recognized standard in the financial planning industry, the CFP degree is achieved by those undertaking a course of study offered by the College for Financial Planning, which is headquartered in Denver, Colorado. The course is studied and exams given in several major sections, and requires two years or more of study, covering all aspects of the financial planning business. See **financial planner; investment advisor.**

charities   recognized as a means for tax shelter, especially for those in the highest brackets. Individuals donate assets to the charity which may have an assessed valuation sufficient to reduce taxes and brackets. See **investment program; tax shelter.**

chartist   the name given to one who watches the movements of a security's price and recommends buying or selling activities based upon those movements. See **point and figure chart; technical analysis.**

Chicago Board of Trade (CBT)   141 Jackson Blvd., Chicago IL 60604; the largest futures trading exchange and parent company of the Chicago Board Options Exchange (CBOE). See **exchange; futures contract.**

Chicago Board Options Exchange (CBOE)   LaSalle at Van Buren, Chicago IL 60605; the national exchange for the trading of option contracts, founded in 1973 specifically to transact calls and puts. See **exchange; option.**

Chicago Mercantile Exchange (CME)   30 S. Wacker Drive, Chicago IL 60606; commodity futures exchange and parent company of the International Monetary Market. See **commodity; futures contract; International Monetary Market (IMM).**

churning   a practice of registered representatives under which the motivation for trading in a client's account is to generate commissions rather than to make a profit in the trade itself. The practice is unethical and may result in penalties to the registered representative upon discovery, resulting from audit or complaint. See **alligator spread; broker; customer complaint; registered representative.**

Cincinnati Stock Exchange (CSE)   205 Dixie Terminal Bldg., Cincinnati OH 45202; an exchange using a fully automated system for all trading. Brokers communicate and place transactions via remote terminals, eliminating the need for a trading floor and on-site activities. See **exchange.**

claim of exemption   a means by which sales of limited partnership units are sold without the otherwise required registration. To qualify, issuers must meet standards as dictated by the state. See **issuer; limited partnership; offering; registration statement.**

class   (1) a term describing groups of options on the same security sharing common features such as exercise limitation.
(2) classification of securities of the same type or sharing some characteristics (classes of bonds or common stocks, for example). See **option; security.**

class life categories of assets under the accelerated cost recovery system (ACRS), each identified by the period of time over which depreciation may be claimed. See **accelerated cost recovery system (ACRS); fifteen-year property; five-year property; ten-year property; three-year property.**

clearance (1) reference to completion of a securities trade, when payment is made and securities are delivered.
(2) netting of trades before settlement is made. See **delivery.**

clearing member a member organization of the New York Stock Exchange whose clearance is handled by the Stock Clearing Corporation. Clearing activities include the handling of trade business by a relatively small number of members representing those trades generated by all clearing members. See **New York Stock Exchange (NYSE); Stock Clearing Corporation (SCC).**

Clifford Trust a short-term trust whereby assets are placed to produce income that is taxed to the trust to beneficiaries in lower tax brackets. The trust must be established for more than 10 years before the grantor may reclaim income-producing assets. See **inter vivos trust; trust.**

climax a substantial change in a security's price, which is characterized by a corresponding increase in volume. See **buying climax; selling climax; volume.**

close (1) the last transaction in a security for a trading day.
(2) the last half minute of a trading day ("the close") for a public exchange.
(3) the transfer of assets after an issue has been underwritten and fully placed with investors.
(4) the price at which a listed security ends a trading day, or the column in a financial listing showing the closing price of a security. See **offering; transfer.**

closed-end (1) an investment or management company which issues a fixed number of shares. These shares may be traded in the secondary market and are not generally redeemed by the management company itself. Closed-end shares are listed and traded on exchanges in most cases.
(2) reference to prior claim by first mortgage holders, prohibiting a property owner from pledging property or collateral already pledged, to obtain additional financing, without prior permission from that mortgage holder. See **investment company; listed stock; mortgage; secondary market.**

closed-end provision allowance favoring the first bondholders in a mortgage bond when the same assets are pledged on more than one issue. The provision entitles first bondholders to seniority in claims, over subsequent bondholders. See **indenture; mortgage bond.**

closed position reference to the status of a risk that has been cancelled by an offsetting transaction. If an investor is "long" (owns the securities), that position may be closed by selling the same securites. A "short" position (in which an investor has sold a security) is closed by purchase of the same security. See **buy; long; sell order; short.**

closing price (1) prices in effect at the end of a trading session (at the close).
(2) Price at which an open position (long or short) is closed and, thereby, eliminated as a position. See **at the close; settlement date.**

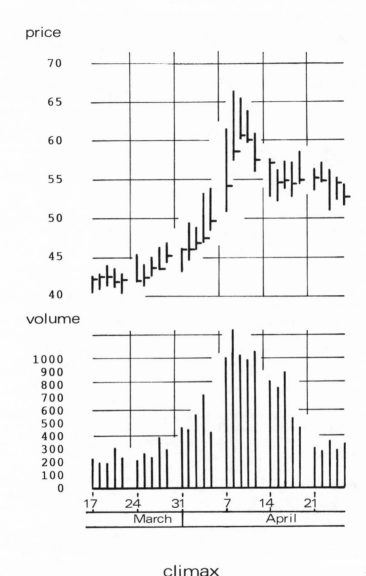

climax

---

closing purchase transaction   action taken by an investor in a short position, whereby that position is eliminated. See **long; short.**

closing quote   the effective asked and bid prices of a security as of the close of a trading session. See **asked price; bid.**

closing sale transaction   action taken by an investor in a long position, whereby that position is eliminated. See **long; short.**

closely-held corporation any corporation in which a substantial portion of the voting shares are held by a small number of shareholders. But, as opposed to a privately-held corporation, there may be trading in the stock in the secondary market by minority shareholders. See **corporation; secondary market; shareholder.**

C.O.D. trade reference used in the securities business to identify a trade in which the securities are paid for upon delivery. See **delivery; delivery versus payment (DVP).**

C.O.D. transaction any transaction made with the stipulation that payment will be made upon delivery of the security, common to institutional orders. See **delivery versus payment (DVP); institutional investor.**

code of arbitration standards guiding the facility established by the National Association of Securities Dealers (NASD) for review, arbitration and settlement of disputes between members and other members or customers. See **board of arbitration; National Association of Securities Dealers (NASD).**

code of procedure guidelines for the actions of NASD District Business Conduct Committees regarding disciplinary proceedings arising from member firm violations of the rules of fair practice. The district in which such actions are taken may be either that district in which the violating party's principal office is located, or the one in which a violation occurred. See **board of governors; District Business Conduct Committee (DBCC); member organization; National Association of Securities Dealers (NASD); rules of fair practice.**

collateral (1) general term used to describe assets that are pledged by a borrower to ensure repayment of a loan.
(2) the loan value of securities that may be used to transact on margin, used in reference to uncovered option writing activities. See **loan value; uncovered option.**

collateral trust bond a type of bond which is secured by securities held in trust as a guarantee of redemption to the bondholders. The trustee may be a commercial bank or other independent agency, and such bond issues may specify that full redemption will occur if the trust-held securities decline to or below the total issue's value. See **debt security; trustee.**

collectibles any tangible asset which may serve as an investment, in the hope that it will appreciate in value. Classified as non-securities for the purpose of jurisdiction by the Securities and Exchange Commission, collectibles as investments contain specific risks: they may be illiquid; valuation can be subjective; and the demand and market are subject to substantial price fluctuations. Most popular among collectibles are rare coins and stamps. See **investment program.**

collection ratio a comparison between accounts receivable and average daily sales, the purpose of which is to determine how many days it takes to collect the average dollar of sales on credit. It is a ratio useful in controlling trends in credit sales, especially when applied over a period of time. Seasonal changes allowed for, the moving trend indicates increasing or decreasing ability of an organization to control the level of outstanding receivables in comparison to the sales volume. See **combined ratios; ratios; sales.**

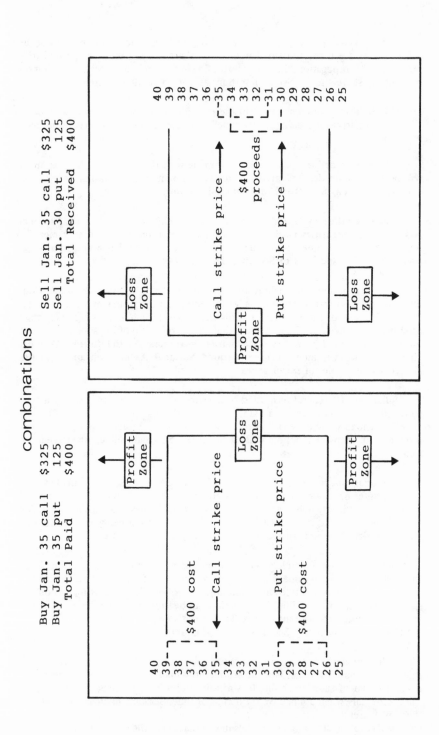

combinations

Buy Jan. 35 call $325
Buy Jan. 35 put   125
      Total Paid $400

Sell Jan. 35 call $325
Sell Jan. 30 put   125
    Total Received $400

$$\frac{\text{Accounts Receivable}}{\text{Average Daily Sales}} = \text{Collection Ratio}$$

$$\frac{\$1,835,000}{\$104,000} = 17.6 \text{ days}$$

collection ratio

combination   any option strategy which combines the purchase or sale of options of the same security, but with different strike prices, different exercise prices, or both. Risks and potential profits are varied by purchasing or selling options relative to strike prices. Combination investors, for example, may buy a call and a put on the same security but with different strike prices, creating profit zones above or below a given point. Or one may sell a call and a put on the same security, creating a restricted profit zone. Any movement of the stock above or below that zone would result in a loss on the strategy. See **expiration date; long; short; straddle; strike price.**

combination program   an oil and gas program which contains elements of exploration and development programs, which reduces the risks and maximizes the potential return of the investment. See **oil and gas; syndicate.**

combined ratios   ratios comparing balance sheet account balances to accounts on the income statement. See **ratios.**

commercial bank   a banking organization engaging in the granting of short-term loans, transactions on checking and savings accounts, trust services and safekeeping facilities, for its customers.
Nationally chartered commercial banks are subject to supervision by the Comptroller of the Currency and regulations of the Federal Reserve. State chartered commercial banks are regulated by the state banking agencies and also by the Fed and the FDIC, if they are members of those agencies. See **demand deposit; Federal Deposit Insurance Corporation (FDIC); Federal Reserve Board (FRB); time deposit.**

commercial paper   bearer obligations that are unsecured and issued for terms of nine months or less. Sold at a discount, they are redeemed for face value, and are issued for amounts between $100,000 and $1 million. See **discount; face value; money market instrument; short-term debt; unsecured debt.**

commercial property   non-residential investment property included as investments in public and private real estate syndications, which include office buildings, hotels and motels, shopping centers and industrial parks. See **private placement; public offering; real estate; syndicate.**

commingled funds   funds and securities mixed in with the funds or securities

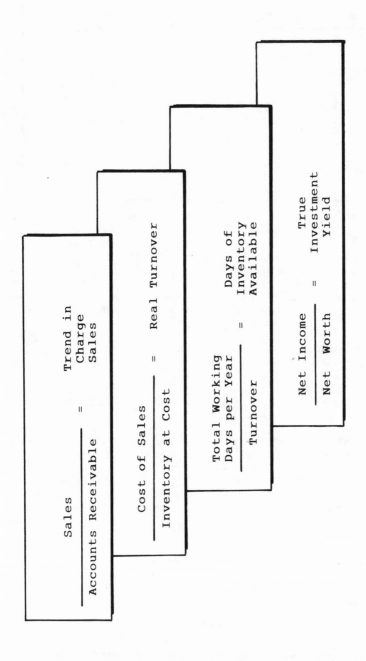

$$\frac{\text{Sales}}{\text{Accounts Receivable}} = \text{Trend in Charge Sales}$$

$$\frac{\text{Cost of Sales}}{\text{Inventory at Cost}} = \text{Real Turnover}$$

$$\frac{\text{Total Working Days per Year}}{\text{Turnover}} = \text{Days of Inventory Available}$$

$$\frac{\text{Net Income}}{\text{Net Worth}} = \text{True Investment Yield}$$

combined ratios

of the brokerage firm or its agent. The practice is prohibited by regulation and by law. See **customer; segregated account.**

commission   a fee representing a broker's income from handling a securities transaction for a client. Commissions are established in advance, and may be modified based upon a dollar amount of number of shares or units purchased or sold. See **breakpoint; broker; concession.**

commission broker   (1) one who acts in an agency capacity for customers in buying and selling securities.
(2) one who transacts in securities for an organization or his or her own account, referred to as a commission house broker. See **broker; concession.**

Committee of Corporate Finance (CCF)   an agency of the NASD, created to review new issues, and approve or reject based upon conditions in submitted documents. See **issue; National Association of Securities Dealers (NASD); new issue.**

Committee on Uniform Securities Identification Procedures (CUSIP)   an NASD agency whose responsibility it is to provide identification numbers for all listed stocks and bonds. The CUSIP number is unique to each security, consisting of seven numbers and two letters for computerized identification. See **National Association of Securities Dealers (NASD); securities.**

commodity   a consumer good, in which investments may be made through transactions in commodity futures contracts. A futures contract is purchased to create a long position, or sold for a short position.
The futures contract is for delivery of a specified amount and grade of a commodity at a time and date in the future. A price is agreed upon in advance by the buyer and the seller, and the value of a futures contract varies with the supply and demand for and in the commodity itself.
Factors such as crop quality and quantity, the weather and its effect on crops, and interest in the general market, will all affect commodities futures. A substantial level of risk is assumed in speculating in futures, and skill, knowledge and experience are required to trade in commodities successfully. See **Commodity Futures Trading Commission (CFTC); futures contract; Kansas City Board of Trade (KCBT); speculation.**

commodity broker   a broker licensed to transact futures contracts and who has passed the NASD Series 3 (National Commodity Futures Exam). See **National Association of Securities Dealers (NASD); registered representative.**

Commodity Credit Corporation (CCC)   an organization which makes loans secured by commodities and assists the commodities market by buying, selling, and transporting. The CCC was organized with a $100 million appropriation to support the farm price support program. See **futures contract.**

Commodity Exchange of New York (COMEX)   4 World Trade Center, New York NY 10048; a major center for transactions in commodity futures contracts. See **commodity; exchange; futures contract.**

Commodity Futures Trading Commission (CFTC)   the regulatory agency of the commodities industry, charged with the responsibility to prevent market corners, manipulation, and communication of false or misleading information about the market. See **corner; futures contract; manipulation.**

commodity spread   a strategy employed by experienced commodities traders, which involves the buy and sell of futures contracts at the same time, to take advantage of price movements in different commodities.

There are three classifications of commodity spread: (a) intra-commodity, involving a buy and sell in the same commodity but in different contract months; (b) inter-market spread, in which the same contract is bought and sold on different exchanges to take advantage of price variations; and (c) inter-commodity spread, the buy and sell of different commodities that are expected to act in relationship to one another. See **long; short; spread.**

commodity spreads

	Jul	Oct	Jan
Intra-Commodity Spread			
Soybeans contract	Sell	Buy	
Inter-Market Spread			
Cotton contract (Chicago)			Sell
Cotton contract (Kansas City)			Buy
Inter-Commodity Spread			
Corn contract	Sell		
Wheat contract	Buy		

common stock   a unit representing partial ownership in a corporation. Common stock provides the owner with voting rights. However, dividends are paid only after preferred stock dividends have been satisfied. In case of dissolution, common stock investors have last claim on the assets of the corporation, after bondholders, creditors and preferred stockholders. See **equity; shareholders' equity; stockholder; voting rights.**

common stock equivalent   (1) any form of security which may be converted into common stock, either at the option of the corporation or the holder of the equivalent. All convertible securities fall into this classification, as do calls, rights and warrants. See **call; convertible security; rights; warrant.**

common stock ratio   a ratio comparing the common stock to total capitalization, to determine the relative ownership of a corporation's equity between bondholders, preferred stockholders and common stockholders (total capitalization). See **capitalization; ratios; total capitalization.**

common stock ratio

```
   Outstanding
   Common   Stock
   ─────────────────    =    common stock ratio
       Total
   Capitalization
```

competitive market maker   an exchange member who transacts in any issue of the NYSE, as requested by another broker or a floor official. The competitive market maker is not restricted to a specified number of securities, as is a specialist. See **floor official; market maker; specialist.**

competitive trader   an exchange member who transacts on the floor of the exchange, for his own account or the account of his firm. See **floor trader; registered trader.**

complaint file   a file maintained in the Office of Supervisory Jurisdiction (branch office) of a broker-dealer, as prescribed by NASD regulations. The file must be maintained, even if there are no actual customer complaints. In the event a complaint is received, it must be kept in the file, and a copy sent to the broker-dealer. See **branch office; broker-dealer; National Association of Securities Dealers (NASD); Office of Supervisory Jurisdiction (OSJ).**

compliance   (1) acting in accordance with the rules, regulations and laws of agencies having jurisdiction over the activities of the entity.
(2) a term used by broker-dealers referring to their activities in determining that all branch office operations, reviews of investment programs, and actions of affiliates and employees, are in accord with broker-dealer and regulatory policies and rules.
(3) an activity of the broker-dealer concerned with ensuring that all employees, officers and affiliates are acting in accordance with the rules and regulations of the industry. An appointed compliance officer ensures full compliance through branch office audits, monitoring of the activities in the branch office, and production of policies and procedures. See **branch office; broker-dealer; due diligence; Office of Supervisory Jurisdiction (OSJ); supervision.**

compliance manual   a policy and procedures document developed and published by the compliance department of a broker-dealer, dictating corporate rules for conduct of branch office affiliates. See **broker-dealer; Office of Supervisory Jurisdiction (OSJ); supervision.**

composite index   an index of the market as a whole, expressed in dollars and cents. The daily composite increase or decrease in overall values does not reflect values accurately, as it is not weighted. But the composite index is referred to often because it is easily comprehended by a large number of investors. See **index.**

compound interest   interest accrued or earned when interest is paid on previously accrued interest in the account. Compounding has the effect of producing a higher rate of return than simple interest, and may be computed under several methods, including daily (based on a 360 or 365-day year); monthly, or quarterly. See **interest; yield.**

$1,000 savings	8% simple	monthly compounding	quarterly compounding
January		$ 6.67	
February		6.71	
March		6.76	$ 20.00
April		6.79	
May		6.85	
June		6.89	20.40
July		6.94	
August		6.98	
September		7.04	20.81
October		7.07	
November		7.13	
December	$ 80.00	7.17	21.22
Total	$ 80.00	$ 83.00	$ 82.43
Annual Yield	8.00%	8.30%	8.24%

compound interest

concession   compensation to a broker-dealer or member of a selling group, based upon the units or shares of an offering that are placed with investment clients. The "dealer gross concession" referred to in offering circulars and prospectuses is the total amount paid. From this, the broker-dealer computes and pays a commission to the brokers or representatives actually selling shares or units to customers. See **broker-dealer; commission; selling group.**

condominium   residential property in which owners of individual attached units share ownership in common areas and land, seen as part of real estate partnerships. See **real estate.**

conduit theory   reference to tax treatment of taxable earnings in real estate investment trusts (REITs) and mutual funds. Taxable earnings are assigned to investors and are not paid by the organization itself. Subchapter M of the Internal Revenue Code allows such treatment for mutual funds and legislation passed in 1960 allowed similar treatment to REITs. See **mutual fund; real estate investment trust (REIT); regulated investment company; Subchapter M.**

confidence index   a measure of investor sentiment in which high-grade and low-grade bond yields are compared. The "Confidence Theory" states that it is the sentiment of investors in the economy which affects prices of securities. The index is published by *Barrons* each week. See **Barron's Confidence Index; technical analysis.**

confirmation   a document prepared and mailed by brokerage houses for every trade executed for a customer. The confirmation states the date, issue trade, whether it was a buy or a sell, the price per share or unit, and the total amount to be paid or received.
The confirmation allows the customer to determine that the right issue was traded for the right price, and also serves as an invoice when settlement is to be made

for a purchase by remitting payment, rather than from deposited funds. Copies of confirmations are retained by the brokerage house as part of its customer filing system. See **broker; order ticket;** SEC **Rule 10b-10.**

conflict of interest   any situation in which someone who has control, influence or authority may also benefit personally from actions or decisions made or taken. In the securities business, a conflict may arise for general partners if they also control or own organizations providing service to a partnership (such as other programs in which the new program may invest; banking and financing relationships; and the negotiation and payment of placement or transaction fees).

Any agent or representative offering and selling investments to customers may have a conflict of interest when that same person is a general partner in an investment program. See **broker-dealer; general partner; registered representative; sponsor.**

conglomerate   a corporation whose operations are diversified over a number of different industries and products. See **corporation; diversification.**

consolidated balance sheet   a financial statement reflecting the status of assets, liabilities and equity for all subsidiaries in the organization. See **balance sheet; financial statement.**

consolidated mortgage bond   a term bond devised and issued to refund previously issued mortgage bonds with varying maturities. The consolidated bond has a single interest rate and may replace a number of other bonds with widely varying rates. See **mortgage bond; term bond.**

Consolidated Tape System (CTS**)**   a coordination service reporting the specifics of all trades, through the major exchanges. Its advantage is the central reporting it provides, regardless of origin (one of the other exchanges or the over-the-counter market).

The system consists of two "networks": network A reports in the New York Stock Exchange and regional exchanges; and network B provides similar reporting for the American Stock Exchange and regional exchanges. Actual name of the system is the Consolidated Transaction Reporting System. See **American Stock Exchange (**AMEX**); New York Stock Exchange (**NYSE**); network A; network B.**

constant dollar plan   a method of investing in which one keeps an established level of funds invested. Depending upon market movements, the dollar amount is kept constant through buying or selling of securities. See **investment; investor basis.**

constant ratio plan   a method of investing in which a constant relationship is maintained between two unlike security categories, most often between stocks and bonds. The percentage maintained in each category is kept constant. As the market changes, the ratio is maintained by buy/sell trades to offset price movements in each. See **investment objective.**

construction and development REIT   a type of real estate investment trust which is structured for the purpose of financing construction activities. Investors' funds are used to provide short-term loans to developers and construction companies. See **real estate investment trust (**REIT**).**

construction bond   a bond issued to ensure completion of construction, also known as a completion bond or a construction completion bond. See **bond; real estate.**

Confirmation

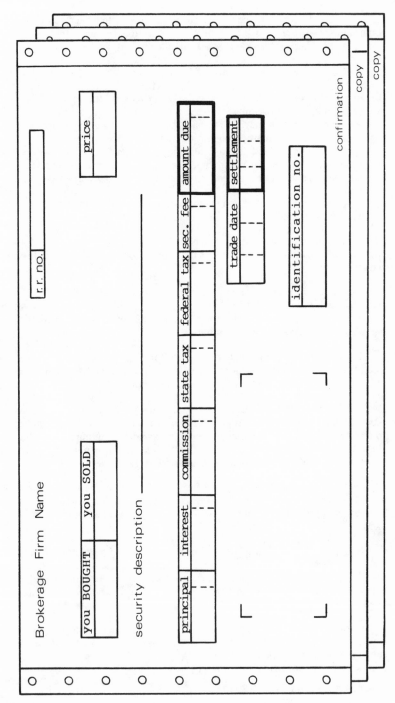

Consolidated Balance Sheet

	Subsidiary A	Subsidiary B	Holding Company	Consolidated Statement
Cash	$ 42,000	$ 827,000	$ 152,000	$1,021,000
Accounts Receivable	525,000	–	–	525,000
Inventory	410,000	385,000	–	795,000
Total Current Assets	$ 977,000	$1,212,000	$ 152,000	$2,341,000
Long-Term Assets	$ 866,000	$ 300,000	$ 42,000	$1,208,000
Less: Reserve for Depreciation	(418,000)	(107,000)	(18,000)	(543,000)
Net Long-Term Assets	$ 448,000	$ 193,000	$ 24,000	$ 665,000
Total Assets	$1,425,000	$1,405,000	$ 176,000	$3,006,000
Accounts Payable	$ 335,000	$ 597,000	$ 49,000	$ 981,000
Accrued Taxes	118,000	80,000	28,000	226,000
Notes Payable	200,000	–	35,000	235,000
Total Liabilities	$ 653,000	$ 677,000	$ 112,000	$1,442,000
Shareholders' Equity	$ 772,000	$ 728,000	$ 64,000	$1,564,000
Total Liabilities and Equity	$1,425,000	$1,405,000	$ 176,000	$3,006,000

Consumer Price Index (CPI) an index published by the U.S. Department of Labor, Bureau of Labor Statistics. Full name is Consumer Price Index for All Urban Consumers (CPI-U). It measures the prices of consumer goods and services, including food, transportation, entertainment, housing and medical care costs.

The Consumer Price Index for Urban Wage Earners and Clerical Earners (CPI-W) measures only those prices paid by salaried and wage-earning employees. See **deflation; index; inflation.**

contingent order an order that is to be executed only if a specified price can be attained. See **buy; sell order; swap order; switch order.**

continuing commissions payments to a registered representative that are made after that individual has left an organization. The vesting of commissions will occur for mutual fund sales where the investor makes a periodic payment, or for investments which are made over several stages, if so specified in a contract with the representative and the broker-dealer.

Continuing commissions are restricted in some cases, when the representative allows an NASD license to lapse, or when the license is taken away for disciplinary reasons. See **broker-dealer; registered representative; staged payment.**

continuous net settlement (CNS) practice of settling daily transactions between brokers, in which the net increase or decrease in accounts is recorded and carried forward. It allows for elimination of paperwork that would otherwise be required. The National Securities Clearing Corporation coordinates and controls CNS reporting. See **National Securities Clearing Corporation (NSCC); net transaction; window settlement.**

contract sheet a report prepared each day by the Securities Industry Automation Corporation (SIAC) reflecting all details of trades that day. It enables brokers to verify information and to correct any errors before settlement dates. See **Securities Industry Automation Corporation (SIAC); trade.**

contractual plan a form of mutual fund investment whereby the customer agrees to deposit a specified sum each month or quarter, over a period of time (commonly 10 or 15 years). It allows for the accumulation of holdings to a specified and desired level. Such plans may include provisions for life insurance which decreases over the term of the savings program. See **investment company; mutual fund; plan company; single purchase contract; voluntary accumulation program.**

control person owner of 10 percent or more of a corporation's stock; who is a corporate officer or director; or who is in a position to control or influence the policies and decisions in the corporation. See **affiliated person.**

control stock the shares of stock held by a control person, or the combined shares held and controlled by members of one family. See **affiliated person.**

controller's department the back office department of an organization responsible for the recording and reporting of transactions, preparation of financial statements, and filing of reports with regulatory agencies. See **back office; financial statement; net capital requirement.**

conventional option an unlisted option, or one not approved by the Options Clearing Corporation. It may have strike price or expiration terms not in standing with those of listed options. See **Options Clearing Corporation (OCC); over-the-counter (OTC); unlisted security.**

conversion   (1) a characteristic of a bond or preferred stock issue, allowing for the exchange of the security for a predetermined number of common shares.

(2) a benefit of real estate investing, allowing the deduction of ordinary losses at full tax rates and the reporting of capital gains at more favorable tax rates.

(3) a provision in some mutual fund contracts for the exchange of one fund's shares for the shares of another fund under the same management, without the assessment of an additional sales charge.

(4) a reference to the taking of a long position in stock when the same investor holds a put option on the same issue.

(5) an illegal practice of using the assets of another, held in trust, for one's own advantage. See **bond; capital gain; conversion ratio; convertible security; family of funds; mutual fund; option; parity; preferred stock.**

conversion arbitrage   a strategy in which an investor who holds shares of an issue sells a call and buys a put with the same expiration date. The premium on each option offsets, so the cost of the strategy is near zero. It is described as "riskless" because the basis of the stock is protected within the term of the options, regardless of market movement. See **arbitrage; option; reversal arbitrage.**

conversion arbitrage

Purchase 100 share
at $33 per share:

38

37

36

(35)   Sell call $ (350)

34

(33) ◄─Current value

32

31

(30)   Buy put $ 350

29
                                    ─────────
Net cost of options $ 0

conversion premium   the difference in value between market value and conversion value in a convertible security. The lower the premium, the more risk is associated with the common stock into which conversion may be made. The higher the premium, the higher the risk of the convertible security itself. See **bond; convertible security; market value; parity.**

Current bond price, 96	$ 960
Conversion parity, 91	910
Conversion premium (5.5%)	$ 50

conversion premium

conversion price   the price of common stock at which conversion can be made, as listed on the indenture at the time of issue. The number of shares of common stock available per $1,000 bond is determined by dividing $1,000 by the conversion price. See **convertible security; market value; par value; underlying security.**

conversion ratio   the comparison of the number of shares of common stock available per share of a convertible security (stock or bond). Investors purchase convertibles to enjoy the privilege of seniority and to maintain flexibility.
Seniority for convertible preferred stockholders relates to the order in which investors are to be paid liquidation values in the case of dissolution. For bondholders, creditor status takes precedence over all stockholders. Yet, the investor has the option to cancel a debt obligation by converting, and becoming a shareholder. Convertibles are then traded for common stock. See **common stock; conversion price; convertible security; parity; preferred stock.**

conversion value   the value of common shares which would be available upon conversion. The value varies as the common stock's value changes. See **market value; par value.**

converted put   a form of investment not involving a listed security. The broker takes a short position and protects the transaction by buying a call on the same issue. The resulting "synthetic" put is taken by the customer representing the broker's position. See **strategy; synthetic put.**

convertible security   a corporate security that can be exchanged for a number of common shares of the same corporation. Convertibles may be bonds or preferred stock. Convertibles are considered a conservative investment, and will yield a lower rate of return than non-convertible bonds or preferred stock. See **bond; parity; preferred stock.**

cooling-off period   a 20-day period which must elapse between the filing date of a new registration and the date that sales may begin. This period was legislated in the Securities Act of 1933. See **issuer; registration statement; Securities Act of 1933; underwriter.**

corner   the ability to influence, control and manipulate the market value of a particular security, through ownership of a substantial portion of the shares outstanding in that security. Cornering a market is illegal. See **manipulation; market place.**

corporate bond   a debt of a corporation issued for a period of five years or more, also broadly referred to as a debt financing device. In order to raise capital without issuing more stock or obtaining financing from a bank or other institution, bond issues are offered. Corporate bonds include the following types: mortgage bond, collateral trust bond, debenture and equipment trust bonds. See **collateral trust bond; debenture; debt security; equipment trust bond; mortgage bond.**

Corporate Financing Committee   a group reporting to the NASD board of governors, whose purpose it is to examine filings and offerings from underwriters, and review for reasonable assumptions and terms of the offering. See **board of governors; National Association of Securities Dealers (NASD); Securities and Exchange Commission (SEC); underwriter.**

corporate income fund   a unit investment trust investing in fixed income securities and providing distributions to investors on a regular basis. See **fixed income fund; income bond; unit investment trust.**

corporate retirement plan   a qualified plan (I.R.S.–approved) established for accumulation of retirement assets in a tax-deferred account; current deductions for the corporation making contributions; and a competitive and valuable employee benefit.
It may take two principal forms: pension plan or profit-sharing plan. Pension plans provide fixed benefits upon retirement, while the benefits of profit-sharing plans vary depending upon the level of profit. Contributions in a profit-sharing plan are assigned to participating employees via a formula, usually based upon income and years of employment. See **defined benefit pension plan; defined contribution pension plan; money purchase plan; pension plan; profit-sharing plan; qualified plan; retirement plans; vesting methods.**

Corporate Services Department (CSD)   a department of the NASD which reviews applications of corporations desiring to become listed publicly on the New York Stock Exchange. This department enforces the policies of the NYSE board of directors.
Minimum requirements are set and revised by the NYSE, and include several minimum criteria: pretax earnings; net tangible assets; the value of common stock held publicly; the number of common shares outstanding; and the number of shareholders. See **board of directors; National Association of Securities Dealers (NASD); New York Stock Exchange (NYSE); publicly held corporation.**

corporation   an entity, other than an individual, recognized legally as a form of business operation. Corporations are chartered by the states, with ownership represented by shares. Shares may be sold in two principal classifications: common and preferred. Common shareholders have voting rights, and preferred shareholders have a prior claim on assets in case of liquidation.
Corporations offer three major benefits to shareholders: limited liability to its owners; a life not limited to the lives of its owners; and the ease of ownership transfer by buying and selling of stock. See **association taxed as a corporation; partnership; proprietorship.**

correspondent   any organization acting in behalf of a remote person or oganization, when the remote entity does not have convenience of direct access to services and facilities. In the securities industry, New York member firms act as correspondents for member organizations not maintaining offices in New York. Banks act as correspondents for out-of-state banks for transactions in other states or cities. See **agency arrangement; bank; member organization.**

cost depletion a method of writing off minerals or natural resources, based upon the number of units removed and sold each year. Cost depletion serves the same purpose as depreciation for other tangible assets. See **depletion; recapture.**

cost overruns the result of underestimating the projected costs of a project or investment program. As a result, profits are lower than as forecast.

Projections given in an offering circular or prospectus should be examined closely before investing, especially the underlying assumptions of program costs. Some unethical sponsors purposely overestimate potential profits to more readily market their programs. See **offering circular; private placement; prospectus; public offering; sponsor.**

cost recovery a concept replacing traditional depreciation rules, legislated under the Economic Recovery Tax Act of 1981 (ERTA).

Under older depreciation rules, assets were to be depreciated over an estimated "useful" life, allowing for a salvage value to be left over. Under the cost recovery provision, depreciation is revised so that the entire cost, without regard to salvage values, is recovered (written off) over a class life (three, five, ten or fifteen years). See **Accelerated cost recovery system (ACRS); Economic Recovery Tax Act of 1981 (ERTA); depreciation; salvage value.**

coupon (1) the interest rate payable on a bearer bond. The term is used in reference to the annual yield (coupon rate), with payments made twice per year.

(2) the detachable portion of a bearer bond certificate, to be mailed in on due dates to receive payment. See **bearer bond; debt security; interest; face value; par value; yield.**

coupon bond a bond with detachable coupons for the purpose of an investor's claim to periodic interest payments. Coupons are used on bonds issued in bearer form. See **bearer bond; par value; yield.**

coupon rate the nominal yield on a bond that will be paid to maturity, based on face value. See **bond; face value; maturity date; yield.**

cover (1) action taken by an investor in a short position in stocks, bonds or futures contracts. A number of shares or units are purchased to close the position and eliminate risks.

(2) reference to an option strategy, in which the writer (seller) of a call also owns 100 shares of stock per short option. In the event the call is exercised, the investor has the shares to deliver.

(3) a corporation's financial ability to pay interest on bonds or notes from current earnings. The ability to "cover" obligations will affect that corporation's bond rating. See **bond; corporation; fixed charge; futures contract; option; position; short sale.**

covered option an option written (sold) by an investor who is long (owns) 100 shares per option sold. In the event the call is exercised, the writer has the shares to deliver, regardless of price changes that have occurred. If the stock's value declines, the selling of a call has discounted the cost of the shares.

covered option

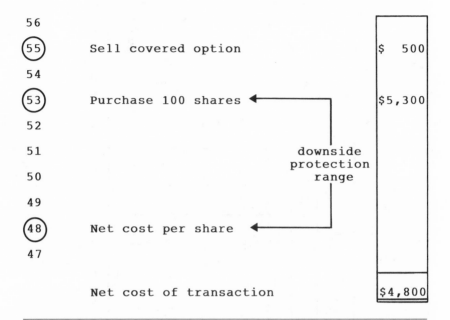

Uncovered (naked) options present unlimited risks to the speculator, as the market value of the stock may increase during the option's life. Covered options build in a predetermined level of profit, but also cap the amount of profit possible in stock investment.

The covered option writer has the advantage over option buyers. As time passes, the time value will decline, so that positions can be closed before exercise date, and profits taken without having the stock called away. See **call; naked option; option; time value; write.**

credit agreement   a document specifying the brokerage's policies regarding margin financing in a customer's account, including provisions for interest charges and other services. See **customer loan consent; margin agreement.**

credit spread   any spread in which the net result is a cash receipt rather than a cash payment, requiring that the sale produce a higher premium than the purchase. See **bear spread; bull spread; debit spread; option spread.**

cross   situation where a separate buyer and seller are matched and stock exchanged at a price and bid acceptable to each. The broker completed the trade representing both parties. See **broker; buy; continuous net settlement (CNS); sell order.**

cum dividend   the status of stock that is traded at a time when the new owner will be entitled to receive the next dividend due. Dividends are declared on one date, payable to holders as of a subsequent date. As long as the purchaser has completed

cumulative vote

shares held	directors nominated						
	3	5	7	9	11	13	15
50	150	250	350	450	550	650	750
100	300	500	700	900	1,100	1,300	1,500
150	450	750	1,050	1,350	1,650	1,950	2,250
200	600	1,000	1,400	1,800	2,200	2,600	3,000

credit spread

	credit spread	debit spread
Sell 50 call	$ 400	
Buy 55 call	(250)	
Net amount received	$ 150	
Sell 45 call		$ 150
Buy 45 put		(225)
Net amount paid		$ (75)

settlement by exdividend date, the upcoming dividend will be credited. See **dividend; exdividend date.**

cum rights   stock that is traded with subscription rights attached, and when the value of those rights has been taken into account in the price per share. See **subscription right.**

cumulative preferred   an advantageous feature of many preferred stock classes, specifying that all current and past dividends will be paid before common stockholders will be paid their declared dividends. Depending upon the results of operations and status of cash flow, some dividends may be omitted. In this case, cumulative preferred owners have the advantage of priority over non-cumulative preferred and common stock owners. See **common stock; dividend; preferred stock; senior security.**

cumulative vote   a feature allowed for the election of board of directors members, in which the stockholders are allowed a total number of votes equal to the number of shares held times the number of board members to be elected. The cumulative vote allows stockholders to cast their total votes in any combination they desire, providing great flexibility and eliminating the need for fractional splitting of total voting rights. See **board of directors; common stock; stockholder; voting rights.**

curb exchange   the American Stock Exchange. It was called "the curb" up until 1921 because it used to conduct business outside. The exchange is the second-largest in the country. See **American Stock Exchange (AMEX).**

current assets   a tangible asset that is held in the form of cash or any form that could be converted to cash within one year. Included are accounts receivable (net of an allowance for bad debts); inventory; marketable securities; and current notes receivable. See **assets; balance sheet.**

current coupon bond   reference to any bond with a coupon rate and yield to maturity that are the same or very close. Such bonds are less sensitive than others to interest rate changes. See **cash flow; coupon bond; yield to maturity.**

current liabilities   the debts of an organization that are due and payable within one year. Included are accounts payable, accrued liabilities and taxes, and current portions of notes payable. See **balance sheet; liabilities.**

current liabilities/tangible net worth ratio   a comparison between the short-term debts and the outstanding equity and capital surplus of an organization. Tangible net worth is the net equity reduced by intangibles (such as goodwill, covenants not to compete, organizational costs, trademarks, patents and copyrights). See **balance sheet ratios; intangible asset; liabilities; net worth; ratios.**

$$\frac{current \quad liabilities}{tangible \quad net \quad worth} \ = \ \underline{\hspace{2cm}} \%$$

current liabilities/ tangible net worth ratio

current market value (CMV)   (1) the closing price of a security, or latest quotation if no sale occurred during the day, as per Regulation T.

(2) assigned value of securities in an account, for the purpose of computing marks to the market and margin status. The closing market values of long positions for listed securities are used, or the bid price for over-the-counter securities. See **bid; closing price; Federal Reserve Board (FRB); market value; marking to the mark; over-the-counter (OTC); quotation; Regulation T.**

current production rate   standard ceiling imposed on the amount of interest that may be paid on GNMA pass-through securities. The rate is set in relation to the mortgage rate, allowing a small retention for processing and administrative costs, with the balance paid to the security holder. See **Ginnie Mae pass-through; Government National Mortgage Association (GNMA); mortgage.**

current ratio   widely used measure of an organization's working capital, especially useful in trend analysis. The total current assets are divided by total current liabilities to determine the relationship. In most industries, a current ratio of 2 to 1 or better is considered positive. Less than a 2 to 1 ratio is a sign that working capital is deficient. See **balance sheet ratios; ratios; working capital ratio.**

current yield   the interest paid per year on a bond, computed by dividing interest rate by the current market price of the bond.

For those concerned with the year-to-year yield more than yield to maturity, current yield is an important measure and means for comparison between issues. See **bond; interest; yield to maturity.**

cushion   (1) the time between a security's issue and its earliest callable date.

(2) the cushion theory: that short selling activity helps to stabilize market movements. See **call protection; callable bond; callable preferred stock; short sale.**

$$\frac{\text{current assets}}{\text{current liabilities}} = \text{current ratio}$$

$$\frac{\$484,600}{\$217,400} = 2.23 \text{ to } 1$$

current ratio

cushion bond a callable bond whose current market value is affected by the call provision. Such bonds may suffer from understatement of value, reflecting investor concern that the bond may be called. See **call protection; callable bond.**

custodian one appointed to protect or manage the assets of another. See **agent; trust.**

customer any person or entity engaged in dealings with a broker-dealer, and for whom the broker-dealer executes transactions in securities, or holds funds intended for use in securities investments. The word is used interchangeably with "client" for the purposes of describing a person who invests or speculates. See **broker-dealer.**

customer complaint a communication from a customer to a broker-dealer, associated registered representative, or a regulatory agency, concerning the practices, methods or statements made to that customer in respect to a securities transaction. All customer complaints made to registered representatives must be maintained in a complaint file, and a copy sent to the compliance officer of the broker-dealer, in accordance with the rules of fair practice, section 21. See **broker-dealer; complaint file; compliance; National Association of Securities Dealers (NASD); registered representative; rules of fair practice; Uniform Practice Code (UPC).**

customer loan consent permission given by margin customers allowing brokers to use securities for delivery on short sales and other uses of the broker-dealer. The consent is often a part of the customer's margin agreement, requiring a separate signature. See **credit agreement; debit balance; margin agreement.**

CUSTOMER LOAN CONSENT

Until you receive written notice of revocation from the undersigned, you are hereby authorized to lend, to yourselves as brokers or to others, any securities held by you on margin for the account of, or under the control of, the undersigned.

Dated,_____, 19__ x_____

_____, _____
        (city)   (state)

Current Yield

coupon rate	when trading at:						
	90	92	94	96	98	100
7.0%	7.70%	7.56%	7.42%	7.28%	7.14%	7.00%
7.5%	8.25	8.10	7.95	7.80	7.65	7.50
8.0%	8.80	8.64	8.48	8.32	8.16	8.00
8.5%	9.35	9.18	9.01	8.84	8.67	8.50
9.0%	9.90	9.72	9.54	9.36	9.18	9.00
9.5%	10.45	10.26	10.07	9.88	9.69	9.50
10.0%	11.00	10.80	10.60	10.40	10.20	10.00
10.5%	11.55	11.34	11.13	10.92	10.71	10.50

cycle (1) one of the three classes of options, identified by expiration periods. Options are issued to expire in the following cycles: Jan/Apr/Jul/Oct; Feb/May/Aug/Nov; and Mar/Jun/Sep/Dec.

(2) an identified period of time required for certain events to occur, such as industry or market trends and movements, inflationary and recessionary activities, and business profitability and production. See **option; technical analysis.**

D

daily bond buyer a publication for the municipal bond industry, containing news and information, notices of sales, and pending offering news. It also contains several important indexes for municipals, including:

20-bond index—an "average" of 20-year maturity bonds with high ratings, producing a "bid" in composite to indicate a trend in the high-quality bond market.

11-bond index—a sampling from the 20-bond index of only the highest rated bonds.

30-day visible supply—a summary of new bond offerings anticipated to be coming up for offer and sale within the next 30 days.

placement ratio—a summary of activity in acceptance by the public of new bond issues. The placement (acceptance) ratio for new offerings is viewed as an indicator of investor sentiment, and a high ratio (90 percent or more) is considered as most favorable. See **acceptance ratio; index; municipal bond.**

daisy chain an illegal technique for the manipulation of a security's value to draw in investors. The person or group trades in the issue, forcing price changes. Interest is generated among buyers, who cannot find a subsequent market for the security, as it was purchased based on manipulated prices. See **manipulation.**

date of record a date of declaration by a corporation's board of directors, on which a transfer agent is to identify the holders of stock. Holders on that date are entitled to receipt of dividends the board declares. See **exdividend date; transfer agent.**

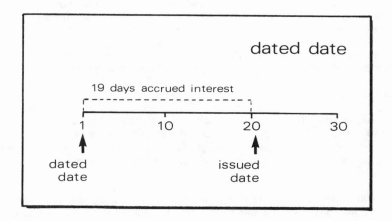

dated date   the date on a bond issue on which interest begins to be calculated. In cases where the dated date precedes the issued date, the buyer pays accrued interest to the issuer, which is regained when the first interest payment is made. See **bond; interest; issued date.**

day order   a type of order which is valid only for a single trading day. If not executed or cancelled on that day, it expires at the close of trading. See **cancellation; execution; order ticket.**

day trade   an activity in which a position is opened and closed on the same trading day, which may consist of a purchase followed by a sale (long); or a sale followed by a closing purchase (short). For investors practicing day trading on margin and on a regular basis, special margin requirements apply. See **buy; margin requirement; sell order.**

dealer   firm or individual buying and selling securities in the capacity of a principal, who subsequently transacts for a marked up price to its customers. Disclosure must be made to the customer that the firm or individual is acting in the capacity of principal in the transaction. See **agent; broker-dealer; principal; specialist.**

dealer bank   a commercial bank acting as a dealer and registered with the Municipal Securities Rulemaking Board (MSRB), or offering a market in agency or government bonds. See **commercial bank; municipal bond; Municipal Securities Rulemaking Board (MSRB).**

debenture   a long-term bond that is unsecured and is backed only by the good faith and reputation of the issuing corporation (maturities of less than 10 years are more correctly called notes). See **bond; collateral; long-term debt; note; unsecured debt.**

debit balance   (1) a balance in a margin account owed by the customer to the broker, created by borrowing on margin or by closing a margin position at a loss, and reflecting balances owed for settled transactions only.
(2) an accounting term referring to the balance of an account netting a left-sided balance (debit) as opposed to a right-sided balance (credit). See **margin account.**

debit spread   an option which results in a debit to the investor, or a net amount due rather than receivable. A debit occurs whenever the net of purchased options exceeds the premium due from written options. See **credit spread; option; option spread; spread.**

debt-equity ratio   a comparison between the liabilities and shareholders' equity of an organization. The purpose of this ratio is to determine the relative ownership of the company, between holders of equity and holders of debt. See **fundamental analysis; ratios.**

debt security   broad term which applies to any investment made by way of a loan of capital. Included are bonds, notes and bills. Debt securities are distinguished from other forms of security investment, such as using capital to borrow more capital (leverage), and taking of an equity position. See **bond; commercial paper; debenture; liabilities; note.**

debt service   the total of interest and principal that must be paid on a mortgage or other note, expressed monthly or annually. Level debt service is a term used to

```
Example A

  Buy  Jun  25  call          $    25
  Buy  Sep  30  call               325

  Debit                       $  350
```

```
Example B

  Buy  Sep  35  call          $  300
  Sell Jun  35  call             (125)

  Debit                       $  175
```

debit spread

describe equal periodic payments, commonly used in regard to fixed mortgage payments. See **interest; level debt service; mortgage principal.**

$1,000 asset	declining balance		
	classification type		
year	3 year	5 year	10 year
1	$ 250	$ 150	$ 80
2	380	220	140
3	370	210	120
4	0	210	100
5	0	210	100
6	0	0	100
7	0	0	90
8	0	0	90
9	0	0	90
10	0	0	90
	$1,000	$1,000	$1,000

```
Current Liabilities:
    Accounts Payable              $    68,400
    Notes Payable                      80,000
    Total Current Liabilities                    $   148,400

Long-Term Liabilities:
    Notes Payable                                $   258,800

Total Liabilities                                $   407,200

Shareholders' Equity:
    Common Stock                  $1,000,000
    Retained Earnings                 384,700

Total Shareholders' Equity                       $1,384,700


Debt-Equity Ratio:

        Long-Term Debt              258,800
        ──────────────────────    ───────────    =    18.7%
        Shareholders' Equity      1,384,700
```

debt-equity ratio

14% mortgage, 30 years	Total Payment	Interest	Principal	Balance
				$80,000.00
January	$ 947.90	$ 933.33	$ 14.57	79,985.43
February	947.90	933.16	14.74	79,970.69
March	947.90	932.99	14.91	79,955.78
April	947.90	932.82	15.08	79,940.70
May	947.90	932.64	15.26	79,925.44
June	947.90	932.46	15.44	79,910.00
July	947.90	932.28	15.62	79,894.38
August	947.90	932.10	15.80	79,878.58
September	947.90	931.92	15.98	79,862.60
October	947.90	931.73	16.17	79,846.43
November	947.90	931.54	16.36	79,830.07
December	947.90	931.35	16.55	79,813.52
		$11,188.32	$ 186.48	
		98.4%	1.6%	
Total Debt Service	$11,374.80			

debt service

declining balance   a method of depreciating capital assets which allows greater deductions in the earlier years of ownership and lesser deductions in later years.

Under the accelerated cost recovery system (ACRS) rules established under the 1981 Economic Recovery Act, distinct class lives are established for all assets. ACRS depreciation rates are set to recognize an amount of depreciation each year on a predetermined schedule, which is a form of declining balance depreciation. Also under ACRS rules, an election may be taken to use straight-line depreciation under one of three methods in each asset class life.

The declining balance method under prior depreciation rules involved computing straight-line rates and then increasing that amount by a given rate. Under the 150% declining balance method, the beginning year's basis would be depreciation at 150 percent of the straight-line amount allowable. The result of declining balance depreciation is to create a higher tax deduction during the early years of an asset's life. See **accelerated cost recovery system (ACRS); depreciation; Economic Recovery Tax Act of 1981 (ERTA); straight-line depreciation.**

deep discount bond   a bond currently valued at less than 80 percent of its par value, assuming it was sold at or near par (does not apply to original issue discount bonds). See **discount bond; original issue discount (OID); par value; premium bond.**

deep discount bond

```
Market Value

$1,200 (120)            p r e m i u m

 1,100 (110)

 1,000 (100)    Par Value ——————————————————

  900 ( 90)            d i s c o u n t

  800 ( 80)
               — — — — — — — — — — — —
  700 ( 70)

  600 ( 60)       d e e p    d i s c o u n t

  500 ( 50)
```

deep in-deep out   an option term for a current premium that is five points or more above or below the strike price.

Deep in the money refers to a call premium above or a put premium below strike. Deep out of the money is the opposite, a call premium five points or more below strike price or a put premium above.

An in-the-money option has intrinsic value, because the option provides its holder with benefit that would be realized upon exercise, as that issue is currently

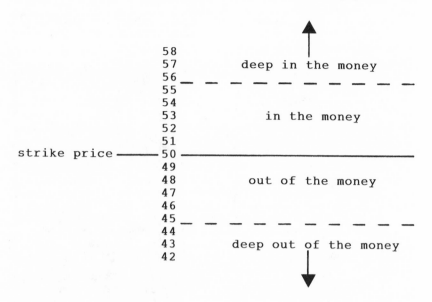

58
57   deep in the money
56 — — — — — — — — — — —
55
54
53   in the money
52
51
strike price ——— 50 ————————————————————————
49
48   out of the money
47
46
45 — — — — — — — — — — —
44
43   deep out of the money
42

deep in - deep out

priced below market value. The difference between intrinsic value and actual premium is time value.

An out-of-the-money option has no intrinsic value because the option provides a strike price above current market value. The entire premium of this option is time value. See **exercise price; intrinsic value; option; strike price; time value.**

default   a failure to meet a financial obligation. The term applies commonly to the situation where an issuer is unable to repay principal and interest on a bond, or fails to pay a declared dividend on preferred stock. A default may also apply to any situation in business where a debt is not repaid by an agreed date. See **bond; interest; note; principal.**

deferral   a delay in payment of liabilities. Commonly applied to taxation and tax shelters, the term describes a reduction in current tax liabilities, to be paid in a later year.

Retirement plans allow the individual to defer taxes on deposited funds and subsequent earnings, all in the current year. Upon retirement or distribution of the funds, the taxes deferred in the qualified plan become payable. See **recapture; tax shelter.**

deferred asset   an asset listed on the balance sheet of an organization, reflecting the unamortized balance of costs or expenses deferred until a later period, and subsequently to be applied against an expense account. See **amortization; assets.**

deferrred payment annuity   a type of contract calling for the payment now of a lump sum or periodic payments, with annuity benefits to begin at a later date. See **annuity.**

deficiency letter a letter sent by the Securities and Exchange Commission (SEC) to an issuer of a registration, informing the issuer of incorrect or incomplete information.

The deficiency letter responds to a preliminary registration statement, and an effective date will not be granted until all deficiencies are corrected. See **effective date; red herring; registration statement; Securities and Exchange Commission (SEC).**

Deficit Reduction Act of 1984 (DEFRA) legislation reducing long-term capital gain periods from one year to six months; creating an income tax on imputed interest for interest-free loans; tightening the requirements for employees claiming deductions for autos and computers used in business; requiring registration of tax shelters with the Securities and Exchange Commission that were previously exempt; and increasing the depreciation on most real estate from 15 to 18 years. See **capital gain; registered security; tax shelter.**

defined benefit pension plan a form of pension plan guaranteeing a specific benefit to be paid at retirement. This benefit may be based upon compensation and years of service, called a "unit benefit" plan.

This plan allows a substantial deduction for the employer, favors older employees, and provides guaranteed benefits. Adjustments are allowed by use of different funding methods. See **Employee Retirement Income Security Act (ERISA); pension plan; retirement plans; vesting methods.**

defined benefit pension plan

Vesting schedule based on total of 400 points

	Years of Service	Salary	Vested Points	Vestation Points	Vestation %
Employee A	3	$ 55,000	58	58/400	14.50%
Employee B	12	22,000	34	34/400	8.50%
Employee C	9	20,000	29	29/400	7.25%
Employee D	10	40,000	50	50/400	12.50%

defined contribution limitations   those limits which apply to the amount which may be placed in a retirement plan and deducted by the employer. See **pension plan; retirement plans.**

defined contribution pension plan   a form of pension plan under which contributions are paid in as a percentage of compensation, regardless of years of service. Retirement benefits are then determined by the amount actually contributed and the investment experience of the plan. See **Employee Retirement Income Security Act (ERISA); pension plan; retirement plans.**

deflation   the opposite of inflation, a condition in which buying power increases and the amount of currency in circulation decreases. See **buying power; inflation.**

delay rental   deductible payments made to the owner of mineral rights in an oil and gas program, so that the period during which drilling takes place can be extended. See **oil and gas; syndicate.**

delayed delivery   a form for delivering securities beyond the regular way. Delayed delivery would be made following the normal settlement date. See **regular way; settlement date.**

delivery   (1) the act of receiving securities in transfer from another individual or firm.
(2) term used to describe the day on which securities are due to be delivered.
(3) action required of an option writen when the option is exercised (assigned), and shares must be delivered in satisfaction of the contract.
(4) settlement of a futures contract, usually meaning transfer of cash and/or documents representing the commodity itself. See **commodity; option; security; settlement date.**

delivery month   the month in which a futures contract expires. See **commodity; futures contract.**

delivery versus payment (DVP)   instructions or terms of a securities transaction, indicating that settlement is to be made upon delivery of those securities, commonly used by institutional traders. See **institutional investor; settlement date.**

delta   a term used in technical analysis to compare the movement in an option's premium to the movement in the underlying security.
Since option premiums do not necessarily move to exactly the same degree as stock prices, different options have different deltas (or are affected in different ways by stock movement). Delta is the measurement of this relationship. See **hedge ratio; option.**

delta spread   the comparison of two delta factors, used to establish the corresponding relationship and trend in the options.
The delta of a purchased option is divided by the delta of a written option to arrive at the delta spread. See **option; ratio spread.**

demand deposit   accounts in commercial banks with check or draft privileges; any account against which funds may be drawn. The term may also apply to certain loans or lines of credit, where funds are available, to be used at the borrower's discretion. See **bank; commercial bank.**

Delta

Delta	stock price movement				
	1	2	3	4	5
1.50	1.50	3.00	4.50	6.00	7.50
1.25	1.25	2.50	3.75	5.00	6.25
1.00	1.00	2.00	3.00	4.00	5.00
.75	.75	1.50	2.25	3.00	4.25
.50	.50	1.00	1.50	2.00	2.50
.25	.25	.50	.75	1.00	1.25

$$\frac{\text{Purchased option's delta}}{\text{Written option's delta}} = \text{delta spread}$$

$$\frac{.75}{1.25} = .60$$

delta spread

democratic rights a policy suggested by the North American Securities Administrators' Association (NASAA), under which limited partners would have voting rights.

Currently, limited partners have no voice in management of the partnership (one of the basic concepts which define "limited"). The granting of democratic rights could curtail the second limitation of this form of investing, the finite liability that limited partners enjoy. See **limited partner; North American Securities Administrators' Association (NASAA); voting rights.**

depletion a form of expense representing the estimated use of a natural resource. From total reserves, an applicable portion is written off by journal entry during each period, reducing income to reflect the use of the resource.

Used by oil and gas and mining companies, depletion can be applied to any investment involving natural resources. See **cost depletion; percentage depletion.**

depository bond a special form of bond issued to commercial banks as compensation for government payroll processing services. Depository bonds cannot be transferred to a third party, but are accepted as collateral for federal funds. See **bond; commercial bank.**

Depository Trust Company (DTC)   a corporation which acts as go-between for securities transfers. Use of the DTC reduces the need for physical transfer of certificates and cash, recording entries on a computerized system. The DTC charges and credits each member's account for net assets changing hands. See **settlement date; stock certificate; transfer.**

depreciation   the periodic write-off of a capital asset, over a class life. Depreciation allows a business to claim a deduction for assets which cannot be claimed as a deduction in a single year.
The accelerated cost recovery system (ACRS) which was enacted as part of the Economic Recovery Tax Act of 1981, replaced previous depreciation procedures, under which assets were written off over an estimated useful life. Under ACRS, all assets are depreciated, or recovered, in one of several specific class lives, with elections for limited alternative methods available. See **accelerated cost recovery system (ACRS); asset depreciation range (ADR); declining balance; straight-line depreciation.**

designated concession   a form of order given to a syndicate, instructing that the total concession to be paid on a transaction is to be paid out to one or more third parties. See **concession; syndicate; trade.**

designated order turnaround (DOT)   the New York Stock Exchange's system for matching of small trades against one another or against the book. See **book; day order; limit order; New York Stock Exchange (NYSE); specialist.**

diagonal spread   an option spread involving a buy and a sell within the same option class. The typical diagonal spread has the following characteristics: the purchased option (long position) expires later than the written option (short position); each option is for a different strike price. See **bear spread; bull spread; option; spread.**

diagonal spread

	Apr	Jul	Oct
a) diagonal bull spread:			
sell call 30		$300	
buy call 25			$(375)
b) diagonal bear spread:			
buy call 60			$(25)
sell call 55	$125		

differential   the amount of commission added to an odd-lot trade to compensate the dealer. Usually one-eighth point, differential is not shown separately, but is added to the cost of the issue. See **commission; confirmation; odd lot differential; round lot.**

dilution   (1) that portion of total interest in a limited partnership that will go to the general partners. The higher the general partners' share, the more diluted the potential earnings to limited partners.

(2) consequence of a stock split on the conversion price of a convertible security. To prevent dilution, the conversion ratio commonly is increased in the event of stock splits or stock dividends (the anti-dilution clause).

(3) decrease in the percentage of ownership in a corporation to an individual stockholder, when more shares are issued to other stockholders. See **convertible security; general partner; limited partner; stock dividend; stock split; stockholder.**

direct participation program   a term used by the National Association of Securities Dealers (NASD) to describe limited partnership investments providing direct benefits to limited partners.

Tax benefits and consequences pass through directly to the limited partners, providing incentives to investors who will benefit from tax losses in the program. See **National Association of Securities Dealers (NASD); tax-advantaged investment; tax shelter.**

direct participation programs registered representative   full title of an individual who has passed the NASD Series 22 examination. This license permits the offer and sale of direct participation programs. See **limited representative; National Association of Securities Dealers (NASD); Series 22.**

director   a member of the board of directors of a corporation, with responsibilities and duties similar to those of a trustee in a trust.

The director, as a member of the board, is to represent the shareholder interest in establishing policies, appointing officers, declaring dividends, and overseeing the management of the company. See **affiliated person; board of directors; corporation; trustee.**

discount   (1) a reduction from face value of a bond. When discounted, the bond sells at less than 100 (par).

(2) discounted options are those with a current premium that is less than intrinsic value.

(3) a discounted security is one which is marketed at less than redemption value, such as treasury bills.

(4) the opinion of market watchers that events or news do not affect the immediate value of the market in general or of a specific security. In such cases, the news is said to be discounted.

(5) applied to commissions, a discount may be granted for unusually large purchases of stocks, bonds, mutual fund shares, or units in direct participation programs. Discount commissions are applied as well to all trades placed through a discount broker.

(6) any reduction in price allowed to a buyer, often as an incentive to pay invoices by a specified date. Terms of "2/10, net 30" mean a two percent discount will be allowed if the bill is paid by the 10th day of the following month. Otherwise, the entire amount, without discount, is due within 30 days. See **bond; option; par value; premium.**

discount arbitrage   the act of buying an option that is currently discounted (selling below its intrinsic value), and at the same time taking a short position in the corresponding issue. This is said to be a riskless transaction because there is more real value in the option that was paid, and any increase in the value of the stock will be reflected in a rise in the option's value to match. See **arbitrage; option; riskless transaction.**

discount bond   a bond available at a price below par value. See **bond; deep discount bond; par value.**

discount broker   brokers providing transaction services only to customers. A discount in the amount of commission is offered, but no investment consultation, advice, literature, or other support is offered.
Discount brokers may offer margin trading, IRA and Keogh account transactions, or custodial services, and are suitable for use by investors desiring to make their own investment decisions. See **broker; commission; exchange business.**

discount rate   (1) the rate of interest charged by a central bank of the Federal Reserve System, available to members who borrow and pledge securities or other assets as collateral. The discount rate also provides a floor. Beneath that rate, member banks will not loan to customers, as it is the rate those banks themselves must pay for funds.
(2) a precise method for computing return on investment, which computes the present value of funds as paid in and as distributed from that investment. The discounted rate of return considers the time value of money in developing the actual yield, and is used commonly in real estate syndication programs. See **accounting rate of return; central bank; collateral; Federal Reserve Board (FRB); interest; present value; time value of money.**

discount window   a Federal Reserve central bank's facility from which member banks borrow from reserves, for the pledge of collateral. See **collateral; Federal Reserve Board (FRB).**

discount yield   a method of computing yield based upon the face amount rather than upon the amount of money invested. If the security is purchased with exactly one year to maturity, the amount of discount is divided by the face amount. For maturities other than one full year, the sum is adjusted to arrive at a true annual yield. The discount yield method is used to compute yields on Treasury bills. See **equivalent bond yield; Treasury bill; yield.**

$$\frac{\text{discount}}{\text{face amount}} \times \frac{360 \text{ days}}{\text{days to maturity}} = \text{discount yield}$$

$10,000 T-Bill, purchased at 97, with 90 days to maturity:

$$\frac{\$300}{\$10,000} \times \frac{360}{90} = 12\%$$

discount yield

discounted cash flow a method for computing return on an investment that allows for the time value of money (computes present value of future investments and distributions), and also includes the estimated tax benefits to arrive at an after-tax yield. See **accounting rate of return; internal rate of return; time value of money.**

discretionary account a type of customer account in a brokerage firm, in which the broker is given control over investment decisions in behalf of that customer. Discretion may be limited in one of several ways.

Limited discretion given verbally relating to specific trades is not included in the definition. A discretionary account must be authorized in writing and approved by an officer of the brokerage firm. See **broker-dealer; customer; power of attorney.**

discretionary order an order placed under a discretionary account agreement. The order must be identified as discretionary, and must be made in accordance with the customer's investment objectives. See **broker-dealer; customer; investment objective.**

discriminatory plan a retirement plan in which the required contributions are considered a burden to some employees, or in which contributions for employees earning different amounts are computed differently. See **Employee Retirement Income Security Act (ERISA); retirement plans.**

disproportionate sharing arrangement (1) a type of agreement in a limited partnership where the general partners invest none of the original capital, or only a small amount, and in return receive a greater share of profits.

(2) reference to NASD guidelines for the quantity of shares that may or may not be sold to customers in a hot issue. The "disproportionate in quantity" rule protects the general public investor from those in a position to benefit from investing in a substantial portion of a new issue or an issue in high demand. See **general partner; hot issue; oil and gas.**

distribution area descriptive of a stock's trading pattern when the range of prices is narrow over an extended period of time. Such a narrow range indicates close resistance and support levels, or the unwillingness of buyers to invest at current prices. See **accumulation area; resistance level; support level.**

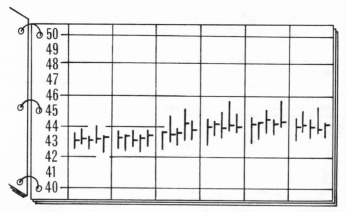

distribution area

distributor   another word for a wholesaler or underwriter of a security, which may apply to new issues, public or private syndications, or mutual fund shares. See **underwriter; wholesaler.**

district bank   one of the 12 Federal Reserve centers. There are 12 districts, each providing services as the central bank for Federal Reserve member banks.
   The twelve district banks are: (1) Boston MA; (2) New York NY; (3) Philadelphia PA; (4) Cleveland OH; (5) Richmond VA; (6) Atlanta GA; (7) Chicago IL; (8) St. Louis MO; (9) Minneapolis MN; (10) Kansas City MO; (11) Dallas TX; and (12) San Francisco CA. See **central bank; Federal Reserve Bank.**

district business conduct committee (DBCC)   a subcommittee of the NASD, which enforces the board of governors' policies and the rules of fair practice, and hears and rules upon complaints against member firms or individuals associated with members in that district. See **board of governors; business conduct committee; code of procedure; National Association of Securities Dealers (NASD); rules of fair practice.**

district uniform practice committee   a subcommittee of the NASD, which keeps members up to date on information about the Uniform Practice Code. See **National Association of Securities Dealers (NASD); Uniform Practice Code (UPC).**

diversification   the practice of placing investment assets into more than one product or issue, to ensure that adverse conditions cannot affect the entire portfolio.
   One may diversify among classifications of investment, industries, or individual issues. The most common forms of diversification are: (a) to place assets into two or more different classifications of investment, such as mutual funds, public syndications, variable annuities, precious metals, or collectibles; or (b) to place funds into a diversified group—a mutual fund or diversified corporation—which in turn will invest its assets in a wide number of other companies. See **investment objective; risk.**

diversified common stock company   a type of mutual fund descriptive of most such funds. All assets available for investment are spread among a large variety of common shares. This diversification may represent several industries and varying levels of risk, depending upon the specific fund's own stated objectives (aggressive growth, income, preservation of capital, etc.). See **common stock; management company; mutual fund; portfolio.**

diversified management company   a mutual fund which maintains at least three quarters of its assets in: cash or receivables; shares of other mutual funds; and government securities. Other securities may be purchased as long as the total holdings do not represent five percent or more of the fund's total assets, and as long as the fund does not control more than 10 percent of the issuer's voting stock. See **management company; mutual fund.**

dividend   (1) income distributed to the stockholders of a corporation, as declared by the board of directors. Dividends paid in this way are taxable, except to the extent tax laws permit an exclusion.
   (2) a stock dividend—crediting of additional shares—is not generally taxed until shares are sold. Stock dividends are given in lieu of cash dividends to expand the earning base and, at the same time, preserve cash for reinvestment. The stockholder receives more shares without tax consequences.

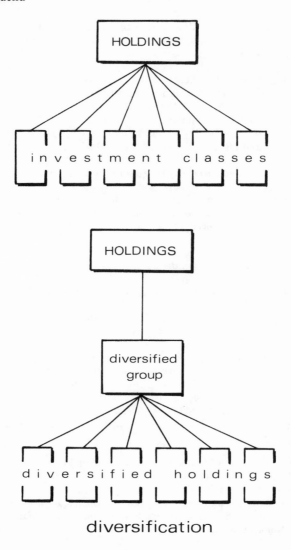

diversification

(3) a distribution from a mutual fund. Dividends may be treated and taxed as dividends, interest, or long or short-term capital gains.

(4) payments from money market funds to shareholders which are actually a form of interest for federal tax purposes. See **board of directors; corporation; stockholder; Subchapter M.**

dividend arbitrage a strategy involving the purchase of stock prior to exdividend date and, at the same time, buying a put contract for each 100 shares. The premium on the put should have a lower time value than the amount of the dividend expected to be declared when the stock goes exdividend. When the exdividend date has passed, the stock and the put contract are sold. See **arbitrage; exdividend date; put; time value premium.**

dividend reinvestment   plans in effect in mutual funds, money market funds, and some individual stock issues, allowing for the purchase of additional shares as an alternative to taking a cash distribution. Dividends reinvested are subject to current tax, but offer several advantages: a reduction of commission costs, a compounding effect on earnings, and an automatic investment without the need to pay in additional funds. See **corporation; mutual fund; shareholder.**

dividend yield   percentage dividend yield, computed by dividing the rate per share by the current market price of the stock. See **stock; yield.**

$$\frac{\text{dividend rate per share}}{\text{market price}} = \text{dividend yield}$$

$$\frac{\$3.00}{\$60} = 5\%$$

dividend yield

divisional bond   a first lien on a portion of a railway system, also called railway mortgage bond. See **bond.**

do not reduce (DNR)   a specification found in stop orders, limit orders, or stop-limit orders, which qualifies that the order is not to be reduced by the effect of dividends on exdividend date. See **exdividend date; limit order; stop-limit order; stop order.**

dollar bond   a serial bond issued in small amounts, traded in dollar value rather than in relation to par. See **bond; serial bond.**

dollar cost averaging   a plan of investing involving the periodic purchase of stock, mutual fund shares, or other security. An established dollar amount is invested, rather than a number of shares or units. See **average down; average up; formula investing.**

don't know (DK)   indicates refusal of payment or delivery on a transaction, because the trade or some of its details are not known, or there is an error or disagreement as to agreed terms. See **broker-dealer; trade.**

double bottom   a term used in technical analysis identifying a strong support level for a stock's price. A support level is seen to occur twice in a period of time,

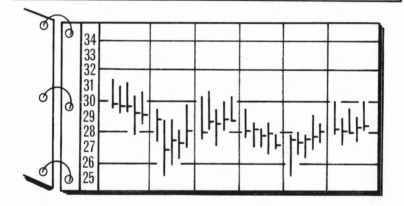

dollar cost averaging

rising prices		dropping prices	
price per share	average cost	price per share	average cost
$25	$25	$25	$25
27	26	23	24
26	26	24	24
30	27	20	23
32	28	18	22
34	29	16	21

double bottom

the implication being that there is support at that price level. See **double top; support level; technical analysis.**

double declining balance a process for the rapid depreciating of an asset, involving 200 percent of the straight-line rate. This method is out of use for assets placed into service since the accelerated cost recovery system (ACRS) was put into effect. Under ACRS, 175% is the maximum percentage that can be used for depreciation.

The "200%-DB" method is computed in the following way: (a) compute the straight-line depreciation on the beginning year's basis; (b) multiply the straight-line depreciation by 2 to arrive at the allowable depreciation; and (c) reduce the basis by the amount of depreciation claimed. See **accelerated cost recovery system (ACRS); declining balance; depreciation.**

double taxation the effect of a corporate dividend. The corporation must pay income tax on its profits. When a portion of those profits are then distributed as dividends, the shareholders are again taxed. See **corporation; dividend.**

double declining balance

Year	Basis	Straight Line	200-DB
1	$10,000	$2,000	$4,000
2	6,000	1,200	2,400
3	3,600	720	1,420
4	2.180	436	872
5	1,308	262	523

total depreciation $9,215

double top a technical analysis term to describe a strong resistance level. When a top — or resistance level — is reached twice within a short period of time, it is pointed to as proof of a strong resistance to prices above that level. See **double bottom; resistance level; technical analysis.**

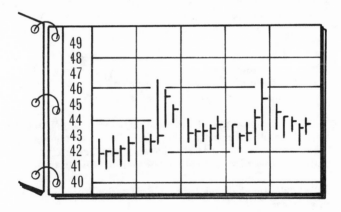

double top

Dow Jones Industrial Average (DJIA) an index of market movement involving 30 industrial stocks. The component stocks represent many of the largest corporations in the United States, and the DJIA is watched daily by investors as an indicator of bullish or bearish sentiment.

While the industrial averages may affect the daily average of other issues, movement in the index does not necessarily show how the market is moving. While more accurate means can be watched to judge the value and sentiment of the market, the

DJIA is the most widely watched of indexes. The index has been in effect since 1884, when it was developed by Charles Dow. See **index; technical analysis.**

Dow Jones Transportation Average   an index of market movement for the transportation industry, involving daily movement of 20 common stocks, including railways, airlines and trucking companies. See **index; technical analysis.**

Dow Jones Utility Average   an index of market movement for public utilities, involving 15 utility stocks representing service to all sections of the United States. See **index; technical analysis.**

Dow Theory   an approach to technical analysis, which contends a primary trend — one that will last for more than one year — will follow the movements in two or more of the Dow Jones Averages. The theory states that trends follow the averages. If one of the three indexes moves substantially and is then followed by a second of the indexes, the market in general should follow. This theory does not identify whether such movements are short-term or truly signals of primary movement. See **index; technical analysis.**

down-and-out option   a form of option trading in which at least 10 identical calls are traded. Included is a provision that the block of options is to be cancelled in the event the value of the underlying stock declines to a predetermined level. See **call; option; up-and-out option.**

downside protection   reference to the range of protection an option writer has. Because the stock is covered and a premium received when the options are sold, the premium reduces the net cost of the stock. The difference between market value at the time of the stock's purchase, and the net cost, is downside protection. A similar safety feature may be obtained by purchasing a put when the stock is held. In this case, the downside protection is effective only until the put option expires. See **call; covered option; option; put; writer.**

downtick   the reduction in the regular-way price of a security. When the latest price is lower than the previous price by one-eighth of a point or more, it is a downtick in value. See **regular way; uptick; zero-minus tick.**

draft   a debt instrument that is to be paid at an identified point in the future, or upon demand, or an instrument for the transfer of funds from one account to another. The account will be debited upon presentation of the draft (a check is a debit upon issue). See **debt security; demand deposit; negotiable instrument.**

dual listing   the simultaneous listing of one security on more than one exchange. See **exchange; listed stock.**

dual-purpose investment company   a so-called leveraged company, one that issues two different classes of shares. Closed-end investment companies may issue capital shares and income shares in a single offering, with each class issued in equal amounts. See **closed-end; investment company; leveraged company.**

due bill   an authorization by which one broker makes legal claim against another for future distributions. It is used when a broker has failed to pay or deliver by settlement date, and takes the form of a postdated check (for cash distributions) or an I.O.U. (for stock distributions). See **delivery; holder of record.**

due diligence   a process of research and analysis of an offering prior to its offer or sale. The process takes place on several levels. First, the sponsor or underwriter must complete economic, tax and regulatory due diligence to ensure that all claims and assumptions of the offering are legal and correct.

The broker-dealer who will participate in placement of the security must determine that its customers will have a reasonable chance to profit from the investment. Due diligence at this level also involves a check into the background and experience of the sponsor, and an investigation of properties involved in the offering.

Finally, the registered representative must ensure that the offering is in line with the customer's investment objectives. See **broker-dealer; investment objective; prospectus; registration statement; sponsor; underwriter.**

E

early exercise   an exercise of an option contract in advance of the due date, often far in advance. See **exercise; expiration date; option.**

earned income   income from salaries, wages, fees and other payments for services rendered. For federal tax purposes, earned income is subject to rules different than those applied to unearned income — including interest, dividends, capital gains, and rents. See **income; tax basis.**

earned surplus   generally, a term meaning the same as retained earnings. Surplus is the amount of earnings which increase tangible capital value in an organization. See **retained earnings.**

earnings   profit from operations. Gross income, less costs, operating expenses, and income taxes is "net" realized earnings. See **net income; retained earnings.**

earnings per share   the amount of net income earned per share of common stock, after payment of dividends to preferred stockholders.

If the corporation has outstanding convertible bonds, the correct reference is "primary" earnings per share. The calculation may be reported on a fully diluted basis — the value that would be available to common stockholders in the event the convertibles were to be called. See **common stock; fully diluted earnings per share; primary earnings per share.**

earnings report   the complete financial statement of an organization, often including explanations or forecasts by the company's senior management. See **balance sheet; financial statement; income statement.**

eastern account   also called a dividend account reference to a form of underwriting agreement. If the entire offering is not sold, each selling member of the syndicate is held responsible for a portion of the total, even if his allotted portion was sold in full. See **severally and jointly; syndicate; united account; western account.**

economic life   term used to describe a property's value due to economics, as distinguished from structural life or value. See **real estate.**

Economic Recovery Tax Act of 1981 (ERTA) a major tax bill which modified significantly the tax and deduction rules for businesses and individuals.

Maximum individual rates were lowered to 50% of taxable income, and capital gains rates were lowered to a maximum of 20%.

For businesses, depreciation was replaced with the accelerated cost recovery system (ACRS), allowing for rapid deductions and first-year expensing of a limited amount, of new assets acquired. See **accelerated cost recovery system (ACRS); capital gain; capital loss; investment tax credit (ITC).**

Edge Act a 1919 bill allowing banks to conduct interstate business for international customers. See **commercial bank.**

effective date the date when a registered offering may be sold to the public. This date generally is the 20th of a month following registration, assuming the SEC does not issue a deficiency letter. See **deficiency letter; offering date; registration statement; Securities and Exchange Commission (SEC).**

effective sale the sale price of a round lot which occurs soonest after the placement of an odd lot sale order. The effective sale price is used to establish the round lot's price with differential added. See **differential; odd lot differential; round lot.**

eighteen-year property a fifth class life under the accelerated cost recovery system (ACRS), added in 1984, as part of the Deficit Reduction Act of 1984 (DEFRA). It increases to 18 years the recovery period for most real estate property. See **accelerated cost recovery system (ACRS); class life; Deficit Reduction Act of 1984 (DEFRA); depreciation.**

eligible security (1) securities defined under Regulation T, which hold loan value in margin accounts.

(2) securities acceptable to the Federal Reserve for collateral on loans.

(3) securities that may be traded over the counter, by exchange members. See **discount window; Federal Reserve Board (FRB); margin account; Regulation T.**

$$\text{earnings per share} = \frac{\text{net earnings} - \text{preferred stock dividends}}{\text{outstanding shares of common stock}}$$

$$= \frac{\$485,000 - \$60,000}{\$250,000} = \$1.70$$

Employee Retirement Income Security Act (ERISA) also called the Pension Reform Act of 1974, ERISA was designed to set standards for retirement and pension accounts. Major provisions include:

a) graded vesting within a maximum of 15 years of employment.

b) enrollment in employer plans for all employees age 25 or over, following one year of service.

c) guidelines for the fiduciary duties of an employer's plan administration.

d) reporting requirements of employers to the Department of Labor.

e) liberalized individual retirement plan rules.

f) funding standards, definition of surviving spouse benefits, and ease of rules when moving from one job to another. See **fiduciary; graded vesting; Pension Reform Act of 1974; vesting methods.**

equipment leasing a classification of tax shelter investment involving formation of a limited partnership to purchase and then lease out business and industrial equipment.

Any form of equipment may be included, although partnerships will frequently specify their emphasis in choosing industries. Examples may include rail cars or containers; aircraft; and high-technology or scientific equipment.

These programs offer several tax advantages: investment tax credit, depreciation, deduction of interest in leveraged programs, and deduction of the program's operating expenses. See **accelerated cost recovery system (ACRS); depreciation; interest; investment tax credit (ITC); syndicate; tax deferral.**

equipment trust bond a form of bond used especially by railroad corporations to fund the acquisition of equipment.

While the bond issue is outstanding, title to the equipment is held in trust. Bondholders hold first claim on equipment in the event of default in most equipment trust bonds.

A typical serial issue would involve a 20% to 25% downpayment, with the balance financed over a 15-year period. If a railroad purchased locomotives for a total of $18,600,000, and put down $3,720,000 (20%), the balance, issued as an equipment trust bond, would see maturity of $992,000 per year for 15 years. See **bond; serial bond; trust.**

equity (1) the net value held by stockholders of a corporation or the owners of unincorporated businesses. Equity is the amount of total assets less total liabilities.

(2) the liquidation value of a customer account, represented by the current value of securities, less any debit balances owed against those securities.

(3) in real property, the market value of property, less outstanding mortgages. On an acquired basis, equity will not show appreciated value, only the difference between cost and debt. See **common stock; corporation; debit balance; margin account; market value; preferred stock; real estate.**

equity build-up the increase over the life period of a mortgage, during which principal payments on the debt increase equity while reducing liability in the property. See **mortgage; principal; real estate; real estate investment trust (REIT).**

equity REIT a real estate investment trust which purchases properties. The equity position the REIT takes in properties produces rental income, offset by deductions for depreciation and operating costs. When properties are sold, capital gains are passed through to investors. Other REITs invest only in mortgages, having no equity position in properties, and others purchase leaseholds or participate as partners in other real estate programs. See **cap rate; depreciation; mortgage REIT; real estate investment trust (REIT).**

T-Bill with 60 days to maturity, discount yield
of 12%, purchased for $98,000 ($2,000 discount)

$$\frac{\text{T-Bill discount}}{\text{T-Bill purchase price}} \times \frac{365}{\text{days to maturity}} = \text{equivalent bond yield}$$

$$\frac{\$2,000}{\$98,000} \times \frac{365}{60} = 12.41\%$$

equivalent bond yield

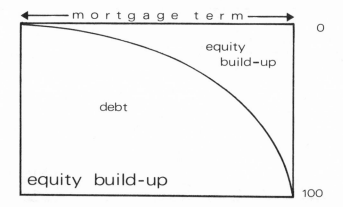

equity requirement   the minimum amount of net equity that must be kept in a customer's margin account in order to pursue margin trading activities. The normal requirement may be increased if customers are writers of uncovered options. See **margin requirement; option; Regulation T.**

equity security   a form of investment that gives its holder equity in a corporation. Common and preferred stock are the most frequent forms equity security will take.

Long call options, warrants and rights, and convertible securities are forms of investments that are equivalent to equity securities, and may be treated as such for tax purposes in case of wash sales. See **common stock; convertible security; option; preferred stock; rights; warrant; wash sale.**

equivalent bond yield   a computation used to compare U.S. Government Security yield to the yield on other securities, notably money market securities.

In the case of a Treasury bill, which is sold at a discount, the equivalent bond yield is computed by dividing the amount of discount by the T-bill purchase price. The sum is then multiplied by the annualized days to maturity. See **coupon rate; discount yield; money market; Treasury bill.**

equivalent positions   a term used to compare two different securities with the same potential for gain or loss. See **profit; securities.**

equivalent taxable yield   the rate of return that must be earned in a taxable investment to equal the return on a non-taxable or tax-deferred investment. The term is applied commonly to municipal securities. The yield is divided by the inverse of the individual's tax bracket. See **break-even interest; tax bracket; tax deferral; yield equivalence.**

ERISA   abbreviation for Employee Retirement Income Security Act, also known as the Pension Reform Act of 1974. See **Pension Reform Act of 1974; retirement plans.**

escheatable funds   monies unclaimed after a number of years. Organizations failing to locate the rightful owner are required to escheat account balances to the state. However, the owner may claim those funds following their escheat. See **abandonment; assets; customer.**

$$\frac{\text{municipal yield}}{1 \;-\; \text{tax rate}} \;=\; \text{equivalent taxable yield}$$

$$\frac{9\%}{1 \;-\; .42} \;=\; 15.52\% \quad \text{equivalent taxable yield}$$

escrow   a type of account established by a third party, to hold funds pending the funding of an investment, purchase of real property, or payment of insurance, taxes and other expenses. See **offering date; real property; syndicate; trust.**

escrow receipt   verification issued by a bank approved by an exchange, that a customer holds securities in that bank's care.

The escrow receipt may be used to pledge securities held in the bank, to write calls. In the event of exercise, the bank promises, through issue of an escrow receipt, to deliver securities in satisfaction of the exercise. See **exercise; underlying security; writer.**

estate planning   term applied to all planning in anticipation of death: investing, retirement and trust fund establishment, writing a will, title to properties, are examples of such planning activities. See **beneficiary; financial planning; inheritance tax; will.**

estate tax   a federal tax on the value of assets of a deceased person. See **assets; inheritance tax; will.**

Eurodollar   description of American dollars in European countries, having arrived there as the result of payments made to overseas companies for delivery of merchandise. See **commercial bank.**

Eurodollar bond   bonds that are issued by European corporations, payable in Eurodollars. They are not registered with the Securities and Exchange Commission and cannot be offered for sale in the United States. See **bond; registered bond; Securities and Exchange Commission (SEC).**

Eurodollar CD   time deposits issued in Eurodollars by banks in Europe. See **London Interbank Offered Rate (LIBOR); time deposit.**

evasion   the act of illegally misrepresenting facts in order to reduce or eliminate income tax liabilities. Evasion may include nondisclosure of information, claiming expenses, deductions or credits that are fictitious, or failing to file an income tax return. See **avoidance.**

excess margin   the amount of equity in a customer's margin account above the Regulation T margin requirement, or above the maintenance requirement of the account. See **initial margin; margin requirement; Reg T excess; Regulation T; special miscellaneous account (SMA).**

excess reserves an amount of cash on hand and funds on deposit with the Federal Reserve, over and above a bank's reserve requirements. When a bank has excess reserves, it may loan those funds to customers or other banks. See **federal funds; Federal Reserve Board (FRB); reserves.**

exchange (1) an auction marketplace where members execute buy and sell orders for their customers or for their own accounts. Exchanges provide an open and continuous market and facilitate an orderly pricing market for publicly traded securities.
(2) the trade of one property for another, of equal or similar value. In some cases, exchanges of property may be tax-free, with capital gains deferred until eventual sale. See **auction marketplace; secondary market; stock exchange; tax deferral.**

exchange acquisition the purchase of a large block of shares through an exchange, in which sell orders are collected and held, to be applied against the buy orders in one transaction. See **auction marketplace; block; exchange distribution.**

exchange business a term used to describe all business transacted on an exchange, including stocks, bonds, options and commodities. See **bond; commodity; option; stock.**

exchange distribution the sale of a large block of shares through an exchange, in which buy orders are collected and held, to be applied against the sell order in one transaction. See **auction marketplace; block; exchange acquisition.**

exchange fund a type of limited partnership investment in which title to securities is transferred in lieu of a cash deposit. The current market value of the securities is used to determine the number of shares the investor is to receive. The exchange fund is used by investors interested in taking paper profits without paying current capital gains taxes. See **limited partnership; market value; paper profit/loss.**

exchange program a feature of some limited partnerships, in which limited partners may exchange their units in the program for an equity position in a sponsor's corporation or in another partnership. See **common stock; limited partnership; sponsor.**

exdividend date "ex," meaning "without," referring to the cut-off date, after which dividends will not be paid to purchasers of stock.
Dividends are declared and scheduled for payment to stockholders as of a date of record (the holders of stock on that date are entitled to the dividend). The actual exdividend date will precede the date of record by four business days, to allow for completion of regular way delivery.
The price of stock is reduced by the amount of dividend on exdividend date, so that stockholders of record after that date purchase stock exdividend. Short sellers must pay dividends against their short shares on the exdividend date. See **dividend; net change; record date; regular way.**

execution completion of a trade, when the buyer and the seller reach agreement as to price and terms. See **buy; sell order; trade.**

exempt security   term used to describe securities not required to comply with registration requirement (U.S. Government securities, for example), proxy rules, margin requirements, or registration of dealers in those securities.

Exemptions are to provisions of two laws, the Securities Act of 1933 (for government bond registration exemption) and the Securities Exchange Act of 1934. See **margin requirement; registered security; Securities Act of 1933; Securities Exchange Act of 1934.**

exercise   the act of demanding rights held under the terms of an option contract, to purchase shares from another investor (call option) or to sell shares currently held (put option). See **assignment; call; called away; option; put; put to seller; strike price.**

exercise limit   limitation placed on the number of option contracts on a single security that can be exercised within a specified time. The limit is placed to prevent an individual, company or group from taking over a corporation through the use of options. See **corner; option.**

exercise notice   notification to the Options Clearing Corporation from a broker, which requires a writer to deliver or accept securities under the exercise provisions of an option contract. See **assignment; buyer; called away; conventional option; Options Clearing Corporation (OCC); put to seller; writer.**

exercise price   same as the strike price for an option contract, the price of an issue at which an option may be exercised. See **strike price; underlying security.**

Eximbank   shortened name of the Export-Import Bank. See **Export-Import Bank.**

ex-legal   designation for a municipal security offered for sale which does not have a legal opinion printed on the certificate. Ex-legal status must be disclosed to the buyer. See **certificate; legal opinion; municipal bond.**

exotic shelter   descriptive of tax shelters not in one of the more common classifications, including highly speculative or unusual ventures involving and often associated with questionable schemes for write-off of deductions, valuation of assets, or greater risk than more traditional shelters. See **risk; speculation; tax shelter.**

expected return   a theoretical return that would or could be made on an investment, *if* the investor would invest over a long period of time, or the type of return that reasonably may be realized from a course of action. See **return on invested capital; yield.**

expense control ratio   a type of ratio involving an expense account's balance or average and another financial result, commonly net sales.

Ratios comparing expenses to sales are of limited value, except as part of an analysis over several periods, the purpose of which is to spot trends in expense levels. See **fundamental analysis; ratios.**

expense ratio   a test applied to mutual funds to determine the cost of operation of the fund. Total operating expenses and management fees are divided by average net assets to determine the cost per $100 of investment. See **mutual fund; net asset value per share (NAV); operating ratios.**

Operating Expense Account
_____ = Expense Control Ratio
      Sales   Volume

$$\frac{\$42,600}{\$804,300} \ = \ 5.3\%$$

expense control ratio

expiration retirement and voiding of an option contract. Upon expiration, the option becomes worthless. If there is value left in a long option, it should be exercised or sold prior to expiration. For writers, expiration is desirable, as the entire amount of premium received becomes income (short-term capital gain) upon expiration. See **option.**

expiration cycle reference to the three established expiration months of options. Options are traded with expirations on one of these three cycles, and will not cross over between the cycles.
The three cycles have expirations in: January, April, July and October; February, May, August and November; and March, June, September and December. See **cycle; FMAN; JAJO; MJSD; option.**

expiration date the actual date on which options expire and become worthless. For listed option contracts, the date is the Saturday immediately following the third Friday of the cycle expiration month. See **option.**

expiration time actual time by which those desiring to exercise an about-to-expire option must submit exercise notices. Since expiration occurs on a Saturday, notices must be completed and submitted on the previous day. See **exercise notice; option.**

exploratory program a type of oil and gas venture concentrating on searching for new wells and reserves in unproven areas, considered the highest risk of oil and gas programs. See **oil and gas.**

exploratory well wells in an exploratory program, known as wildcat wells. See **oil and gas; risk.**

Export-Import Bank an independent government agency formed in 1934. The Eximbank finances exporting and importing activities, provides insurance to overseas companies, and grants loans for related activities. See **Eximbank.**

ex-rights "without" rights, a reference to a rights offering that cannot be transferred. When stock is sold ex-rights, the rights cannot be traded or must be traded in a separate transaction. See **rights; underlying security.**

extra   a form of dividend, correctly known as "extra dividend," offered above and beyond the normal or expected dividend. See **dividend.**

extraordinary item   entry on a financial statement for income, cost or expense material enough to deserve special mention, that is not part of normal operations, and thus is not expected to recur in future years. See **balance sheet; financial statement; income statement.**

ex-warrant   a form of warrant that, upon sale, will not include any attached warrants as part of the transaction. See **underlying security; warrant.**

F

face amount certificate   a form of debt issued with the promise to pay an established amount — the face amount — at a set date two years or more in the future. In return, the investor makes a deposit or a series of payments and receives a fixed interest rate. See **debt security.**

face value   the par value of a bond, as printed on the certificate, representing the amount the issuer promises to pay upon maturity. See **certificate; maturity date; par value; redemption.**

facilitation   making available a market for the trading of securities, which may take one of many forms of reducing risks on large block trades. For example, one may purchase put options to protect a long position in a large number of shares of a company, thus facilitating the purchase and its related risk. See **bid; institution; offering price.**

fail contract   securities not delivered or paid as per the agreed terms or by the settlement date. See **delivery; payment date; settlement date.**

fail position   status of a broker-dealer unable to satisfy the terms of an agreed trade by the settlement date. See **broker-dealer; delivery.**

fail to deliver   securities are not delivered as agreed under the terms of a trade, specifically when a seller does not produce securities for payment to the buyer. See **broker-dealer; delivery.**

fail to receive   the opposite side from fail to deliver, in which a buyer withholds payment because the seller has failed to deliver securities. See **broker-dealer; payment date.**

fair, just and equitable   descriptive of standards applied to offerings. Regulatory agencies of the states may force sponsors to rework the terms of an offering if, in their opinion, the terms as presented for registration do not meet the fair, just and equitable standards they enforce. See **offering; registration statement; sponsor; syndicate.**

fair market value (FMV)   the price established in a free and open market, which is the result of supply and demand, representing the agreed buy and sell price at which current market value is set. See **current market value (CMV); free and open market.**

fair treatment   reference to the fiduciary and business interaction between brokers and customers. See **fiduciary; rules of fair practice.**

fair value   option term sometimes used to identify the market worth of a contract, and sometimes used in place of the phrase "intrinsic value." See **intrinsic value; option.**

family of funds   the collective funds offered by investment companies, each with a distinct makeup and investment objective. Some mutual funds are designed strictly to maximize current income; others seek tax-free returns or growth; funds may be classified as conservative, speculative, or aggressive, again depending upon the management philosophy and objective behind each fund. See **investment manager; investment objective; mutual fund; switching.**

family partnership   a form or organization in which members of the same family form a partnership, the objective often being that the original company owner desires to eventually pass ownership to others in the family, while reducing taxes at the same time. See **financial planning; partnership.**

Fannie Mae   abbreviated name of an organization marketing debt securities, the Federal National Mortgage Association (FNMA). See **Federal National Mortgage Association (FNMA).**

farm corporation   partnerships in farming activities that include a corporation as a partner, or corporations themselves farm directly. A farm corporation must report income on the accrual basis and must capitalize all costs and expenses incurred prior to production of its first crop.
Exempted from these rules are S Corporations (Subchapter S); family corporations; and those with less than $1 million of gross income per year since 1975. See **corporation; Subchapter S.**

Farm Credit Act of 1933   law that established the Farm Credit Administration (FCA) and a Co-Op bank in 12 farm credit districts. See **Bank for Cooperatives (CO-OP); Farm Credit Administration (FCA).**

Farm Credit Administration (FCA)   supervising agency of the Bank for Cooperatives (CO-OP) and the Federal Intermediate Credit Bank (FICB). See **Bank for Cooperatives (CO-OP); Federal Intermediate Credit Bank (FICB).**

Farm Loan Act of 1916   legislation which credited the Federal Land Banks. See **Federal Land Bank (FLB).**

farm out   the act of continuing drilling in an oil and gas program by assignment of a lease to another operator. See **oil and gas.**

farm syndicate   a farm entity which is not a regular corporation and either is required to register with a federal or state regulator, or has 35 percent or more of its losses allocated to limited parters. See **corporation; partnership; Subchapter S.**

Farmers Home Administration (FmHA)   an agency of the U.S. Department of Agriculture, which grants mortgage loans to farmers. See **Federal Financing Bank (FFB).**

federal debt the amount of money owed by the federal government, including marketable and nonmarketable securities: Treasury bills, notes and bonds as well as U.S. Savings Bonds and government account series. See **debt service; marketable securities; nonmarketable securities.**

Federal Deposit Insurance Corporation (FDIC) insurance organization protecting depositors in member banks, in the event of the banks' becoming insolvent. See **savings deposit; time deposit.**

Federal Farm Credit Banks an agency supervised by the Farm Credit Administration (FCA), organized to consolidate three other agencies: the Bank for Cooperatives (CO-OP), Federal Intermediate Credit Bank (FICB), and the Federal Land Bank (FLB). See **Bank for Cooperatives (CO-OP); Farm Credit Administration (FCA); Federal Intermediate Credit Bank (FICB); Federal Land Bank (FLB).**

Federal Farm Mortgage Corporation (FFMC) an organization which may issue loans for defaulted farm mortgages, established in 1932. See **default; mortgage.**

Federal Financing Bank (FFB) a consolidation formed in 1974 of a number of other agencies. The FFB is able to obtain rates more competitive than the individual agencies, lowering interest costs. See **financing; interest.**

Federal Financing Bank Act of 1973 law which established the Federal Financing Bank, with authorization to purchase obligations of other federal agencies and finance those purchases by issues similar to Treasury debts. See **guaranteed bond; marketable securities.**

federal funds (1) excess reserves of Federal Reserve member banks.
(2) funds available for payment of money market instruments.
(3) available net funds in margin accounts, special miscellaneous accounts (SMAs), and other brokerage client accounts. See **central bank; excess reserves; Federal Reserve Board (FRB).**

federal funds rate the daily computed rate applied to excess reserves loaned from one bank to another. See **commercial bank; excess reserves; interest.**

Federal Home Loan Bank (FHLB) an agency which loans money for the home building industry, through savings and loan associations and savings banks. See **mortgage bond; savings and loan association; savings bank.**

Federal Home Loan Mortgage Corporation (FHLMC) organization which buys existing home mortgages from its members, and resells to the general investing public. See **Freddie Mac; mortgage.**

Federal Income Tax Act of 1913 the law which established a tax on income in the United States. See **income.**

Federal Intermediate Credit Bank (FICB) an agency supervised under the Farm Credit Administration (FCA), which loans money to finance agricultural endeavors. See **Farm Credit Administration (FCA); Federal Farm Credit Banks.**

Federal Land Bank (FLB) part of the Farm Credit Banks Consolidated System-Wide Banks, which originally was created under the Farm Loan Act of 1916.

The FLB grants real estate first mortgage loans to farmers and ranchers for agricultural purposes. See **Farm Loan Act of 1916; Federal Farm Credit Banks.**

Federal National Mortgage Association (FNMA)   a corporation which buys existing mortgages of the Federal Housing Administration (FHA), the Farmers Home Administration (FmHA), and the Veterans Administration (VA), financed by the sale of notes and debentures. See **Fannie Mae; Farmers Home Administration (FmHA); mortgage.**

Federal Open Market Committee (FOMC)   a committee of the Federal Reserve board of governors which carries out policies of the Federal Reserve System in control of money supply and credit supply. See **board of governors; Federal Reserve Board (FRB); open market operation.**

Federal Reserve Bank   a bank acting as agent for the U.S. Treasury in the marketing of government securities, and one of the components of the Federal Reserve System. See **commercial bank; Federal Reserve Board (FRB); primary market.**

Federal Reserve Banking Act of 1913   law devised to regulate financial policies of commercial banking industry. See **commercial bank; district bank.**

Federal Reserve Board (FRB)   a board which regulates and monitors the banking industry by setting of reserve requirements, the discount rate and credit controls. The seven-member board is appointed by the President. See **board of governors; central bank; commercial bank; discount rate; district bank; Federal Open Market Committee (FOMC); reserve requirement.**

Federal Savings and Loan Insurance Corporation (FSLIC)   organization providing insurance that is required of federally chartered associations. See **savings and loan association.**

fidelity bond   a form of insurance coverage protecting broker-dealers against theft, the loss of cash or securities, fraud, and other losses and activities of agents or employees. See **blanket bond; broker-dealer.**

fiduciary   a person or firm acting in a capacity of responsibility for the handling of funds for other persons or firms. See **agent; custodian; general partner; trustee; Uniform Gift to Minors Act (UGMA).**

FIFO   abbreviation of an inventory valuation method, first in, first out (FIFO). See **first in, first out (FIFO).**

fifteen-year property   one of four class lives developed for depreciation purposes under the accelerated cost recovery system (ACRS). The other classes are three, five and ten years. Real estate, originally included under the 15-year class, was subsequently increased to 18 years, under the Deficit Reduction Act of 1984 (DEFRA). See **accelerated cost recovery system (ACRS); class life; declining balance; Deficit Reduction Act of 1984 (DEFRA); depreciation.**

fill or kill (FOK)   condition added to a limit order which specifies the order is to be filled immediately and completely, or not at all. See **limit order; order ticket.**

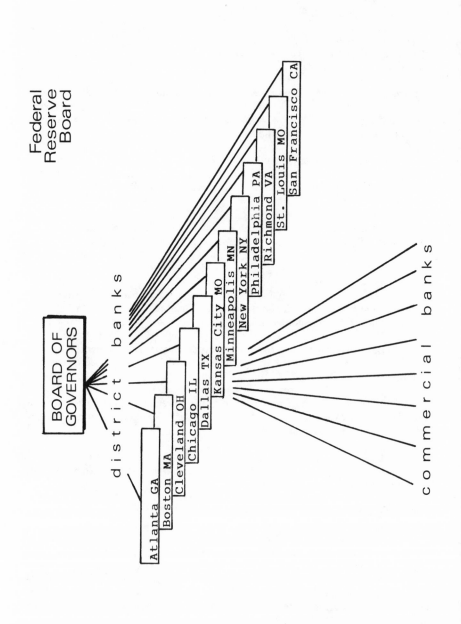

Federal
Reserve
Board

BOARD OF
GOVERNORS

district banks

Atlanta GA
Boston MA
Cleveland OH
Chicago IL
Dallas TX
Kansas City MO
Minneapolis MN
New York NY
Philadelphia PA
Richmond VA
St. Louis MO
San Francisco CA

commercial banks

Financial Accounting Standards Board (FASB)   organization of certified public accountants which evaluates and sets standards for reporting and for the preparation of financial statements. See **financial statement.**

Financial and Operations Combined Uniform Single Report (FOCUS)   a report filed with regulatory agencies by broker-dealers, on a monthly or quarterly basis, which includes summaries of operations, net capital computation, and a breakdown of volume. See **broker-dealer; financial statement; FOCUS Report.**

financial and operations principal   often called "financial principal," this is the designation for one who has passed the NASD Series 27 Examination. The license must be held by at least one individual in each broker-dealer. The financial principal prepares financial statements and computes monthly net capital and signs for the broker-dealer. See **financial statement; National Association of Securities Dealers (NASD); net capital requirement.**

financial futures   futures contracts involving interest rates. Trading involves futures of treasury security rates, certificates of deposit and GNMA pass-throughs. Trading is regulated by the Commodity Futures Trading Commission (CFTC). See **Commodity Futures Trading Commission (CFTC); futures contract; Ginnie Mae pass-through; interest.**

financial institution   an organization which provides financial services or products, or whose assets consist of financial instruments. The term applies to investment companies; mortgage companies; real estate investment trusts; life and property/casualty insurance companies; commercial banks; mutual savings banks; savings and loan associations; credit unions; finance companies; federal credit agencies; state and federal government pension funds; and private pension funds. See **commercial bank; investment company; savings and loan association.**

financial plan   a course of action that is designed specifically for an individual, family, or organization, which identifies investments, strategies and placement of assets to maximize returns, reduce or eliminate taxes, and ensure adequate retirement income and insurance coverage. The term is associated with a written document, often prepared formally by a financial advisor or planner. See **estate planning; investment objective; retirement fund.**

financial planner   an individual providing services to customers in the preparation and planning of personal or business finances. The planner may have certification and registration in order to provide services, or may use the title without special licenses.
   The planner may be compensated by a consultation fee, or may provide services without direct charge, being paid by sales commissions. See **Certified Financial Planner (CFP); investment advisor; registered investment advisor (RIA).**

financial planning   the process of preparation relating to finances — investment, insurance, taxes and the management of assets and liabilities.
   The term as applied to an occupation has several meanings. Planning as an occupation may refer to an individual with many years' experience providing tailored services to individuals, or may be a term used by someone with little or no experience and with no education, licenses or registrations. See **assets; estate planning; inflation; investment objective; liabilities; tax preference.**

financial statement a report of an organization summarizing the status or results of operations. The two most common types of statements are the balance sheet (reporting assets, liabilities and net worth as of a specific date) and the income statement (summarizing income, costs and expenses for a period of time). The two statements may be referred to collectively as a single financial statement. See **balance sheet; income statement.**

financing the raising of cash to fund the operations of a company. Debt financing includes the obtaining of a loan or an issue of bonds. Equity financing is the sale of stock (in a corporation) or the taking in of a partner (partnership). See **capitalization; equity; SEC Rule 10b-16.**

firm commitment a form of offering in which the underwriter actually buys securities to be sold to the public. The public offering price is the maximum price the underwriter may charge so that profits have a ceiling, although lower prices may be charged if the underwriter cannot sell shares or units at that price. See **freeriding; public offering price; underwriter; withholding.**

firm market a quotation price at which a market maker is prepared immediately to trade, used in the over-the-counter market. See **market maker; over-the-counter (OTC); quotation.**

firm order (1) a buy or sell order placed with finite terms and conditions and a time to place, which is to be placed as specified or will expire.
(2) an order placed for a broker-dealer's own account. See **broker-dealer; buy; sell order.**

firm quote a price for buy or sell of a round lot that a market maker is prepared to execute. See **buy; market maker; round lot; sell order.**

first call date the earliest date at which the issuer of a callable security may exercise a call of all or part of the issue. See **call feature.**

first in, first out (FIFO) method of inventory valuation in which it is assumed the first manufactured or purchased stock is also the first to be sold. This method is presumed in effect by the Internal Revenue Service unless another method is chosen by the organization. See **FIFO; inventory; last in, first out (LIFO); LIFO.**

first mortgage bond a type of bond having first claim against property in the event of default. See **junior lien; mortgage; open-end mortgage; senior lien.**

fiscal year a twelve-month business year chosen by an organization for tax and financial reporting. The fiscal year may end at any month, but is chosen most frequently to correspond with the natural business cycle. See **financial statement; fundamental analysis; tax basis.**

Fitch Investors Service an organization providing corporate bond ratings, along with Standard and Poor's and Moody's. See **corporate bond; rating systems.**

five-hundred dollar rule a general guideline stating that sell-out procedures should not be invoked against an account when the deficiency is less than five-hundred dollars. See **broker-dealer; Regulation T; sell-out procedures.**

five percent rule a guideline under the rules of fair practice which provides general definition of fair and reasonable markups that should and should not be

```
┌─────────────────────────────────────────────────────┐
│  Fitch Investors  Service                           │
│                                                     │
│  highest quality          AAA    AA    A           │
│                                                     │
│  medium quality           BBB    BB    B           │
│                                                     │
│  low quality              CCC    CC    C           │
│                                                     │
│  questionable value       DDD    DD    D           │
└─────────────────────────────────────────────────────┘
```

applied in transactions and the level of profits that are thought to be expected. See **fair treatment; National Association of Securities Dealers (NASD); rules of fair practice.**

five-year property   class of ACRS depreciation which includes most machinery and equipment, under which assets are recovered—depreciated—over a five-year period.

An election may be made in this class to take straight-line depreciation over 5, 12 or 25 years as an alternative to the accelerated five-year ACRS method. See **accelerated cost recovery system (ACRS); class life; declining balance; depreciation.**

fixed annuity   a type of annuity which promises to pay a set amount of money to the annuitant, either for life or for a certain number of years. See **annuity; variable annuity.**

fixed assets   properties of an organization which must be capitalized, or written off over a period of years known as class life. Any property puchased which has value for more than the current year may be considered as "fixed," or long-term.

See **class life; long-term assets; depreciation; financial statement.**

fixed charge   a formula comparing an organization's net profits before interest and taxes, to the amount of interest paid on debts that are "fixed"—bonds, for example. The calculation indicates the level at which earnings are adequate to fund their debt obligations. See **interest; net income.**

$$\frac{\text{income from operations}}{\text{interest payments}} = \text{fixed charge}$$

$$\frac{\$742,600}{\$199,300} = 3.7$$

fixed charge

Fiscal Year

Fiscal Year	1st Quarter	2nd Quarter	3rd Quarter	4th Quarter
Jan 31	Apr 30	Jul 31	Oct 31	Jan 31
Feb 28	May 31	Aug 31	Nov 30	Feb 28
Mar 31	Jun 30	Sep 30	Dec 31	Mar 31
Apr 30	Jul 31	Oct 31	Jan 31	Apr 30
May 31	Aug 31	Nov 30	Feb 28	May 31
Jun 30	Sep 30	Dec 31	Mar 31	Jun 30
Jul 31	Oct 31	Jan 31	Apr 30	Jul 31
Aug 31	Nov 30	Feb 28	May 31	Aug 31
Sep 30	Dec 31	Mar 31	Jun 30	Sep 30
Oct 31	Jan 31	Apr 30	Jul 31	Oct 31
Nov 30	Feb 28	May 31	Aug 31	Nov 30
Dec 31	Mar 31	Jun 30	Sep 30	Dec 31

fixed dollar annuity   another term for "fixed annuity," an agreement for the payment of a fixed dollar amount upon annuitization. See **deferred payment annuity; fixed annuity; immediate payment annuity; joint and survivor annuity; life annuity; life insurance; single purchase contract.**

fixed income fund   a type of closed-end mutual fund seeking the objective of maximum income to investors, usually from high-yielding debt securities and, in some cases, from common stocks with a high dividend payment. See **closed-end; investment objective; mutual fund; yield.**

fixed rate mortgage   a real estate mortgage with a rate of interest that does not change over the duration of the contract. See **adjustable rate mortgage (ARM); mortgage; real estate.**

fixed trust   a unit investment trust which identifies in advance the securities or classes of security in which it will invest. See **mutual fund; participating trust; plan company; unit investment trust.**

flat bond   a bond that trades with no adjustment for accruals of interest from earned date to effective date of issue. See **accrual; and interest; bond.**

flat defined pension plan   a format not in common use, where all employees of the organization will receive the same amount of retirement benefit. See **pension plan; percentage defined pension plan; retirement plans.**

flat market   descriptive of the market for a security or in general, in which there is little activity and, thus, little movement. See **bear; bull; price.**

flexible rate mortgage   a term used interchangeably with adjustable rate mortgage (ARM). See **adjustable rate mortgage (ARM).**

float   (1) shares or units of a security available for buying or selling. They may be in the hands of the public as opposed to closely held.
(2) the amount of yet uncleared checks or drafts drawn against a deposit and not yet posted by the bank. See **bank float; cash flow; closely-held corporation; outstanding stock.**

floating an issue   term meaning the same as public offer and sale of securities. See **offering; underwriter.**

floating debt   municipal security debts scheduled for maturity within five years. See **funded debt; long-term debt; municipal bond; short-term debt.**

floating rate note (FRN)   a type of note whose interest rate varies with a predetermined index such as T-bill rates. See **index; interest; note.**

floating supply   (1) the number of listings found in the *Blue List*, showing the availability and size of the current bond market.
(2) number of shares available for trading on a particular issue, representing publicly held outstanding shares. See **Blue List; bond; index.**

floor   the trading market's exchange area where auction activities are conducted in securities. See **auction marketplace; exchange; trading market.**

floor broker   a commission broker or trader who transacts in securities on the floor for a member firm or its customers. See **broker; commission broker; stock exchange; two-dollar broker.**

floor official   individual who settles disputes during the auction process. See **auction marketplace; stock exchange.**

floor ticket   an order ticket placed for the buy or sell activity of a customer. The ticket must contain the customer's name; date, time, and effective length of the order; type (buy or sell; short or long); number of shares or units to be traded; name or symbol of the security; order terms or conditions; and the price. See **buy; office ticket; order ticket; sell order; trade.**

floor trader   a competitive trader trading for his or her own account. See **competitive trader; registered trader; specialist.**

flower bond   a type of Treasury bond which may be used to pay estate taxes following the death of the owner, granted full par value even though current value is discounted. Flower bonds were issued prior to April, 1971 and all will have reached maturity by 1998. See **discount bond; estate tax; par value; Treasury bond.**

FMAN   identification of one of the three option cycles, those with expiration dates in February, May, August and November. See **cycle; expiration cycle; JAJO; MJSD; option.**

FOCUS Report   shortened name for the Financial and Operational Combined Uniform Single Report (FOCUS). See **broker-dealer; Financial and Operational Combined Uniform Single Report (FOCUS); financial statement.**

forced conversion   status of convertible securities when selling above call price. With the market value of common stock considered, the issuer calls convertibles. The owner is forced to convert or, to avoid conversion, to sell convertibles. See **call price; convertible security; underlying security.**

foreclosure   the process of removing the rights to property ownership because of mortgage default, in which the loan is liquidated by repossession of the property. See **mortgage; real estate.**

Form 3   a report that officers and directors of a corporation, or those with 10 percent or more of its stock, file with the SEC. The report summarizes all stock under direct ownership; beneficial ownership; convertible holdings; rights, warrants and options. See **control person; Securities and Exchange Commission (SEC); stockholder.**

Form 4   a report that officers and directors of a corporation, or those with 10 percent or more of its stock, file with the SEC. The report deals with changes in securities owned, and is filed within 10 days following a month in which the change occurs. See **control person; Securities and Exchange Commission (SEC); stockholder.**

Form 8K   a report filed by corporations with the SEC, summarizing material events that would affect an investor's decision to buy, sell or hold stock in that company. See **corporation; Securities and Exchange Commission (SEC).**

Form 10K a report filed annually with the SEC by all listed corporations; those with more than 500 stockholders; and those with assets over $2 million. The 10K is included with the annual report sent to stockholders. See **corporation; publicly held corporation; Securities Act of 1933; Securities and Exchange Commission (SEC).**

Form 10Q a quarterly report filed with the SEC by corporations, containing interim information similar to that contained on Form 10K. See **corporation; publicly held corporation; Securities and Exchange Commission (SEC).**

Form 1065 a federal partnership return, filed with the Internal Revenue Service. No tax is paid at this level, but summaries indicate those other partnerships, corporations and individuals earning portions of taxable income. See **partnership.**

formula investing any form of investing in which a formula determines the level of participation, such as the constant dollar plan and dollar cost averaging. This strategy involves following a set of rules established and followed, regardless of outside influence, such as market movement in a security. See **constant dollar plan; dollar cost averaging (DCA).**

Fortune 500 an index published by *Fortune Magazine*, rating the top 500 corporations in the United States, in terms of net income, total sales, and stockholders' equity. See **corporation; index.**

forward contract practice in futures trading in which a buyer and seller agree on a sale price, but with a future settlement date. See **commodity; futures contract.**

forward pricing the method used to set the value of buy and sell orders of mutual fund shares. Orders received are assigned a value based upon the next net asset valuation, less redemption charges. See **mutual fund; net asset value per share (NAV); public offering price.**

fourth market computerized trading system used by institutional traders dealing directly with one another. See **instinet system.**

fractional point discretion condition attached to an order allowing execution within a specific range. If discretion is granted for one-half of a point, the trade can be executed within a half-point difference from the preferred price. See **buy; discretionary order; sell order.**

Freddie Mac abbreviated name of Federal Home Loan Mortgage Corporation securities. See **Federal Home Loan Mortgage Corporation (FHLMC).**

free and open market a type of market in which prices are set by supply and demand. See **auction marketplace.**

free crowd individuals involved in the trading of active bonds. See **active bond.**

free right of exchange the right held by a bond owner if allowed to change from registered to bearer form or from bearer to registered form. See **registered form.**

free security any security upon which no liens are placed. See **lien; securities.**

freeriding (1) activity in a customer's account in which a security is transacted without having shown evidence of cash to back a trade. When freeriding has been identified, accounts may be frozen for 90 days under Regulation T.

(2) term applied to underwriters who hold a portion of a public offering, to later sell it at a profit. See **frozen account; National Association of Securities Dealers (NASD); Regulation T; underwriter.**

front-end load (1) form of mutual fund which charges a fee at the time an investment is made, to pay for sales charges (commissions) paid to those placing orders.

(2) fees charged by a syndicate to pay sales commissions or fees to the general partners, which reduce the amount of capital that actually goes into the investment. Front-end loads vary greatly between programs, and should be examined before a limited partnership is selected. See **limited partnership; load mutual fund; load spread; no-load (NL); sponsor; syndicate.**

frozen account a customer account suspended from trading because of Regulation T violations, such as delay in payment for trades, or freeriding. See **freeriding; Regulation T.**

frozen capital ratio a comparison between net fixed assets (long-term assets) and tangible net worth, showing the relationship between a company's total investment in assets and equity ownership. See **balance sheet ratios; fundamental analysis; ratios.**

$$\text{frozen capital ratio} = \frac{\text{long-term assets} - \text{depreciation}}{\text{tangible net worth}}$$

Balance Sheet	
Current Assets	$1,386,000
Long-Term Assets	1,945,600
Less: Depreciation	(295,500)
Intangible Assets	50,000
Total Assets	$3,086,100
Liabilities	$1,840,300
Net Worth	1,245,800
Total	$3,086,100

$$\frac{(\$1,945,600 - \$295,500)}{(\$1,245,800 - \$50,000)} = 1.38 \text{ to } 1$$

frozen capital ratio

$$\frac{\text{earnings}}{\text{outstanding shares} + \text{convertible shares}} = \text{fully diluted earnings per share}$$

$$\frac{\$1,845,650}{\$1,000,000 + \$750,000} = \$1.05$$

fully diluted earnings per share

full disclosure concept embodied in the Securities Act of 1933, that all facts which may affect an investor's decision to select a particular security must be disclosed prior to the final decision. See **Securities Act of 1933.**

full vesting a vesting method under which no partial vestation is allowed until the end of the period, after which 100 percent is accrued. See **retirement plans; vesting methods.**

full vesting	
Year	Amount of Vesting
1	0
2	0
3	0
4	0
5	0
6	0
7	0
8	0
9	0
10	100%

fully diluted earnings per share a way of reporting the per-share value of net earnings, but reported as though all convertible securities outstanding had been converted to common stock at the beginning of the earnings period. See **common stock; conversion; earnings per share; primary earnings per share.**

fully distributed description of a public offering that has been placed with customers. See **public offering; underwriter.**

fully registered an individual who has all of the NASD licenses required to transact each type of business in the securities business or as offered by a firm. See **broker; trader.**

functional allocation sharing a form of oil and gas offering in which the general partner capitalizes the tangible costs that are not deductible to the limited partners. The deductible intangible costs are funded by the limited partners and are fully deductible by them. See **intangible drilling costs; oil and gas; tangible drilling costs; tax preference.**

fundamental analysis   a technique employed by investors who believe a company's future stock value is determined by information to be found solely in financial statements: earnings, dividends, assets, and financial strength. The fundamentalist also considers economic influences, government policies, and the state of the industry. See **financial statement; quantitative analysis; technical analysis.**

funded debt   a company's liabilities with maturities beyond five years. See **floating debt; long-term debt; short-term debt.**

funded debt ratio   a comparison between working capital (current assets less current liabilities) and long-term liabilities. The ratio indicates how well the company is able to pay obligations from working reserves. See **balance sheet ratios; ratios.**

future time value   option premium that has no intrinsic value, but reflects the additional amount investors will pay to obtain a contract. See **option; time value premium.**

futures contract   an agreement for purchase and sale of a commodity at an established price and delivery date in the future. See **commodity; forward contract; index.**

G

gap financing   a form of short-term loan used by real estate investment trusts (REITs), to pay construction lenders, and repaid upon finalization of a mortgage loan. See **mortgage; real estate investment trust (REIT); short-term debt.**

garage   common name for an annex to the trading floor of the New York Stock Exchange. See **floor; stock exchange.**

$$\text{funded debt ratio} = \frac{\text{funded debt}}{(\text{current assets} - \text{current liabilities})} = \frac{\$427,300}{(\$612,400 - \$291,100)} = 75.2\%$$

funded
debt ratio

gemstones   a non-security identified by rarity, color and clarity. Investors may purchase gemstones hoping for eventual increases in value, over time. Some tax shelter schemes have been devised to purchase stones, and then donate them to a charity at an inflated valuation. However, the I.R.S. maintains that only the investor's basis is deductible. Gemstones are risky because valuation is subjective, and there may be a limited or non-existent market when the investor desires to sell. See **investment program; precious gemstones; tax shelter.**

general mortgage bond   a bond which does not necessarily have seniority of claims on a property, but is secured by real estate. See **junior lien; mortgage bond; senior lien.**

general obligation bond (GO)   type of municipal security that is backed by the full faith and credit, and by the taxing power of the issuer, including limited tax bonds and special assessment bonds. See **limited tax bond; municipal bond; special assessment bond; tax-exempt security.**

general partner   (1) in a general partnership, one of the business owners, who holds a portion of equity and shares with other general partners in profits and losses of the business.
(2) in a limited partnership, the person, firm or group representing limited partners in the management of partnership assets. General partners have unlimited liability, while limited partners may be liable only to the extent of their committed investment basis. See **direct participation program; limited partner; partnership; private placement; public offering.**

general partnership   a form of business organization in which an unincorporated entity is formed, consisting of two or more persons, corporations or other partnerships. Each general partner holds a share of equity, profits and losses and liabilities. See **limited partnership; partnership.**

general securities principal   a person who has passed the NASD Series 24 examination. The management of broker-dealers are required to hold the general securities license, as are branch office managers and others who will supervise in the capacity of an Office of Supervisory Jurisdiction. See **branch office manager; broker-dealer; National Association of Securities Dealers (NASD); Office of Supervisory Jurisdiction (OSJ); Series 24.**

general securities registered representative   a person who has passed the NASD Series 7 examination. The license entitles its holder to offer and sell direct participation programs, mutual funds, stocks and bonds and variable annuities. See **broker-dealer; National Association of Securities Dealers (NASD); registered representative; Series 7.**

generally accepted accounting principles (GAAP)   a set of standards established by the Financial Accounting Standards Board (FASB) for the consistent reporting of financial data and preparation of financial statements. See **Financial Accounting Standards Board (FASB); financial statement; fundamental analysis.**

geothermal energy   an investment in programs designed to explore for and produce and develop energy sources from geothermal deposits such as heated steam or water. Many of the same tax preference treatments of drilling costs that are common to oil and gas programs are allowed for geothermal programs. See **investment program; tax-advantaged investment; tax preference.**

120 / gift-leaseback

gift-leaseback   a method of operation in which a trust is established to accept gifted business equipment. The grantor then leases back the equipment and claims a deduction for it.

To qualify for a tax write-off, the grantor must deal with an independent trust. The grantor may keep no equity in the property, and the lease must occur for a bona fide business purpose. Also, there must be a written lease, and the amount of rent must be in line with lease prices otherwise charged for similar equipment. See **sale-leaseback; trust.**

gift tax   a tax on the giver of a gift. To the recipient, a gift is tax-free. But a federal gift tax, less an annual exclusion, is charged to gifts between any two people except spouses. See **tax basis; value.**

gilt-edged   any security with a reputation for consistent high earnings, payment of dividends or interest, and prompt payment to investors of earnings. See **dividend; high-grade security; interest.**

Ginnie Mae   abbreviation for securities of the Government National Mortgage Association (GNMA). See **Government National Mortgage Association (GNMA).**

Ginnie Mae pass-through   a part interest in a mortgage pool of residential properties. The earnings of each investor are passed through from the homeowner to a bank, then through to the investor in a GNMA program. See **Government National Mortgage Association (GNMA); mortgage; real estate.**

give up   (1) a term used to describe a broker acting in behalf of another, such as a member firm. In placing orders, the broker "gives up" the name of the firm, indicating he is acting on that firm's behalf.

(2) sharing part of a commission or fee with another broker, or "giving up" a portion of earnings. In some situations, the practice is illegal. See **agent; commission; broker.**

Glass Steagall Act   a federal law applying to commercial banks. It states a commercial bank may not own a broker-dealer, or form trading or underwriting securities or most municipal bonds. However, bank holding companies may hold a subsidiary broker-dealer organization. See **bank holding company; broker-dealer; commercial bank; revenue bond.**

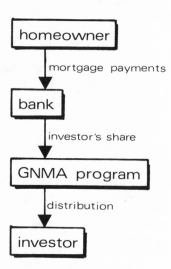

ginnie mae
pass-through

GNP deflator index   an index which measures the dollar's loss of purchasing power since its base year of 1972. In that year, the index was set at 100.0. If the current index sits at 156.3, it will cost 156.3% more to purchase an asset than it would have cost in 1972. See **inflation; index.**

going concern value   valuation of an active business based on earning power rather than book or market value if liquidated. See **earnings; liquidation value.**

GNP deflator index

$$\$8,000 \quad \times \quad \frac{156.30}{100.00} \quad = \quad \$12,504$$

going public the act of selling securities to the public for the first time. See **public offering.**

gold a non-security investment thought to be a hedge against inflation, which may be purchased directly (taking possession of bullion or coins, for example) or indirectly (by buying shares of gold-producing companies or gold mutual funds). See **investment program; precious metals.**

good delivery standards that must be met before a certificate must be accepted in a security transaction, as specified by the Uniform Practice Code (UPC). See **certificate; negotiable instrument; Uniform Practice Code (UPC).**

good faith deposit (1) deposit placed by a customer with a broker, often applied when a new customer purchases securities for the first time.
(2) deposits by members of an underwriting group, given to a syndicate as assurance of their performance under the terms of the agreement.
(3) deposit made by municipal bond underwriters with the issuer. See **customer; municipal bond; syndicate; underwriter.**

good money term meaning federal funds, so called because they do not need bank clearance prior to application. See **clearance; federal funds.**

good til cancelled (GTC) an order specifying a price, limit or stop, that stays in effect until cancelled or executed. In practice, the order, if left unexecuted, will be checked and renewed periodically. See **limit order; stop-limit order; stop order.**

government bond the highest rated bonds available, those issued by the U.S. Government. See **bond; high-grade security.**

Government National Mortgage Association (GNMA) organization developed to buy mortgages from private sources and guarantee payment to investors who subsequently purchase securities in the mortgage pool bonds offered by the association.
GNMA (also called "Ginnie Mae") originally was part of the Federal National Mortgage Association and is directed by the Department of Housing and Urban Development (HUD). Activities of GNMA are intended to encourage construction in the housing market. See **Federal National Mortgage Association (GNMA); Ginnie Mae; mortgage pool.**

graded vesting a method of vesting in a retirement plan in which a set percentage is added after each qualified year of service. For example, the plan may call for no vesting until completion of five years of service; five percent per year through the 10th year; and ten percent per year (of total employer contributions) through the 15th year. See **retirement plans; vesting methods.**

Graded Vesting

Employer's Accumulated Contributions	Employee's Age	Years of Service	% Vested	Graded Vesting
$ 4,500	32	1	0%	$ -0-
9,000	33	2	0	-0-
13,500	34	3	0	-0-
18,000	35	4	0	-0-
22,500	36	5	25	5,625
27,000	37	6	30	8,100
31,500	38	7	35	11,025
36,000	39	8	40	14,400
40,500	40	9	45	18,225
45,000	41	10	50	22,500
49,500	42	11	60	29,700
54,000	43	12	70	37,800
58,500	44	13	80	46,800
63,000	45	14	90	56,700
67,500	46	15	100	67,500

graduated payment mortgage a mortgage with provisions for a low monthly payment at the beginning of the contract, with periodic increases and, after five to ten years, a leveling off for the duration. See **mortgage; real estate.**

grantor trust a trust established and controlled by the individual who will place assets into that trust. See **reversionary interest; trust.**

gross margin ratio a ratio comparing gross profits to total sales, expressed as a percentage and useful when comparing results between operating periods. See **income account ratios; ratios.**

gross
margin
ratio

$$\frac{gross\ profit}{sales} = gross\ margin$$

$$\frac{863,000}{1,928,300} = 44.75\%$$

gross multiplier one method used in real estate investments to estimate the value of properties, especially in evaluating assumptions about future property value growth. It is based upon estimated rental increases. The multiplier is a factor used in comparing gross rents to property value. See **cap rate; real estate.**

Annual Rental Income	Gross Multiplier	Value
$ 50,000	8.5	$425,000
100,000	8.5	850,000
$ 50,000	9.0	$450,000
100,000	9.0	900,000
$ 50,000	9.5	$475,000
100,000	9.5	950,000

gross multiplier

Gross National Product (GNP) a measure of activity in buying and selling markets in the United States during a given period of time. It is the value of goods and services bought and sold, containing personal consumption, government purchases, investment in business equipment, and the net difference between foreign

gross national product

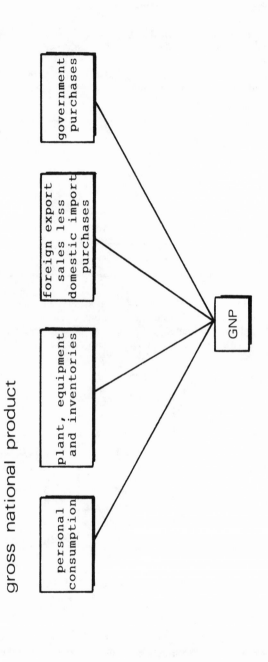

purchase of American exports and domestic purchase of foreign imports. See **fundamental analysis; index.**

gross profit the amount of profit realized after deducting all direct costs — materials used from inventory, purchases, and other costs of acquiring or manufacturing product — from sales, but before deducting selling or administrative expenses. See **financial statement; income statement.**

growing equity mortgage a mortgage with a fixed rate of interest but varying principal payments, based upon a predetermined index or schedule. See **mortgage; real estate.**

growth stock a stock with a record of rapid growth, or expectation of rapid growth, in terms of price and market value. See **dividend yield; market value; price-earnings ratio (P/E).**

guaranteed bond a bond which has its interest and/or maturity payments guaranteed by another organization, often a parent company. See **bond; guaranteed stock; safety.**

guaranteed income contract a type of agreement granted by an insurance company to an institutional investor (often a profit-sharing or pension plan). The investor agrees to deposit a substantial sum of capital as an investment, and the insurer guarantees a minimum rate of return, for a period up to 10 years. See **collateral; institutional investor; rate of return; yield.**

guaranteed payment a payment to the general partner, such as salary, in a limited partnership. Such payments usually are deductible to the limited partners. See **capital expenditure; deferred asset; general partner; limited partnership; partnership.**

guaranteed stock used in reference to the promise of one organization (often a parent company) that dividends will be paid by another (a subsidiary), seen frequently regarding preferred stock. See **guaranteed bond; preferred stock; safety; stock.**

H

haircut the requirement that a broker-dealer reduce the valuation of securities held on its balance sheet. The haircut is set up to 30 percent of book value, and is to reflect the risk of loss associated with that security. Up to a 100 percent haircut can be required for securities held for which a complete loss is possible. See **broker-dealer; net capital requirement.**

half-life an estimate of the date on which one-half of the mortgages in a mortgage pool will have been paid by the homeowner, considering prepayments and defaults. See **Ginnie Mae pass-through; mortgage pool.**

half-year convention standard practice under which a half-year's depreciation may be taken on an asset acquired, no matter what month the actual purchase was made. See **accelerated cost recovery system (ACRS); depreciation.**

top (bear trend)

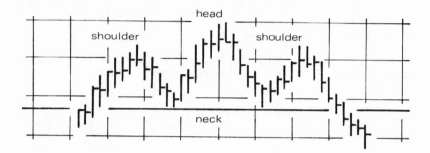

bottom (bull trend)

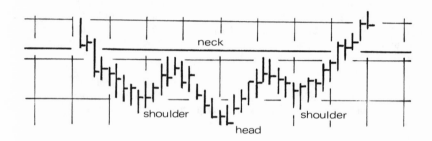

head and shoulders

head and shoulders   reference to the appearance of a stock's movement in which a series of upward or downward trends combine to make a head and shoulders appearance just prior to a breakout. Stock chartists contend that plotting a head and shoulders pattern can predict future movement of the issue. See **bear; bull; chartist; technical analysis.**

head cost averaging   technique used by investors in cattle feeding programs, involving investment in several programs to average out the price of feed, and to protect against wide price variances that can be experienced in a single program. See **cattle feeding; diversification; leverage.**

hedge   a strategy involving two different securities purchases or sales, which are intended to limit losses. Potential gains are reduced by hedge positions, an exchange made for the safety the strategy allows. See **arbitrage; option; risk; short against the box.**

hedge clause   a disclaimer made in a report or market letter, that conclusions or recommendations are made depending on information supplied by others and, therefore, the producer of the document does not claim total accuracy. See **market letter.**

hedge fund a type of partnership formed just to invest in securities, especially when the type of activity involves hedge transactions. See **investment program; limited partnership.**

hedge ratio another term for an option's delta. See **delta.**

hedged tender term for action taken by one who offers a security for sale. Anticipating that the full amount will not be purchased, a portion of the total is sold short, protecting against being unable to dispose of the whole block. See **short sale.**

highballing an illegal action which occurs between a dealer and a customer. Securities held at a loss position are bought by the dealer for a price above market value. At the same time, a separate security is sold to the customer, also for a price above market value. The dealer recognizes a gain on the sale of new securities and the customer moves from one paper loss to another. See **manipulation; market value; paper profit/loss.**

highest and best use general description used in real estate offerings of utilization of property in a way that produces maximum return to the investor. See **investment income; real estate.**

high-grade security a type of security that offers the lowest possible risks; best possible chance for prompt payment of interest or dividends; and greatest likelihood for return of capital. See **rating systems; risk; safety.**

historical yield (1) at one time, the method by which mutual funds were required to set comparative value, involving the dividing of dividends by the average offering price.
(2) any reasonable formula for computation of yields on mutual funds.
(3) record of earnings, usually expressed as a percentage of return to the investor, in any security. Direct participation programs offer the historical yield of the sponsor in past programs as proof of their ability to successfully offer viable investments to the public. See **direct participation program; mutual fund; public offering price; yield; yield to maturity.**

hobby losses according to the Internal Revenue Service, a non-deductible loss from a hobby or any other activity "not engaged in for profit."
Presuming a profit motive, the general guideline for a small business is that a profit should be shown in any two years of a consecutive five-year term. The burden of proof is on the individual to establish that an activity is a business for profit, and not a hobby. See **losses; profit.**

holder of record the owner of a security recognized on the record date, especially for the purpose of accruing and then paying dividends. See **record date; stockholder of record.**

holding company an organization which controls the voting stock of another organization, or is formed to manage and control related companies. See **investment company; voting privilege.**

holding period   the period of time a capital asset is owned, referred to for the purpose of deciding whether a gain or loss is short-term or long-term. See **capital gain; capital loss; long-term assets.**

Homeowner's Land Corporation (HLC)   a federal agency formed in 1932 to issue bonds guaranteed by the government. The bonds are used in exchange for defaulted mortgages. See **default; government bond; mortgage.**

Honolulu Stock Exchange (HSE)   843 Fort Street, Honolulu HI 96813; a regional exchange which is exempted from SEC registration, upon request and due to minimal trading activity. See **regional exchanges; Securities and Exchange Commission (SEC); Securities Exchange Act of 1934; stock exchange.**

horizontal spread   another term for a calendar spread, in which two or more options are bought or sold, with the same strike price but different expiration dates. See **calendar spread; diagonal spread; expiration date; option; strike price.**

```
horizontal spread

1)  Sell Oct 35 call        $    25
    Buy Jan 35 call             (225)

    Net cost                $ (200)


2)  Buy Mar 25 put          $ (100)
    Sell Jun 25 put             350

    Net proceeds            $  250
```

hot issue   any security about to be offered for sale that will trade above the public offering price, and subject to protective and special rules to prevent freeriding and withholding. See **freeriding; premium; public offering price; rules of fair practice; withholding.**

house of issue   an organization acting as underwriter of a security issue. See **floating an issue; underwriter.**

house rules   the policies and procedures of a broker-dealer, also called compliance rules, that are imposed upon registered representatives and employees. See **broker-dealer; compliance manual.**

housing authority bond   a revenue bond which has special features. The U.S. Government pledges its full faith and credit that contributions will be adequate to pay principal and interest, but which are intended to be repaid by collection of rents from properties constructed from bond proceeds. See **municipal bond; revenue bond.**

hundred dollar rule   a policy which allows exemption from Regulation T margin requirements when different securities are bought and sold on the same day, when the net debit balance is $100 or less. See **margin requirement; Regulation T.**

hybrid annuity   a type of annuity which has combined features of fixed and variable contracts. See **fixed annuity; variable annuity.**

hydro-electric energy   a category of alternate energy that, as an investment program, provides tax preference benefits from depreciation and credits. See **alternate energy; direct participation program; investment program; tax preference.**

hypothecation   a pledge of securities as collateral when the customer owns the securities but allows them to be held by the broker-dealer. Margin purchases are held under a hypothecation agreement and may be re-pledged (rehypothecated) for additional financing by the broker-dealer, yet still remain the property of the customer. See **broker-dealer; collateral; customer; margin account; rehypothecation; SEC Rule 15c2-1.**

I

immediate-or-cancel (IOC)   a type of limit order specifying the buy or sell of securities, with the condition that any portion that cannot be executed at the price is to be cancelled. See **execution; limit order; order ticket.**

immediate payment annuity   a single purchase contract made currently, with annuity benefits beginning at retirement, and continuing for the lifetime of the annuitant, or for a number of years. See **annuity; single purchase contract.**

implied volatility   a method of judging a security's volatility by current activity and price, in consideration of market conditions, rather than by that security's historical performance. See **BETA; technical analysis; volatility.**

in and out   trading activity which takes advantage of short-term price changes rather than holding on for the long-term appreciation potential or dividends. An in-and-out trader may buy and sell within a short period of time, often in a single trading day. See **day trade; trade.**

in the money   term describing any option when the value of the underlying security is higher (for calls) or lower (for puts) than the strike price. An option consists of intrinsic value and time value. For an in-the-money option, that portion of the call premium equal to the points above (or put premium equal to the points below) strike price is intrinsic value. See **intrinsic value; option; out of the money; strike price.**

in the money

inactive bond bonds that are expected to have a low level of trading activity. See **active bond; bond; cabinet crowd; debt security.**

inactive stock issues which trade on a very low volume, to the extent that many are bought and sold in 10-share lots rather than the traditional round lot of 100. See **round lot; stock; volume.**

incentive stock option a benefit provided under the Economic Recovery Tax Act of 1981, allowing employees of corporations to exercise options granted on their employer's stock, without incurring a tax liability. Only when stock bought through incentive options is sold, is a capital gain recognized for tax purposes. See **capital gain; Economic Recovery Tax Act of 1981 (ERTA); exercise price.**

incidental life insurance life insurance purchased within a qualified retirement plan, allowed only if "incidental," or minor in comparison to the benefits provided through an annuity contribution, or to the level of premium paid. See **defined benefit pension plan; defined contribution pension plan; individual retirement account (IRA); Keogh plan; life insurance; retirement plans.**

income (1) for individuals, earnings from employment, self-employment, or investment; cash received for services rendered; or assets or benefits credited in place of cash.
(2) for businesses, the profit realized after costs, expenses and taxes, from enterprise; return on stockholders' equity; or net profit to partners in a partnership.
(3) for investors, the interest, dividends or capital gains realized from taking risks through lending capital, purchasing equity positions, or speculating through options, warrants, or commodity futures. See **earned income; earnings; equity; investment income; net income.**

income account ratios comparisons between classifications of income, costs, expenses or net income for the purpose of spotting trends or in performance of fundamental analysis. See **expense control ratio; fundamental analysis; gross margin ratio; margin of profit.**

income bond another term of an adjustment bond, an instrument offered in exchange for outstanding debts, with interest and principal promised only as earned. See **adjustment bond.**

income company a mutual fund seeking the objective of income, often the highest possible income regardless of the risk level. See **investment company; investment objective; mutual fund.**

income shares type of equity offered through dual-purpose investment companies, often including a minimum guaranteed payment. In such a company, investors may purchase income shares or capital shares. All income is earned by the income shareholders, and all capital gains by capital shareholders. See **dividend; dual-purpose investment company; interest.**

income statement one of the two major financial statements (the other being the balance sheet), which reports total revenues, costs, expenses and net earnings from operations.
While a balance sheet reports the status of assets, liabilities and net worth as of a specific date, the income statement shows results for a period of time, commonly

income account ratios

$$\frac{\text{Gross Profit}}{\text{Sales}} = \text{Gross Margin Ratio}$$

$$\frac{\text{Operating Expenses}}{\text{Sales}} = \text{Expense Control Ratio}$$

$$\frac{\text{Net Income}}{\text{Sales}} = \text{Margin of Profit}$$

one year. A comparative income statement shows results for the current year and for the previous year. See **financial statement; net income; sales.**

Income Statement

Sales	$2,840,300
Direct Costs	1,698,000
Gross Profit	$1,142,300
General Expenses	930,500
Income from Operations	$ 211,800
Income Taxes	47,100
Net Profit	$ 164,700

incremental return

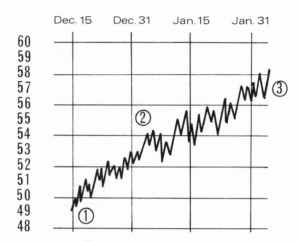

1,000 shares bought at $49, with
target sales price of $60 per share

		credit	debit
①	December 15 – stock value $49 per share		
	▶sell 2 calls, Feb 50	$ 350	
②	January 1 – stock value rises to $53		
	▶Buy 2 calls, Feb 50 and sell 5 calls, Feb 55	$1,000	$ 800
③	February 1 – stock value rises to $58		
	▶Buy 5 calls, Feb 55 and sell 10 calls, Feb 60	$3,750	$3,500
	Total	$5,100	$4,300
	Net income from covered calls	$ 800	

incremental return   a covered call-writing strategy which realizes the full appreciation value of the underlying stock while also profiting from the option premiums, even though the stock is moving in an upward pattern.

The strategy works when several contracts can be written, and begins with the sale of options against only a portion of the portfolio. When the stock rises in price, the positions are closed, and a higher number of new positions are opened at a higher strike price. This is repeated until the target sales price is reached, continually rolling up and producing a net credit in option premiums. See **covered option; strike price; write.**

indenture   a name for the deed of trust which spells out the terms of a bond contract, including the appointment of a trustee, terms and conditions of repayment, rate of interest and maturity date, and priority of claims. See **debt security; Trust Indenture Act of 1939; trustee.**

indenture qualification statement   a statement required to be filed with the Securities and Exchange Commission for debt securities that are not required to be registered. See **debt security; Securities Act of 1933; Securities and Exchange Commission (SEC); Trust Indenture Act of 1939.**

independent broker   exchange members who trade for other brokers who do not have a member on the floor, or for brokers with more workload than they can handle. See **commission broker; two-dollar broker.**

index   a measure of performance of a broad class of securities or economic conditions, usually weighted to reflect fairly how individual components of the index affect the overall performance. An index may be used to show market price activity, volume or economic conditions that will affect markets. See **American Stock Exchange Market Value Index; American Stock Exchange Price Change Index; averages; NYSE composite index.**

index fund   a type of mutual fund that invests in the same securities included in a specific index, and in the same mix, so that performance in the fund will reflect closely the movement of the index. See **mutual fund; portfolio.**

index of leading indicators   collective index of a series of economic conditions, which together are believed to affect the performance of markets, and is viewed by many as the primary summary of the state of the American economy. Included in the index, among other indicators, are steel, auto and oil production, employment, the money supply, currency in circulation, personal income, the Consumer Price Index, inventories, and the comparison of exports to imports. See **Consumer Price Index (CPI); fundamental analysis; inflation.**

index option   an option contract written against an accepted index, rather than against a specific issue. The same strategies of trading may be used as those for stock options, except that index options cannot be used to protect or offset positions in an account. Upon exercise, in-the-money options are settled by cash payment for the difference between closing market value and exercise price. See **closing price; exercise; settlement price.**

indicated gain   a portion of total proceeds from sale of an asset that will be subject to capital gains tax treatment. See **assets; capital gain.**

indication of interest   expression used to describe the limited discussions that may be held with customers before approval of registration with the Securities and Exchange Commission, of an offering. The customer may be approached for an indication of interest, which is neither a commitment to buy nor a purchase, nor a promise by the underwriter to sell interest in a program. See **customer; offering; registration statement; SEC Rule 10b-6; underwriter.**

individual proprietorship   a form of business organization in which a sole individual operates an unincorporated concern. All net income is reported on an individual tax return, summarized on Schedule C, and the proprietor must also pay self-employment (social security) tax on net income. See **corporation; partnership; Schedule C.**

individual retirement account (IRA) a benefit allowed to any individual with earned income (such as salaries and wages, fees, or self-employment income, but excluding interest, dividends, and capital gains). An amount of money may be invested in an IRA each year, regardless of what other retirement plans the individual has. Earnings are not taxed until withdrawn upon retirement. See **Keogh plan; qualified plan; retirement plans; tax deferral.**

individual retirement annuity an annuity issued on a single life or as a joint and survivor benefit, sold within the rules of an individual retirement account and subject to annual premium limitations. See **annuity; joint and survivor annuity; life annuity; qualified plan; retirement plans; tax deferral.**

industrial development bond a type of municipal revenue bond subject to special rules for tax exemption of interest. Since financing is for a corporation outside of the municipality, proceeds of the issue must be used for renovation, construction or improvement of civic facilities or pollution control. See **bond; revenue bond; tax-exempt security.**

industrial mortgage type of financing for industrial properties, and a form of lending that is seen as a replacement of corporate bond financing. The industrial mortgage may have as short an amortization period as ten years. See **corporate bond; mortgage bond.**

industrial revenue bond a form of municipal bond in which an independent corporation is responsible and liable for payment to bondholders. The municipality sponsors the issue, which is to be used for construction or development of facilities for the corporation, and the level of tax exemption may be restricted. See **bond; municipal bond; tax-exempt security.**

inflation economic environment in which prices rise and, as a result, the buying power of the dollar declines. See **buying power; Consumer Price Index (CPI); deflation.**

inheritance tax a state tax levied against the individual shares of an estate after that estate has been divided. See **beneficiary; estate planning; estate tax.**

initial margin the amount of equity that must be put up by a margin account trader, applying to both long and short trading, or trading in a margin account with borrowed funds. See **margin requirement; Regulation G; Regulation T; Regulation U.**

inside information a term describing news or knowledge that is not available to the public at large, and is of a nature that may influence an investor's decision to buy, sell or hold a security. See **insider; securities; trade.**

inside market the wholesale, inter-dealer market, or pricing structure of trading used between dealers. See **dealer; market maker; quotation.**

insider (1) officer or director of a corporation.
(2) a control person, one who owns 10 percent or more of the voting stock of a corporation, including members of the immediate family of such stockholders.

(3) anyone with inside information. See **control person; corporation; director; inside information; principal stockholder.**

Insider Trading Sanctions Act of 1984 legislation allowing the Securities and Exchange Commission (SEC) to impose fines and penalties against insiders who trade based on information not available to the public. See **Securities and Exchange Commission (SEC).**

installment sale a type of sale of capital assets, in which proceeds are paid over a period of time. If all tests are met, capital gains are realized over the period of payment, rather than at the time the sale is completed. See **recognized gain; tax basis.**

instate bond a bond purchased by an investor who resides in the state of the issuer. See **municipal bond; tax-exempt security.**

instinet system a registered stock exchange which handles trades strictly through an automated system, whose full name is the Institutional Networks Corporation.
Also known as the fourth market, Instinet serves primarily institutional investors, and eliminates the cost of brokerage fees for subscribers. See **fourth market; institutional investor; stock exchange.**

institution descriptive of an organization involved solely in financial instruments, assets or transactions, such as a commercial bank, mutual fund or savings and loan association. See **commercial bank; mutual fund; savings and loan association.**

institutional investor a large company or institution trading in high volumes and receiving discounted commissions for block trading, acting in behalf of a large number of customers or investors, or investing its own assets. See **commercial bank; mutual fund; savings and loan association; trust.**

insubstantial quantity an amount of shares or units that can be allocated to restricted persons, even for hot issues, limited to 100 shares of stock or $5,000 face value of bonds. See **hot issue; National Association of Securities Dealers (NASD).**

intangible asset an asset reported on the balance sheet of an organization with a value that is difficult to determine, because there is no physical asset. Examples include goodwill, covenants and patents. See **tangible value; value.**

intangible drilling costs type of expenses in oil and gas, geothermal energy, and other energy programs, which may be capitalized or deducted in the year incurred, representing potentially substantial deductions for investors in those programs. See **amortization; capital expenditure; geothermal energy; oil and gas; tangible drilling costs.**

Inter-American Development Bank (IADB) an international organization whose purpose is to aid its members in economic development, through financing via issue of international bonds. See **bond; debt security.**

inter-bank rate the rate at which banks trade excess reserves among themselves. See **excess reserves; federal funds rate; interest.**

installment sale

Sale price $80,000; Basis, $55,000:

Year		Total	Return of Capital (55/80)	Capital Gains (25/80)
0	25 percent at sale	$20,000	$13,750	$ 6,250
1	7.5% payment	6,000	4,125	1,875
2	7.5% payment	6,000	4,125	1,875
3	7.5% payment	6,000	4,125	1,875
4	7.5% payment	6,000	4,125	1,875
5	7.5% payment	6,000	4,125	1,875
6	7.5% payment	6,000	4,125	1,875
7	7.5% payment	6,000	4,125	1,875
8	7.5% payment	6,000	4,125	1,875
9	7.5% payment	6,000	4,125	1,875
10	7.5% payment	6,000	4,125	1,875
	Total	$80,000	$55,000	$25,000

inter vivos trust   a living trust, one established for the benefit of someone who is still living. See **living trust; testamentary trust; trust.**

interest   (1) the cost of borrowing money; a rate that must be paid by a borrower to a lender for the use of funds.
(2) a holding in a security, usually a long position. One has an "interest" represented by a number of shares or units of that security. See **compound interest; earnings; investment income; return on invested capital; simple interest.**

interest averaging   a computation of interest when two or more loans or mortgages are in effect, to determine the actual annual interest cost. See **debt service; mortgage.**

---

(1) Annual percentage rate (APR)xBalance=Weighting

(2) Total Weighting/Total Balances=Interest Average

	Balance	Annual Percentage Rate	Weighting
First mortgage	$22,000	7.25%	1,595
Second mortgage	5,000	10.00	500
Third mortgage	45,000	14.50	6,525
Totals	$62,000		8,620
Average		13.90%	

interest averaging

---

interest coverage   a ratio comparing total earnings to interest payable on a bond, used as a measurement of the earnings' ability to "cover" the interest expense. See **fixed charge.**

$$\frac{Earnings}{Bond\ Interest} = Interest\ Coverage$$

$$\frac{\$830,200}{\$92,800} = 8.9\ times$$

interest coverage

Internal Rate of Return

$10,000 investment, assuming 11% return:

Year	Expenses	Net Return	Present Value Factors	Present Value
1	$2,100	$ 0	0.9009	$(1,892)
2	0	300	0.8116	243
3	0	350	0.7312	256
4	0	350	0.6587	231
5	0	400	0.5935	237
6	0	14,000	0.5346	7,484
Totals	$2,100	$15,400		
Net return		$13,300		
Net return in Present Value				$ 6,559
Average return per year (net / 6)		$ 2,217		
Annual straight return		22.2%		
Annual internal rate of return				10.9%

interest-free loan   a loan given, often to a trust or a family member, without charging interest. The interest-free loan has been used as a device to transfer taxable income without tying up capital for several years, as would be required by a Clifford Trust or similar arrangements. See **Clifford Trust; tax bracket; trust.**

interim bond   a temporary certificate given pending production of permanent negotiable instruments on regular bonds, which may be transferred as easily as may the final certificate forms. See **bond; certificate; transfer.**

interim financing   a type of financing intended to be replaced by permanent financing following construction, or repaid by proceeds after sale of a property. See **lending institution; real property.**

interim report   a quarterly summary of operations, issued for stockholders and reporting in an abbreviated form the same information given on an annual report. Financial statements will not be the result of a full, independent audit, but may be prepared on a compiled basis. See **annual report; balance sheet; financial statement; fundamental analysis; income statement.**

intermediary   (1) an organization or person assisting investors in creation or implementation of investment programs, such as a mutual fund or insurance company (portfolio intermediary).
(2) an individual who completes transactions for customers or provides advice on security selection (marketing intermediary). See **broker-dealer; commercial bank; portfolio manager.**

intermediate trend   the second of three steps in the Dow Theory, following a minor trend and preceding a major trend. The intermediate stage should last for several weeks or months. See **Dow Theory; major trend; minor trend; secondary movement; technical analysis.**

Intermountain Stock Exchange (ISE)   39 Exchange Place, Salt Lake City UT 84111; a regional exchange registered with the Securities and Exchange Commission and located in Salt Lake City. See **regional exchanges; Securities and Exchange Commission (SEC); Securities Exchange Act of 1934; stock exchange.**

internal rate of return   known as discounted cash flow, this is a method for computing return which takes the present value of future receipts and payments into account in computing average annual returns. See **discounted cash flow; present value; time value of money.**

International Association of Financial Planners (IAFP)   an organization for financial planners which presents regional and national conventions and refers clients to area members. See **Certified Financial Planner (CFP); financial planner.**

International Bank for Reconstruction and Development (IB)   international organization which aids its members in development of modern industrial capability. See **bank; capital market.**

International Monetary Market (IMM)   a specialized agency of the Chicago Mercantile Exchange specializing in financial futures on foreign currencies, bills and notes. See **Chicago Mercantile Exchange (CME); financial futures; futures contract.**

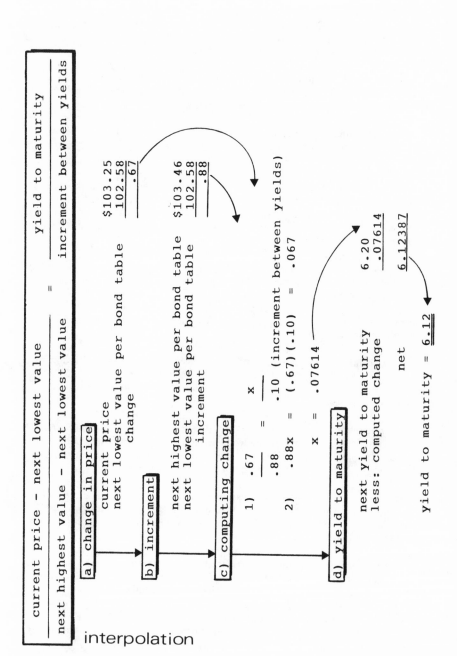

$$\frac{\text{current price} - \text{next lowest value}}{\text{next highest value} - \text{next lowest value}} = \frac{\text{yield to maturity}}{\text{increment between yields}}$$

a) change in price

current price	$103.25
next lowest value per bond table	102.58
change	.67

b) increment

next highest value per bond table	$103.46
next lowest value per bond table	102.58
increment	.88

c) computing change

1) $\dfrac{.67}{.88} = \dfrac{x}{.10}$ (increment between yields)

2) $.88x = (.67)(.10) = .067$

$x = .07614$

d) yield to maturity

next yield to maturity	6.20
less: computed change	.07614
net	6.12387

yield to maturity = 6.12

interpolation

interpolation   a method of estimating the yield to maturity, or the price when a bond's maturity is not listed exactly on bond tables, but falls between two listed dates. The next highest and next lowest values are computed and factored against the increment between yields to compute yield to maturity. See **bond; market value; yield to maturity.**

interpositioning   an action intended to create a double commission to a customer. A second broker is used to complete a trade which could be completed singularly, so that double billing of commissions results. See **broker; commission.**

Interstate Commerce Commission (ICC)   a federal agency that, in addition to its jurisdiction over the transportation industry, is the regulator of equipment trust bond offerings. See **equipment trust bond.**

intrastate exemption   a provision under SEC Rule 147 that when a securities offering is made in one state and investors reside in that same state, the offering may be exempt from registration. See **SEC rule 147; Securities Act of 1933.**

intrinsic value   the amount of premium for an in-the-money option which represents tangible value. The number of points between the current value of the stock and the strike price is intrinsic, with any balance being time value. See **cash value; option; premium; time value.**

intrinsic value

option	option premium	stock price	intrinsic value
Call, Feb 35	$ 8	$41	$ 6
Put, Apr 20	4	18	2
Call, Sep 60	6	61	1
Call, Mar 40	5	39	0

inventory   (1) for dealers or specialists, the net long and short positions held in securities.
(2) for businesses, the value of investment in goods for manufacture or resale. See **dealer; first in, first out (FIFO); last in, first out (LIFO); specialist.**

inventory ratios   ratios used to analyze inventory trends and efficiency. Traditional turnover compares inventory to sales, but is inaccurate. Sales reflect marked up results, while inventory is reported at cost. "Real" turnover compares average inventories to the cost of goods sold. Turnover, the result of the equation, is the number of times average inventory was completely sold or replaced.
The number of days of inventory available is an average computed by dividing turnover by the number of working days in one year, and is useful in trend analysis. See **fundamental analysis; ratios; real turnover.**

inventory turnover   ratio comparing average inventory to sales or to the cost of goods sold. The "average" inventory is computed by taking beginning and ending

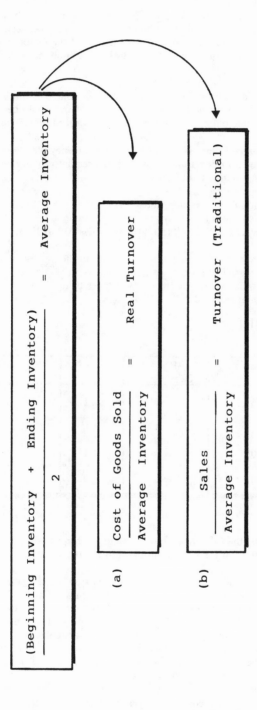

$$\frac{(\text{Beginning Inventory} + \text{Ending Inventory})}{2} = \text{Average Inventory}$$

(a)
$$\frac{\text{Cost of Goods Sold}}{\text{Average Inventory}} = \text{Real Turnover}$$

(b)
$$\frac{\text{Sales}}{\text{Average Inventory}} = \text{Turnover (Traditional)}$$

inventory turnover

$$\frac{\text{Cost of Sales}}{\text{Inventory at Cost}} = \text{Real Turnover}$$

$$\frac{\text{Total Working Days In One Year}}{\text{Turnover}} = \begin{array}{l} \text{Days of} \\ \text{Inventory} \\ \text{Available} \end{array}$$

inventory ratios

figures only, although more frequent counts or estimates may be used when seasonal changes would materially affect the average. See **fundamental analysis; ratios; real turnover.**

inverted scale   description of a serial bond offering when short-term yields are greater than long-term yields. See **bond; long-term debt; serial bond; short-term debt; yield.**

investment   (1) utilization of capital to leverage (obtain more capital), or to take equity or debt positions in securities, with the intention of gaining an increase in that capital from growth or income.
(2) general term applied to a program designed as an investment, offering the chance for gain against risks of loss.
(3) description of a business purchase of fixed assets or in speculative ventures related to the purposes of the operation. See **debt security; equity security; investment objective; leverage; speculation.**

investment advisor   a title used by a variety of individuals providing financial consultation, including financial planners, registered investment advisors, or securities or insurance salespeople. See **financial planner; Investment Advisors Act of 1940; registered investment advisor (RIA).**

Investment Advisors Act of 1940   legislation requiring SEC registration for individuals selling investment consultation services on a fee basis. See **financial planner; registered investment advisor (RIA).**

investment banker   another term for underwriter, or any person or firm aiding an issuer in the preparation and distribution of a securities offering. See **broker-dealer; syndicate; underwriter.**

investment club   an organization formed by a limited number of people, for the purpose of pooling their investment capital and making collective investments. Formed as a corporation or a partnership, most clubs contain between 10 and 25 members. For purposes of securities regulation, an investment club is considered as a single investor. See **corporation; National Association of Investors Corporation (NAIC); partnership.**

investment company   an organization whose purpose is to invest the pooled capital of many other investors, which specializes in trading securities within the definitions of an investment objective. Included are face amount certificate companies, open-end and closed-end investment companies, and unit investment trusts. See **closed-end; face amount certificate; management company; mutual fund; open-end management company; unit investment trust.**

Investment Company Act of 1940   legislation to protect investors against unfair activities by investment companies. The act sets standards for the prices and operation of investment companies and their securities. See **investment objective; Securities and Exchange Commission (SEC); underwriter.**

Investment Company Amendments Act of 1970   legislation which sets limitations on the charging of sales fees by investment companies. The act directs the methods under which sales charges may be computed and sets the maximum load at nine percent. It also sets a 45-day cancellation provision, during which an investor may cancel and receive a refund of all sales charges plus the current value of shares invested. See **contractual plan; penalty plan; sales charge.**

investment company products/variable contracts limited representative   title for a person who has passed the NASD Exam Series 6. This individual may sell mutual funds and variable annuities. See **mutual fund; National Association of Securities Dealers (NASD); Series 6; variable annuity.**

investment company products/variable contracts principal   title for a person who has passed the NASD Exam Series 26. This individual may sell mutual funds and variable annuities, and supervises registered representatives with the NASD license Series 6. See **mutual fund; National Association of Securities Dealers (NASD); Series 26; variable annuity.**

investment contract   an agreement under which investors agree to pool funds and place them under the management of a management company or another individual, for the purpose of making selections of securities or properties. See **offering; Securities and Exchange Commission (SEC); state securities agency.**

investment grade   distinction assigned to bonds assigned one of the top four ratings by one of the three primary rating services, as the safest and least speculative bonds available. See **bond; Fitch Investors Service; Moody's Investors Service; rating systems; Standard and Poor's Corporation.**

investment history   a guideline used to set limitations on the amount of a hot issue that may be sold to customers who might otherwise be freeriding or withholding in the issue. If, over a three-year period, the customer has had at least 10 purchases of a dollar value equal to the amount of the hot issue to be acquired, it generally will be acceptable. See **freeriding; hot issue; withholding.**

investment income   defined range of earnings used to set the limit on interest deductions for borrowings to subsequently invest. For this purpose, interest, dividends, some recaptures, and short-term capital gains are included. See **dividend; interest; recapture; short-term capital gain.**

investment interest   interest earned from investments, for the purpose of determining deductibility when borrowed funds are used to make those investments. See **interest; yield.**

investment interest limitations the limit on deductibility of investment interest. See **interest; investment program; tax basis.**

investment letter a written document from the buyer to the seller in a private placement, stating the intention to hold units in the program for a period of time, commonly two years, and that within that time, those units will be offered for resale. See **direct participation program; offering; private placement.**

investment manager a general term that may refer to a money manager, a person or firm offering asset management services, investment advisors, and others acting in a fiduciary capacity. See **fiduciary; investment advisor; Investment Advisors Act of 1940; Registered Investment Advisor (RIA); Securities and Exchange Commission (SEC).**

investment market a broad reference to the capital and the money markets, from which investment funds are drawn. See **capital market; money market.**

investment objective identification of an individual's or institution's purpose in engaging in investment activities, defining acceptable levels of risk, safety, and liquidity, as well as a personal comfort level with decisions reached. The objective may be influenced by knowledge, experience and the ability to devote funds to an investment program.
The objective may aim toward retirement savings, protection against unexpected and premature death, college financing, and a number of other end uses. Common objectives include return of capital; growth; income; tax-free income; and preservation of capital. One may take an aggressive, conservative or speculative approach to investing within an objective. See **inflation; liquidity; risk; tax deferral.**

investment program a classification of investment, broken down by medium of trading or by industrial emphasis. Common programs include stocks, bonds, mutual funds, real estate, oil and gas, alternate energy, collectibles, cattle, agriculture, real estate investment trusts (REITs), variable annuities, commodities, options and warrants. See **bond; commodity; direct participation program; exchange business; mutual fund; option; private placement; public offering; real estate investment trust (REIT); stock; variable annuity.**

investment tax credit (ITC) a credit allowed as a reduction of net tax liability for the purchase of assets used in business. The credit can be claimed in the year during which assets are placed into service, and a portion must be recaptured (taken back) if assets are sold before expiration of the class life. See **recapture; tangible value; tax preference.**

investment value a value, expressed as a percentage of par applied against a convertible bond. The formula attempts to describe a convertible's value in comparison to a non-convertible bond of equal quality. See **bond; conversion; maturity date.**

investor basis an investor's total equity in a partnership, for the purpose of setting a maximum deduction allowable. The basis consists of total contributed capital plus share of recourse loans. See **losses; nonrecourse loan; partnership; recourse loan.**

involuntary underwriter also called a statutory underwriter, one who purchases and resells securities that have not been registered. See **public offering; registration statement; statutory underwriter.**

IRA abbreviation for Individual Retirement Account. See **Individual Retirement Account (IRA).**

IRA rollover a provision allowing the acceptance of a lump-sum distribution from a pension plan (commonly that of an employer), without being taxed on the proceeds. The distribution must be for the entire vested interest, and must be placed into an IRA within 60 days to avoid tax. See **lump-sum distribution; retirement plans; tax deferral.**

issue (1) a specific security or class of securities of a corporation.
(2) to make available for investment the securities of a corporation, or to create an offering such as a bond issue. See **offering; securities.**

issued and outstanding the total number of shares of a corporation that are held by stockholders, excluding treasury stock (stock repurchased by the company). See **authorized shares; corporation; outstanding stock; treasury stock; unissued stock.**

issued date the date from which interest is accrued on a bond, also known as the dated date. See **bond; dated date; interest.**

issuer an organization making available an investment, in its own equity or debt securities, or in units of a partnership it sponsors. See **distributor; partnership; sponsor.**

J

JAJO one of three option expiration cycles, with expiration months falling in January, April, July and October. See **cycle; expiration cycle; FMAN; MJSD; option.**

joint account an account in which two or more persons have interests. See **joint tenants with rights of survivorship (JTWROS); tenants in common.**

joint and survivor annuity a type of annuity contract promising periodic payments which may continue until both have died. See **annuity; life annuity.**

joint bond bonds guaranteed by two or more agencies or companies, or issues that are joint obligations. See **bond; corporate bond; debt security.**

joint tenancy a form of registration in a securities account or within a contract for business or property holding. In this form of ownership, each participant owns a share of the entire property, rather than an identified portion, changing the way that assets would be redistributed in the event of death, and the level of contingent liabilities in the event of litigation. See **tenants in common; unity of ownership; unity of possession.**

joint tenants with rights of survivorship (JTWROS)   a form of registration of a securities customer account, bank account, or business account, in which two or more people may have interests. In the event of death of one of the holders, all rights to the assets pass to the remaining holders. See **joint account; tenants in common.**

joint venture   a finite business structure that operates like a partnership, with the understanding that its purpose is for certain projects and will terminate or be modified at completion of those projects. See **general partnership.**

jointly and severally   form of identification used in accounts where each member is responsible for proportionate shares of the entire account, regardless of involvement levels. In eastern account underwritings, each member must absorb severally the unsold portion of an offering, even if a specific share was sold or over-sold originally. See **eastern account; municipal bond; severally but not jointly.**

junior lien   a type of mortgage or bond issue not having first right to assets in the event of default. See **bond; second mortgage; senior lien.**

junior preferred   a class of preferred stock when more than one such class is issued. In this case, all preferred stock has priority of claim over common stockholders. However, junior preferred classes would have claims secondary to the senior classes. See **preferred stock; prior preferred; senior preferred.**

junk bond   expression used to describe any bond with a rating of BB (or Bb) or below. The lower the rating, the more speculative the investment. See **bond; rating systems; speculation.**

jurisdiction   the regulatory right to hear and decide cases or issues. State securities agencies claim jurisdiction in their own states, while several federal agencies regulate entire industries or activities. See **regulation; state securities agency.**

K

Kansas City Board of Trade (KCBT)   4800 Main Street, Kansas City MO 64112; a regional exchange in Kansas City, Missouri, specializing in agricultural commodities. See **commodity; futures contract; regional exchanges.**

Keogh plan   a retirement plan designed for self-employed individuals and the employees of that individual. The legislation, also referred to as HR-10, was enacted by Congress in 1962 under the title, "Self-Employed Individual Tax Retirement Act." The name of these plans is derived from the bill's sponsor, Congressman Eugene J. Keogh of New York.
Keogh legislation was created to provide benefits to the self-employed comparable to those available to employees of corporations offering retirement and tax-deferred benefits. The self-employed person may establish a profit-sharing or pension plan with a qualified trustee, and is allowed to invest in a variety of assets (mutual funds, money market accounts, common stocks, corporate bonds, variable annuities, public limited partnerships, and combinations of these).
Anyone with income from self-employment activities may establish a Keogh plan. The trust agreement must be established by December 31 of a qualifying year,

with contributions for that year made by the due date of the tax return, including allowed extensions. The total amount of contributions is deductible from gross income on the individual's federal income tax return.

Benefits of establishing a Keogh plan include:

a) reduction of current income taxes through deductibility of current year's contributions

b) accumulation of retirement funds without tax liability on contributions or earnings

c) flexibility in the choice of tax-deferred investments and trustee arrangements

d) self-direction of investment choices.

Individuals may contribute up to 25 percent of net earnings from self-employment, to a maximum annual contribution of $30,000. The same person may participate as well in an Individual Retirement Account and a corporate plan offered by an employer.

Funds accumulated in a Keogh plan must be withdrawn between the ages of 59½ and 70½. The account may be distributed earlier in case of permanent and total disability or upon death. Otherwise, early withdrawals are subject to immediate taxation and a tax penalty. See **Individual Retirement Account (IRA); retirement plans; tax deferral; trustee.**

know your customer   SEC Rule 405, a dictate that brokers should be familiar enough with the financial situation, goals and objectives, and preferences of each customer on an individual basis, before investment advice and recommendations are given. See SEC **Rule 405.**

L

land contract   a mortgage arrangement in which the seller retains the original mortgage and title does not transfer until the loan is paid in full. See **mortgage; real estate.**

lapsed option   an option that has been allowed to expire without being exercised or cancelled by closing of the position. See **exercise; option.**

last in, first out (LIFO)   inventory valuation method which assumes the latest items purchased are the first to be sold. This has the effect of continually adjusting the overall value of stock on hand to reflect the latest market prices. See **first in, first out (FIFO); inventory; LIFO.**

last sale   (1) the last trade in a trading day.

(2) the most recent price of a security, used to determine uptick rules for short selling and restrictions of specialist activities. See **short sale; specialist; trade; uptick.**

last trading day   the last day in an option expiration cycle, which is the third Friday of the expiration month. See **expiration; option.**

late tape   situation where trading volume on the exchanges is heavy to the extent that reporting of transactions is running late. See **stock exchange.**

lay-off a contingency allowing an issuer to sell unsubscribed shares or units to the underwriter in a rights offering. See **issue; rights offering; standby underwriter.**

lead underwriter the firm that will take responsibility for placement of shares or units of an offering and who may also be the sponsor of that offering. See **managed offering; selling group; sponsor; underwriter.**

Legal Advisory Committee (LAC) a group of attorneys which advises the New York Stock Exchange board of directors on a variety of matters, especially regarding legal jurisdiction, the securities industry and other matters in the capital markets. See **board of directors; capital market; New York Stock Exchange (NYSE).**

legal description the proper identification of a real property. See **real estate.**

legal investment a highly rated security acceptable for the portfolios of fiduciaries falling under the jurisdiction of banking, insurance and securities agencies. See **fiduciary; institutional investor; investment grade; rating systems.**

legal opinion (1) a letter from counsel to the issuer of securities stating that the terms of the offering are in compliance with specific rules and regulations, or that regulators will respond to an offering in a certain way.
(2) a letter prepared by an attorney as part of the due diligence process, verifying that the assumptions in an offering are within the law and the rules and regulations of the industry. See **direct participation program; due diligence; syndicate.**

legal transfer description of a security that cannot be sold without special documentation, due to the form of registration or other circumstances. Such securities cannot be sold until the seller provides this documentation and legal transfer requirements have been met. See **bond power; registered form; stock power; transfer.**

lending at a premium situation in which a short seller pays a lender an additional fee, above and beyond collateral, for the right to use certificates to back the short sale. See **collateral; marking to the mark; short sale.**

lending at a rate situation in which a short seller demands interest on the collateral left on deposit with the lender. See **collateral; margin account; short sale.**

lending institution an organization whose business includes the lending of cash to other firms, institutions, or individuals. See **capital market; commercial bank; money market; mutual savings bank; savings and loan association.**

letter bond issues that may be resold, subject to the provisions of an investment letter. See **bond; investment letter; transfer.**

letter of guarantee a document supplied by a bank or other institution, to a broker-dealer. The letter states that an option writer has securities on deposit, and that the securities will be delivered in the event an option is exercised. See **assignment; brokerage house; commercial bank; covered option; writer.**

letter of intent a contract signed by a customer and given to a mutual fund, promising to purchase a specific number of shares during a period of time (commonly 13 months), in order to qualify for a breakpoint — reduced commissions — and used in lieu of a single lump-sum purchase. See **breakpoint; load mutual fund; mutual fund; sales charge.**

letter of transmittal   a broker-dealer form to be completed by a representative and signed by a customer upon investing. The letter specifies the terms of the investment and becomes the file document for the broker-dealer. See **broker-dealer; customer.**

letter security   a privately sold security that is not registered, and that requires an investment letter. See **investment letter; private placement;** SEC **Rule 144;** SEC **Rule 237.**

level debt service   (1) a provision that a municipal bond issue shall be retired in approximately level annual payments, including both principal and interest.

(2) the most common type of payment on a mortgage or other debt, in which monthly or periodic payments are made for the same amount, with a portion applied to interest, and the balance to principal. See **interest; mortgage; municipal bond; principal.**

Level Debt Service

	Level Payment	7.25% Interest	Principal	Balance
				$22,000.00
January	$165.00	$132.92	$ 32.08	21,967.92
February	165.00	132.72	32.28	21,935.64
March	165.00	132.53	32.47	21,903.17
April	165.00	132.33	32.67	21,870.50
May	165.00	132.13	32.87	21,837.63
June	165.00	131.94	33.06	21,804.57

Level I Service   a subscription service offered through the NASDAQ system, which provides electronic bid and offer price information to brokerage firms. See **brokerage house; National Association of Securities Dealers Automated Quotations (NASDAQ).**

Level II Service   a variation of the subscription service offered through the NASDAQ system, giving electronic bid and offer prices for institutional investors and member organizations. See **institutional investor; member organization; National Association of Securities Dealers Automated Quotations (NASDAQ).**

Level III Service   the highest level of subscription service offered through the NASDAQ system, providing electronic bid and offer prices for market makers, and

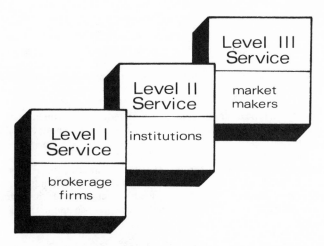

allowing for trades between market makers, as a market in and of itself. See **market maker; National Association of Securities Dealers Automated Quotations (NASDAQ).**

leverage   one of the three uses of investment capital (the other two being lending through the purchase of debt securities and equity positions through ownership purchases like common stock). With leverage, the amount of capital is used to borrow additional funds, usually with a property as collateral. The principal works the same way in margin transactions (with stock and bond holdings offered as collateral) or syndicated investments (with real property, for example, made subject to a mortgage for leveraged portions of the purchase).

Leverage increases potential profits, because a larger position may be taken in an investment. It also increases risks, as debt service must be allowed for from the investment's cash flow or from additional capital paid in by the investors. See **collateral; debt service; margin transaction; risk; syndicate; trading on equity.**

leveraged company   (1) a dual-purpose investment company, offering investors both income and capital shares. All capital gains are earned by the capital shareholders, and dividends or interest is paid to income shareholders.

(2) an open-end management company allowed to borrow money as part of its approved charter, to take a higher position in securities, increasing potential return and risks to investors.

(3) any business whose capital consists both of equity and debt capitalization. A "highly" leveraged company is one with a substantial portion of debt, in comparison to equity. See **capitalization; debt security; dual-purpose investment company; equity security; long-term debt; open-end management company; return on equity; risk.**

leveraged lease   a type of contract allowing investors to take a position without committing a large amount of capital. In its place, a nonrecourse loan is signed. See **depreciation; equipment leasing; investment tax credit (ITC); nonrecourse loan.**

liabilities   the debts of a person or of an organization. Liabilities represent the commitments made against the assets of a company, and on a balance sheet, are the difference between assets and net worth. See **assets; balance sheet; current liabilities; financial statement; long-term liabilities.**

lien a claim against tangible property. Mortgages are granted upon property, and are subject to the liens made by lenders in the event of default. Bond issues of corporations unable to honor their commitment are subject to liens from bond-holders. And customers trading on margin may have their securities liquidated to satisfy a lien. See **bond; junior lien; margin call; mortgage; real estate; senior lien.**

life annuity a type of annuity contract with terms that payments will be made to the annuitant for the remainder of his or her life. See **annuity; fixed annuity; variable annuity.**

life annuity with payments certain a type of annuity contract guaranteeing payments for a specific period of time, no more and no less. Common terms call for 10, 15 or 20 years of continuing payments. In the event of death, the beneficiary or the estate continues to receive the balance of payments. See **annuity; fixed annuity; variable annuity.**

life annuity with payments certain

annual payments

	life annuity	life annuity with payments certain, 10 yrs.
a) death after seven years		
Year 1	$ 4,800	$ 4,800
Year 2	4,800	4,800
Year 3	4,800	4,800
Year 4	4,800	4,800
Year 5	4,800	4,800
Year 6	4,800	4,800
Year 7	4,800	4,800
Year 8	0	4,800
Year 9	0	4,800
Year 10	0	4,800
Year 11	0	0
Year 12	0	0
b) death after 11 years		
Year 1	$ 4,800	$ 4,800
Year 2	4,800	4,800
Year 3	4,800	4,800
Year 4	4,800	4,800
Year 5	4,800	4,800
Year 6	4,800	4,800
Year 7	4,800	4,800
Year 8	4,800	4,800
Year 9	4,800	4,800
Year 10	4,800	4,800
Year 11	4,800	0
Year 12	0	0

life insurance

whole life

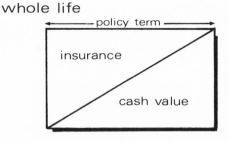

level term   ## decreasing term

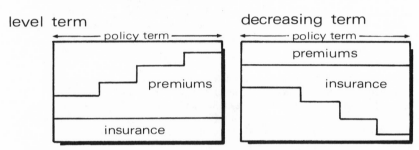

life insurance   a contract made between a life insurance company and an individual. In return for the payment of premiums over a period of time, the insurer promises to pay a specified amount of money to a beneficiary upon death.

A whole life policy is one offering cash value for the higher premiums charged. This combines life insurance coverage with an investment. Over a period of time, the amount of true insurance coverage decreases while the cash value increases, until the policyholder owns the entire face value of the policy.

Term insurance, for lower premiums, offers insurance coverage only, without provision for any cash value. Decreasing term coverage is a type where coverage decreases over a period of time, but premium payments remain level. Level term provides the same amount of insurance, with periodic adjustments in the amount of premium to be paid, as determined by the age of the insured person. See **cash value; estate planning; investment; whole life insurance.**

life insurance trust   a type of trust whose assets consist of life insurance policies on the life of the trust's creator. When claims are made, payment goes to the trust, where a trustee may manage funds for less experienced investor/beneficiaries.

Alternatives to a life insurance trust include establishing a testamentary trust, or the choosing of a settlement option with the insurance company other than cash payment of proceeds. See **estate planning; testamentary trust; will.**

LIFO   abbreviation for last in, first out, a type of inventory valuation assuming the latest goods purchased are the first ones sold. See **last in, first out (LIFO).**

limit order   an order which establishes specific limits for the broker.

Sell orders may have a limit to the lowest acceptable price. Actual sale may be higher, but not lower than the limit order specifies.

Buy orders may have a limit to the highest acceptable price. Actual purchase may be lower, but not higher than the limit order specifies.

A limit order may also specify the time by which the order may be executed. See **buy; order ticket; secondary market; sell order.**

limit-or-market-on-close order   a form of limit order which reverts to a normal market order, for execution at or near that day's close of the market. See **close; limit order; market order; order ticket.**

limit price   the highest buy limit or lowest sell limit a customer places as part of a limit order. See **buy; order ticket; sell order.**

limited discretion   written permission given to a broker to use best judgement in a particular set of circumstances. Unlike a discretionary account, which allows unlimited judgement to the broker, limited discretion is given for a specific time and condition. It is seen commonly in option trading, for a period of time close to expiration date. See **broker; discretionary account; expiration date; fiduciary; option; registered representative.**

limited partner   an individual who purchases units in a partnership, in the hope of economic gain or tax benefits. The limited partner has little or no influence upon general partners in the management of the partnership; he is potentially liable only to the extent of the amount at risk, in the event of litigation against the partnership. See **general partner; private placement; public offering; silent partner.**

limited partnership   a form of business organization including both general and limited partners. The general partners assume unlimited business liability, while limited partners are at risk only to the extent of their contributed capital and committed capital (via notes).

Limited partners have little or no voice in the management of partnership business, and are also called passive — or silent — partners in the venture. The partnership is finite. It will dissolve upon mutual agreement or upon final sale of invested assets as specified in the original agreement. This is unlike a corporation, which is assumed to have an infinite life.

Limited partnerships are formed frequently to enable the limited partners to obtain a pass-through of tax losses, especially in the early years of the business. See **general partnership; Uniform Limited Partnership Act (ULPA).**

limited principal general securities sales supervisor   title of an individual who has passed the NASD Series 8 examination. The license is held by branch office and sales managers and other supervisors and allows no offering or sales privileges beyond the supervisory aspects of a job. See **National Association of Securities Dealers (NASD); Series 8.**

limited representative   abbreviated title for an individual who has passed the NASD Series 6 examination. See **investment company products/variable contracts limited representative; Series 6.**

limited reversionary interest   a sharing arrangement in oil and gas programs in which the sponsor shares a limited portion of the completion costs of wells. See **oil and gas; reversionary interest; sponsor.**

limited tax bond   a general obligation bond issued at the city, county or other local level, which will be repaid from a specified portion of real estate taxes devised to repay the issue. See **assessed valuation; general obligation bond (GO); municipal bond.**

limited trading authorization   a discretionary account in which a broker is given the authority to transact in a customer's account. The funds are used at the discretion of the broker, but may not be withdrawn from the account or pledged by the broker. The written authorization may further restrict the broker's actions by excluding certain types of transactions. See **brokerage house; customer; discretionary account.**

liquid market   description of a market in which buying and selling is made easy by the volume of activity, or facilitated by an exchange absorbing the inbalances between buyers and sellers. See **auction marketplace; price.**

liquidation   (1) the sale of securities when cash is required for other purposes. Such a liquidation may be involuntary, as in the case of a broker's selling securities of a customer to meet a margin call.
(2) general description of the dissolution of a business. All assets are liquidated — turned to cash — and used to satisfy creditors, lenders and shareholders. See **conversion; margin call; priority; shareholder.**

liquidation value   the value of securities or other assets that would be realized if the asset were converted into cash. See **conversion; priority.**

liquidity   (1) an investment objective in which the customer desires the ability to convert holdings into cash in a short period of time and without substantial loss.
(2) a condition for a security in which the market may experience a high level of volume without a significant change in market value.
(3) a high presence of liquid assets — cash or cash equivalents — in a business, especially as reported on a financial statement. See **balance sheet; financial statement; investment objective; volatility.**

liquidity ratio   also known as the acid test or quick asset ratio, the comparison of current assets without inventory, to total current liabilities. Liquidity refers to the ready conversion to cash of assets included, and a ratio of one to one or better is considered the minimum acceptable liquidity ratio for most industries. See **acid test ratio; quick asset ratio; ratios.**

$$\frac{(\text{current assets} - \text{inventory})}{\text{current liabilities}} = \text{liquidity ratio}$$

$$\frac{(\$850,400 - \$300,600)}{\$433,100} = 1.28 \text{ to } 1$$

liquidity ratio

listed company   a corporation whose stock is traded on a public exchange. See **New York Stock Exchange (NYSE); stock exchange.**

Listed Company Advisory Committee (LCAC)   an advisory group to the board of directors of the New York Stock Exchange. The LCAC includes members of listed companies – chief executive officers and presidents – and advice is given on matters of concern or interest to listed organizations. See **board of directors; New York Stock Exchange (NYSE).**

listed option   an option traded on the public exchanges. Unlisted options are also traded in the market, but without as liquid a market. Options may be traded on the New York, Chicago, Pacific, American and Philadelphia exchanges. See **exchange; option.**

listed stock   stock of a corporation listed on one of the major exchanges. To become listed and to maintain a listing, companies must meet minimum criteria for the number of publicly held shares, the number of stockholders, and annual volume of sales. See **New York Stock Exchange (NYSE); Securities and Exchange Commission (SEC); stock exchange.**

living trust   a trust created during the lifetime of its creator. It may be revocable or irrevocable, and the creator may also be the trust's beneficiary. See **beneficiary; life insurance trust; revocable trust; testamentary trust.**

load   the sales charge assessed against investors in mutual funds, direct participation programs, and other programs. Load is applied to the payment of sales commissions or fees of various kinds collected by the general partners.

Reviewing the front-end load (the amount taken from proceeds as they are paid in) of direct participation programs is one way to qualify the value of a direct participation program.

Some mutual funds are no-load, since sales commissions are not paid. Others are back-load funds. In this case, no load is charged upon deposit of funds. However, if the investment is withdrawn within a specified period, a declining load will be assessed at that time. See **direct participation program; no-load (NL); open-end management company; sales charge.**

load mutual fund   a mutual fund assessing a load fee at the time an investment is made, most of which will be used to pay a sales commission to the salesperson recommending the fund to the investor. See **mutual fund; open-end management company; sales charge.**

load spread   a treatment of sales load in which the early years' contributions are subject to assessment of a load exceeding the maximum allowed by law of nine percent. The balance exceeding the maximum is applied against future periods in which the investor remains with the program. See **contractual plan; mutual fund; sales charge.**

loan value   the amount, set by the Federal Reserve Board under Regulation T, that a broker may allow a margin account customer to use securities or cash for purchases of additional securities.

Loan value is subject to change by the Federal Reserve, and may vary between different types of securities. See **current market value (CMV); eligible security; Federal Reserve Board (FRB); margin account; Regulation T.**

local government bond   a municipal bond issued by a city, county or other local government. See **municipal bond.**

locked in   (1) descriptive of an investor unable to sell because to do so would produce a capital gain that he or she does not want to recognize in the current year; or when closing a position would create a greater loss than the investor is willing to absorb.

(2) situation when an investor cannot sell stock because an option is written covering the issue. To sell, the option position would have to be closed, or allowed to expire or be exercised; or the option would revert to uncovered status.

(3) an illiquid situation in which an investor owns shares or units, especially in a private placement, for which there is no market (the units cannot be sold). The lack of a market may be due to the lack of economic substance of the units, or due to an expiration of any tax benefits realized in the early years of the program. See **capital gain; covered option; direct participation program; paper profit/loss; private placement.**

London Interbank Offered Rate (LIBOR)   the rate used on floating rate notes issued in Eurodollars or to set the exchange value of U.S. dollars on deposit in a European bank. See **Eurodollar bond; floating rate note (FRN); interest.**

long   (1) an investor is long when he or she has purchased securities, options or futures contracts. A long position signifies ownership, while a short position is the opposite. One who is short in a security has sold the stock, option or future, with the obligation to buy it (close the position) at a later date or, in the case of options, to wait for expiration.

(2) a broker-dealer is "long" when it holds more securities than it has promised to deliver. See **bond; futures contract; option; short; stock.**

long bond   (1) a bond owned by an investor.

(2) a description of an issue that will mature in 10 years or more in the future. See **debt security; long-term.**

long coupon   (1) a situation in which the first coupon date of an interest-bearing bond is longer than six months from issued date. First payment will normally fall within the first six months, with subsequent payment dates at six-month intervals.

(2) sometimes used to describe long bonds — with maturities of 10 years or more. See **coupon; interest; maturity date.**

long hedge   (1) a strategy used to protect a short seller's position. A call option is purchased for every 100 shares on which the investor is short.

If the stock declines in value, the call will expire worthless but a profit will be realized by going short. If the stock increases in value, losses in the short position are offset by gains in the option.

(2) a strategy used to protect a purchaser's position. A put option is purchased for every 100 shares owned by the investor.

If the stock increases in value, the put will become worthless but a profit will be realized from the stock investment. If the stock declines in value, losses in the stock will be offset by gains in the put option. See **call; interest; put; short.**

long market value (LMV)   the current market value of securities held in long position in a customer's margin account. See **margin account; short market value (SMV).**

long straddle   the simultaneous purchase of a call and a put on the same security, at the same strike price and with the same expiration date. The strategy

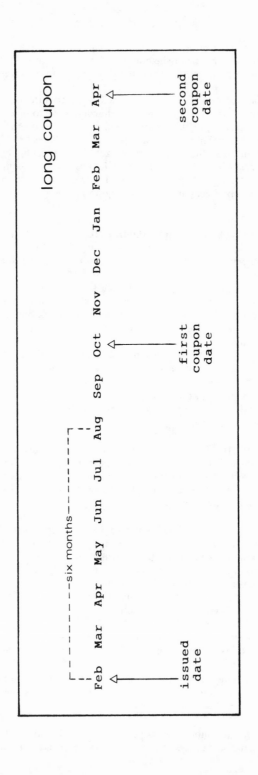

long coupon

long hedge call

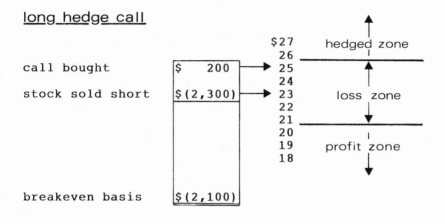

call bought	$ 200
stock sold short	$(2,300)
breakeven basis	$(2,100)

$27 hedged zone
26
25
24
23 loss zone
22
21
20
19 profit zone
18

long hedge put

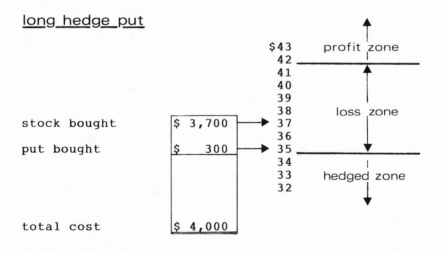

stock bought	$ 3,700
put bought	$ 300
total cost	$ 4,000

$43 profit zone
42
41
40
39
38 loss zone
37
36
35
34
33 hedged zone
32

long hedge

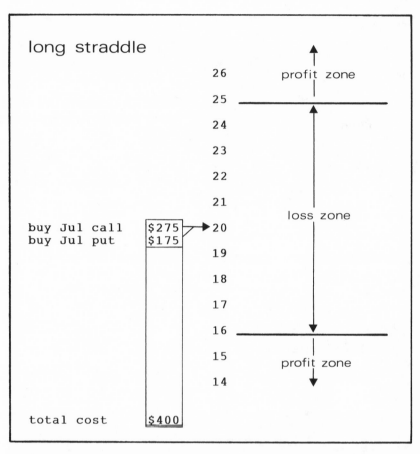

long straddle

buy Jul call	$275
buy Jul put	$175
total cost	$400

26 — profit zone

25

24

23

22

21

20

loss zone

19

18

17

16

15 — profit zone

14

assumes a wide price swing before expiration. See **exercise price; expiration date; option; put; straddle; underlying security.**

long-term   (1) a type of capital gain or loss held long enough to qualify for long-term tax rates. With a gain, only a portion is taxable, and with a loss, only a portion is deductible.

(2) a type of bond with a maturity greater than one year.

(3) liabilities or the portion of liabilities that are not due and payable until a year or more has passed. Long-term liabilities are reported in a separate section of the balance sheet than current liabilities.

(4) assets that are not convertible to cash within one year (such as cash, accounts receivable and inventories), and generally must be set up as capital assets and depreciated over a class life. See **short-term.**

long-term assets   also called "fixed," any asset that must be written off (depreciated) over a class life, and cannot be recognized as an expense in the year acquired. See **assets; depreciation; fixed assets.**

long-term capital gain   the gain on the sale of a capital asset (property or securities, for example), where the holding period was greater than the short-term maximum. Long-term gains are subject to favorable tax rates. See **capital gain; short-term capital gain; tax basis.**

long-term capital loss   the loss on the sale of a capital asset, where the holding period was greater than the short-term minimum. Only a portion of a long-term capital loss can be deducted. See **capital loss; short-term capital loss; tax basis.**

long-term debt   (1) that portion of a debt that is payable in more than one year. On a balance sheet, the long-term portion is reflected separately from the current portion.
(2) a bond which will mature in more than 10 years. See **bond; liabilities; short-term debt.**

long-term debt		
Total note balance		$85,000.00
Monthly payments one year	$1,294.34 x 12	
Current debt		15,532.08
Long-term debt		$69,467.92

long-term liabilities   any liability not due and payable within 12 months. See **balance sheet; current liabilities; financial statement.**

losses   reduction of a capital base due to unprofitable operations or untimely or poorly chosen investments. See **capital loss; profit.**

lowest net interest cost (NIC)   the bid placed by an underwriting group through whom a bond issuer will offer its securities. Competitive bids are placed by all underwriters desiring to handle the issue, and the one offering a bid that will produce the lowest net cost to the municipality wins the bid. See **bond; general obligation bond (GO); municipal bond; underwriter.**

lump-sum distribution   an amount of money paid out to an individual from a retirement account, which may be rolled over into an individual retirement account to defer tax, or may be recognized and taxed at lower rates by using a special 10-year averaging provision. See **IRA rollover; retirement plans; rollover; tax deferral; vesting methods.**

M

M1   also known as the "basic" money supply, including all deposits in checking accounts, NOW accounts, and demand deposits; drafts on credit union shares; travelers checks issued by non-banks; and cash in the hands of the general public. See **commercial bank; demand deposit; NOW account; savings bank.**

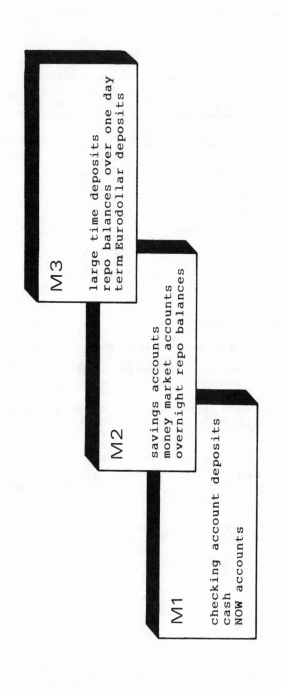

M3

large time deposits
repo balances over one day
term Eurodollar deposits

M2

savings accounts
money market accounts
overnight repo balances

M1

checking account deposits
cash
NOW accounts

M2   an extension of the money supply, made up of M1 plus all personal savings accounts, money market fund balances, and repurchase agreements held on an overnight basis. See **commercial bank; money market fund; savings deposit; time deposit.**

M3   a further money supply extension, including M2 plus all large certificates of deposit, term Eurodollar deposits and repurchase agreements longer than one day. See **certificate of deposit (CD); money market fund; repurchase agreement; time deposit.**

main room   the New York Stock Exchange floor, where most issues traded are assigned for trading. See **blue room; floor; garage; New York Stock Exchange (NYSE).**

maintenance call   notification to a margin customer that additional collateral must be placed in the account by a specified time, to meet minimum requirements of the exchange or the broker-dealer. Failing to meet this requirement will result in a liquidation of positions to satisfy the requirement. See **broker-dealer; customer; liquidation; margin call; minimum maintenance.**

maintenance requirement   a dollar amount or percentage of security values held in a margin account representing the margin capital that must be held by the customer. See **broker-dealer; minimum maintenance; Regulation T.**

major trend   in the Dow Theory, the third phase of an overall market trend, following the minor and then the intermediate trend. A major trend may last for several years, and is characterized by a series of progressively higher or lower tops or bottoms. See **Dow Theory; intermediate trend; minor trend; secondary movement; technical analysis.**

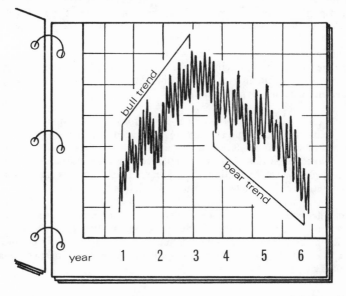

major trend

Maloney Act   a 1938 amendment to the Securities Exchange Act of 1934, under which the NASD and the MSRB were created and registered with the SEC. See **Municipal Securities Rulemaking Board (MSRB); National Association of Securities Dealers (NASD); Securities and Exchange Commission (SEC); Securities Exchange Act of 1934.**

managed offering   a form of offering where the sponsor assigns one organization as lead underwriter. See **lead underwriter; offering; sponsor.**

management company   an organization which accepts pools of capital from investors and conducts discretionary investment activities in their behalf. See **closed-end; diversified management company; investment company; mutual fund; non-diversified management company; open-end management company.**

management group   an investment advisor to a management company, used for the purpose of making recommendations for the purchase or sale of securities. See **investment advisor; open-end management company.**

manipulation   the creation of artificial price movement, volume, or interest in a security, done for the purpose of inducing others to invest in that security; or the falsification of financial information created to deceive investors or prospective investors. See **price; value; volume.**

margin   the capital placed into a margin account or good faith deposit put up for a futures contract, representing the equity portion of an investment when the balance is loaned to the customer. See **collateral; Federal Reserve Board (FRB); good faith deposit; leverage; Regulation T.**

margin account   a type of account in which the customer trades partly on collateral and partly on equity borrowed from the broker-dealer. See **broker-dealer; Federal Reserve Board (FRB); Regulation T; SEC Rule 10b-16; SEC Rule 15c2-1.**

margin agreement   a contract between the customer and the broker-dealer, specifying the terms of margin activities; the limits to which the customer agrees; and the uses to which securities in a margin account may be put by the broker-dealer. See **broker-dealer; customer; hypothecation.**

margin call   a demand by the broker-dealer for more cash or securities to be placed as collateral in a margin account, by a specified deadline.
The margin call may result from a purchase or a short sale, or from a movement in price that affects the value of collateral in the account. If the margin call is not met, the broker-dealer may close positions in the account to eliminate the call or to satisfy the margin requirement. See **broker-dealer; Regulation T.**

margin department   a broker-dealer department that deals with the business of margin accounting and compliance, including computation of maintenance requirements in the account, updating for market value of margin securities and customer transactions, and the granting of credit. See **broker-dealer; compliance; Regulation T.**

margin of profit   the dollar amount of profit after all costs or expenses, or the profit expressed as a percentage of gross sales. See **financial statement; fundamental analysis; net income.**

$$\frac{\text{Net Income}}{\text{Sales}} = \text{Margin of Profit}$$

$$\frac{\$430,100}{\$5,143,600} = 8.4\%$$

margin of profit

margin of profit ratios correctly used to describe the comparison of net income to total sales, and reported as a percentage. The term "margin of profit" is also confused with the term "gross profit," which is the profit after costs of goods sold have been subtracted, but before administrative expenses have been taken into account. The gross profit margin, also reported as a percentage of sales, is incorrectly but commonly called the "margin of profit." See **financial statement; fundamental analysis; gross margin ratio; ratios.**

margin requirement the amount or percentage required to be deposited with the brokerage firm as collateral for margin account activities. The requirement must be met at all times. In case of activity in the account or price movement in deposited securities, the actual amount of requirement may vary, resulting in excess margin or in a margin call. See **broker-dealer; excess margin; Federal Reserve Board (FRB); Regulation T.**

margin security any security that may be pledged as collateral in a margin account. This will include the stock of companies traded on a registered stock exchange; debt securities that are convertible to or carry warrants for subscription to a margin stock; or an over-the-counter security that has been approved for margin inclusion by the Federal Reserve. See **debt security; equity security; Regulation G; Regulation T; Regulation U.**

margin substitution the closing of a position in one customer account to cover the margin requirement in another. Substitution may be equal (of the same value) or unequal (of a value higher or lower than required by the margin terms).
Both long and short positions may be used as margin substitution, depending upon the nature of the margin requirement. A purchase of securities or a short sale may be substituted against a long sale, for example. See **customer; long; Regulation T; short; special miscellaneous account (SMA).**

margin transaction the action taken by a broker-dealer in extending credit to a margin customer or arranging for a stock loan against that customer's margin account. See **broker-dealer; customer; Regulation T.**

mark down (1) the difference between the bid and asked price absorbed by the seller of the security.
(2) the process of lowering the sales price in an underwriting when market

response is unfavorable. See **as principal; asked price; bid; five percent rule; market maker; market value; syndicate.**

mark up   (1) same as mark down, but from the dealer's perspective, representing the profit in a security trade; also called the spread.
(2) increase in the asked price of an offering when the market value increases.
(3) an accounting term for the difference between cost of goods or merchandise and the sale price. See **asked price; bid; five percent rule; spread; underwriter.**

market data system (MDS)   an automated system used by the New York Stock Exchange to communicate trade and volume data internationally. See **New York Stock Exchange (NYSE); trade; volume.**

market if touched   a type of order used on the Chicago Board Options Exchange (CBOE) only, which instructs that a buy or sell order is to be executed only if a series of options rises or falls to a specified price. See **Chicago Board Options Exchange (CBOE); option series.**

market letter   a communication mailed from a broker-dealer to subscribers or customers, giving economic or market news or opinions. The letter must conform to standards for all advertising and sales literature, and must be retained by the issuing broker-dealer in its files. See **advertising; broker-dealer; compliance.**

market maker   an exchange member who acts as a dealer in trading on his or her own account. The market maker may not participate as an agent for another. See **fair value; over-the-counter (OTC); SEC Rule 15c2-11.**

market-on-close order   a trading order which is to be executed at or as close as possible to the day's close of business. See **at the close; order ticket.**

market order   the most common form of trading order, specifying a desire for immediate execution at the best available price. See **good til cancelled (GTC); limit order; order ticket; stop order.**

market-out clause   a provision in an underwriting agreement allowing the underwriter to withdraw from the commitment in the event the market proves unfavorable for the offering. See **underwriter.**

market oversight surveillance system (MOSS)   an automated system operated by the Securities and Exchange Commision (SEC) to regulate trading activities and monitor the actions of those active in it. See **Securities and Exchange Commission (SEC).**

market performance committee (MPC)   a group consisting of institutional traders, allied members, commission brokers and specialists, whose function is the evaluation of specialist organizations and their performance within the New York Stock Exchange. See **institutional investor; New York Stock Exchange (NYSE); specialist.**

market price   the current, or latest reported price of a security; or, historically, a reference to the market value of securities at a specific moment. See **closing price; quotation.**

market value the current price of a security purchased over an exchange and in the auction marketplace. Market value is the value reflecting the willingness of buyers and sellers to agree upon a price in order to complete a transaction. It bears no direct relationship to book value, the tangible worth of a corporation on a per-share basis. See **auction marketplace; book value; price; value.**

marketability description of conditions in which a security or a group of securities may be bought or sold easily, without a drastic effect on the market price. See **auction marketplace; liquidity; secondary market.**

marketable securities those issues that are bought and sold quickly and easily in the open market. See **certificate of indebtedness; government bond; Treasury bill; Treasury bond; Treasury note.**

marking to the mark adjusting the amount of collateral in a margin account because of changes in the market value of securities positions transacted on margin. See **margin account; market value; settlement date.**

married put the purchase of a put option at the same time 100 shares of stock are bought. The action hedges against downward movement of the stock price beyond the strike price of the put, but raises the basis in stock by the amount of the premium paid. See **hedge; long hedge; option; premium; strike price.**

master lease the agreement in effect when one intends to sublet the property to other tenants. See **operating leaseback; real estate; sale-leaseback.**

matched and lost a response from the exchange floor advising brokers that a particular transaction was not executed at the ordered price, even though that price was available. This happens when other orders with priority of time are executed first, and the opportunity to meet the same price again does not materialize. See **market order; price.**

matched book situation when the borrowings and loans of a broker-dealer are equal. Financial matching can be achieved through the use of repurchase agreements and reverse repurchase agreements. See **broker-dealer; repurchase agreement; reverse repurchase agreement.**

matched orders (1) a market order for immediate execution, at whatever price available.
(2) the pairing of buy and sell orders for the same security, for an equal number of shares, and at the same price.
(3) Illegal practice of simultaneously buying and selling the same security on different exchanges, for the purpose of creating the appearance of high volume and market interest in the security. See **buy; Securities Exchange Act of 1934; sell order.**

matrix trading buying and selling related securities of the same class but with different maturity or exercise dates, to take advantage of temporary fluctuations in relative market values. See **income; option; trade.**

maturity date (1) the precise date on which the issuer of a debt security is committed to repayment of face value and accrued interest.
(2) the date assigned for income shares by a dual-purpose investment company as maturity for the issues from which income is to be derived.

married put

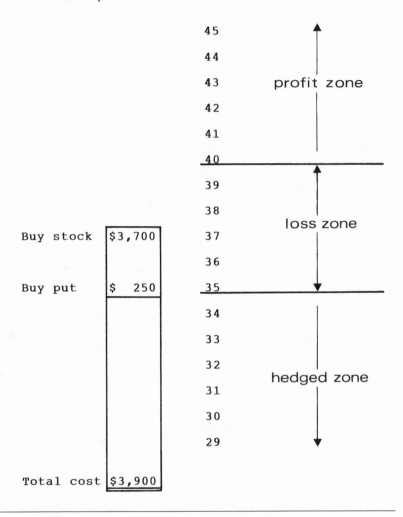

		45	
		44	
		43	profit zone
		42	
		41	
		40	
		39	
		38	
Buy stock	$3,700	37	loss zone
		36	
Buy put	$ 250	35	
		34	
		33	
		32	hedged zone
		31	
		30	
		29	
Total cost	$3,900		

(3) the due date of a note or other liability. See **bond; debenture; dual-purpose investment company; face value; income shares; interest; principal.**

medium-term bond   generally, any bond that will mature in two to ten years. See **bond; long-term debt; note; short-term debt.**

member firm regulation and surveillance division   the New York Stock Exchange department which oversees the conduct of member organizations. See **New York Stock Exchange (NYSE).**

member organization (or member firm)   a company with a principal who is a member of the New York Stock Exchange or one of the regional exchanges. See **clearing member; New York Stock Exchange (NYSE); stock exchange.**

merger term describing two or more organizations becoming one, usually by mutual agreement. See **conglomerate; corporation; take-over.**

Mid-America Commodity Exchange (MACE) 444 West Jackson Blvd., Chicago IL 60606; a regional commodity exchange located in Chicago. See **commodity; regional exchanges.**

Midwest Stock Exchange (MSE) 120 South LaSalle Street, Chicago IL 60603; one of the registered regional exchanges, located in Chicago. See **regional exchanges; stock exchange.**

mill (or **mil**) one one-thousandth. The term is used in assessing property valuation and to determine subsequent property taxes (the rate may be expressed in mills). It may also be expressed as .1%; .001; or 1/10 of one cent. See **assessed valuation; real estate; value.**

mill

Valuation	Tax Rate	Tax Amount
$ 60,000	8 mills	$ 480
90,000	10 mills	900
120,000	5 mills	600
150,000	7 mills	1,050

mineral acquisition costs the rights to acquire minerals in an investment program. These cannot be deducted as current costs, but must be amortized through cost depletion allowances. See **cost depletion; rights.**

minimum maintenance the specific requirement for equity in a margin account, representing collateral for margin trading. The term may refer to a broker-dealer's own requirements, or those of the Federal Reserve Board, the National Association of Securities Dealers, the New York Stock Exchange, or a regional exchange.

Minimum maintenance may consist of a percentage of various types of securities, as well as a minimum dollar amount that must be placed via securities or cash, regardless of the level of margin trading. See **broker-dealer; Federal Reserve Board (FRB); margin requirement; National Association of Securities Dealers (NASD); New York Stock Exchange (NYSE); regional exchanges; Regulation T.**

minimum tax a special tax that must be computed in some circumstances (such as when a certain level of taxable income and preference income has been reached).

minimum maintenance

Example

```
$2,000 minimum on all accounts
25% on long positions
35% on short positions
```

| Account Balance | | Minimum |
Long	Short	Maintenance
$ 8,000		$ 2,000
7,000		2,000
24,000		6,000
	$ 8,000	2,800
	3,800	2,000
6,000		2,000
	23,000	8,050

The tax is designed to ensure that everyone with substantial earnings will be liable for some income tax.

The tax applies to dividends under the dividend exclusion, accelerated depreciation and amortization, exploration and development costs, percentage depletion, intangible drilling costs, long-term capital gains, and the savings realized in basis when exercising incentive stock options. See **add-on minimum tax; alternative minimum tax; tax preference.**

Minneapolis Grain Exchange (MGE) 150 Grain Exchange Building, Minneapolis MN 55415; a regional commodity exchange located in Minneapolis. See **commodity; regional exchanges.**

minor an individual who has not yet reached the age of majority under state law, and who may make a contract voidable (cancel its terms after signing). Accordingly, brokerages will not allow a minor to open a trading account and transact business except through a custodian or guardian. See **customer; Uniform Gift to Minors Act (UGMA).**

minor trend one of three components in market movements as described under the Dow Theory. Following the minor trend—which may last only a few hours or days—is an intermediate and then a major trend. See **Dow Theory; intermediate trend; major trend; technical analysis.**

minus tick reference to a current price below the previous traded price. See **downtick; zero-minus tick.**

missing the mark   the failure by a member to execute a transaction for a customer at the instructed and available price, when a subsequent price is less advantageous. When this occurs, the member is obliged to reimburse the difference to the customer. See **broker; customer; price; trade.**

mixed account   description of a trading account containing long and short positions, usually referring to a margin account. See **customer; long; margin account; short.**

MJSD   identification of one of the three option cycles, those with expiration dates in March, June, September and December. See **cycle; expiration cycle;** FMAN; JAJO; **option.**

mobile home certificate   a type of Government National Mortgage Association (GNMA) mortgage security, on mobile homes rather than on traditional homes. The same guarantees for payment of principal and interest are applied, although maturity may be for a shorter term. See **Government National Mortgage Association (GNMA); mortgage.**

money market   short-term investments and the collective institutions and organizations involved in that market. See **banker's acceptance; capital market; certificate of deposit (CD); commercial paper; federal funds; short-term debt; Treasury bill.**

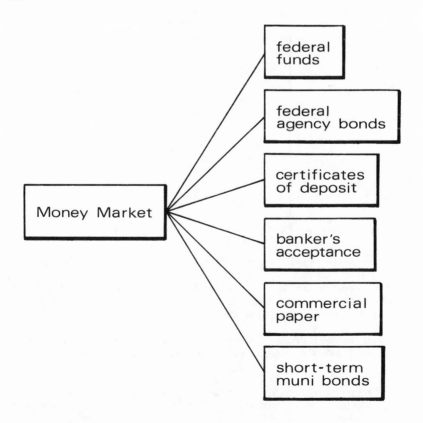

money spread

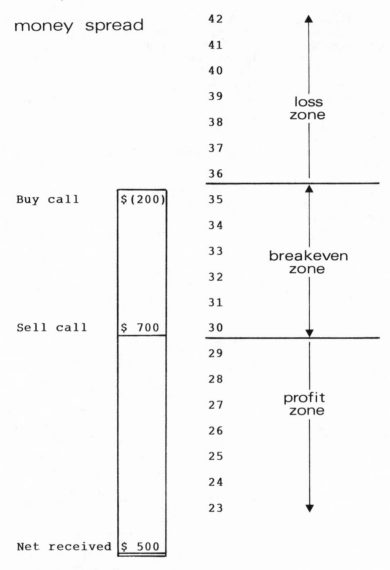

	42	
	41	
	40	
	39	loss zone
	38	
	37	
	36	
Buy call $(200)	35	
	34	
	33	breakeven zone
	32	
	31	
Sell call $ 700	30	
	29	
	28	
	27	profit zone
	26	
	25	
	24	
	23	
Net received $ 500		

money market fund   (1) a no-load mutual fund that invests only short-term money market securities and pays daily interest to investors.

(2) a money market "account" offered through a commercial bank that invests in the same money market securities as a money market fund. See **commercial bank; debt security; interest; mutual fund; short-term.**

money market instrument   a money market debt security, often issued at a discount. See **banker's acceptance; commercial paper; discount; interest; Treasury bill.**

money purchase plan   a type of pension plan in which a fixed percentage of each employee's salary is contributed each year. Benefits tend to increase when investment performance is favorable; younger participants in the plan are favored; and contributions are not increased when investment results are poor. Contributions may be lower than those under a defined benefit plan; a large portion of benefits go to rank and file employees; and there is a penalty against the employer for failing to meet minimum funding requirements. See **defined benefit pension plan; defined contribution pension plan; pension plan; retirement plans.**

money spread　also known as a vertical spread, an option strategy under which two or more options are purchased or sold at the same time. Expiration is identical but strike price is different, creating the potential for profit or loss in case of wide movement in the underlying issue. See **option; spread; vertical spread.**

month order　a type of market order that expires on the last day of the month in which the order is placed. See **market order; order ticket.**

Moody's investment grade　a rating system that places a quality valuation upon short-term municipal notes. The four ratings—MIG1 through MIG4 are all considered as investment grade. The system is published by Moody's Investors Service. See **bank quality; investment grade; municipal note; rating systems.**

MIG1	best quality
MIG2	high quality
MIG3	favorable quality
MIG4	adequate quality

Moody's Investment Grade (MIG)

Moody's Investors Service　a registered investment advisor that publishes a rating service on corporate bond issues and preferred stocks (as well as on certain common stocks). See **corporate bond; rating systems.**

Moody's Investors Service

Top quality	Aaa	Aa	A
Medium quality	Baa	Ba	B
Low quality	Caa	Ca	C

moral obligation bond   a bond issue passed by one legislature but not legally binding upon a subsequent legislature. There is an implied obligation upon the current legislature to honor the commitment made by its predecessor. See **municipal bond.**

moral suasion   the Federal Reserve Board may influence and persuade member banks to comply with its wishes regarding financial policies, based upon the leverage and broad power of the board. See **commercial bank; compliance; Federal Reserve Board (FRB).**

mortgage   a debt instrument in which real estate is pledged as security. Title to properties remains with the lender (mortgagor) until the entire debt has been satisfied. See **foreclosure; long-term debt; real estate; secured debt.**

mortgage banker   a mortgage company acting as conduit between investors and lenders, by purchasing mortgages from lenders and assuming the risks against the security of real property. See **real estate; secured debt.**

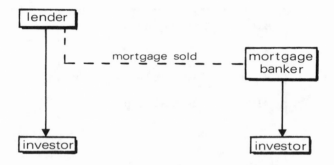

mortgage banker

mortgage bond   the most common type of corporate bond, which is secured by collateral in the form of tangible real property of the corporation, wholly or in part. The assets so pledged are specified in the indenture. See **bond; collateral; corporate bond; debt security; long-term debt; real property.**

mortgage company   an organization in the business of originating interim financing and reselling subsequent mortgages to banks and other institutions. See **financial institution; interim financing; mortgage banker; real estate.**

mortgage-participation certification (MP)   a pass-through security underwritten and purchased by the Federal Home Loan Mortgage Corporation, and consisting of interests in mortgage pools. See **Federal Home Loan Mortgage Corporation (FHLMC); pass-through security; residential mortgage.**

mortgage pool   an investment made up of a number of similar mortgages, usually having the same interest rate and the same or a similar maturity period. See **maturity date; real estate.**

mortgage REIT   a real estate investment trust (REIT) that has the primary objective of providing mortgages to finance new construction. The REIT may also participate in equity or as a partner in other programs, or may own lease rights to land and structures. See **construction and development REIT; equity REIT; real estate investment trust (REIT).**

mortgage wraparound   a financing arrangement in which the buyer makes a single payment to the seller, who in turn pays existing individual mortgages. See **financing; real estate.**

mortgage wraparound

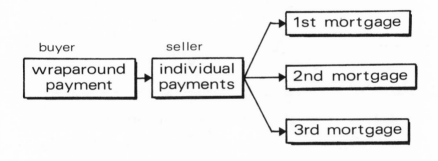

MSRB financial principal   the title of an individual who has passed the Series 54 examination, licensing one to compute net capital and oversee marketing activities in an organization marketing municipal bonds. See **municipal bond; Municipal Securities Rulemaking Board (MSRB); Series 54.**

MSRB registered representative   the title of an individual who has passed the Series 52 examination, licensing the marketing of municipal securities. See **municipal bond; Municipal Securities Rulemaking Board (MSRB); Series 52.**

MSRB supervisory principal   the title of an individual who has passed the Series 53 examination, licensing the supervision over municipal securities marketing activities. See **municipal bond; Municipal Securities Rulemaking Board (MSRB); Series 53.**

multiplier   the leverage commercial banks may use in setting reserves for outstanding loans, expressed as a percentage of loan amounts. For example, if a 20 percent reserve requirement is in effect, the bank is required to establish a reserve equal to 20 percent of the amount loaned. If borrowed funds are deposited in another member bank, it is conceivable that the leverage from a multiplier could result in loans of four times or more over the original deposit. See **commercial bank; leverage; reserve requirement.**

multiplier effect   the result of leveraged application of reserve requirements; or when applied to economic analysis, the effect of a small change in one factor upon a larger index. See **Gross National Product (GNP); inflation.**

Multiplier

Bank	Deposited Balance	Amount Loaned	Reserve (20%)
1	$10,000	$8,000	$2,000
2	8,000	6,400	1,600
3	6,400	5,120	1,280
4	5,120	4,096	1,024
5	4,096	3,277	819
6	3,277	2,622	655
7	2,622	2,598	524
8	2,598	2,078	520
9	2,078	1,662	416
10	1,662	1,330	332

municipal bond   a bond issued by a state, county, city or other political subdivision, or a non-federal agency. Interest on muni bonds is exempt from federal tax and from state income taxes in the state of issue. See **bond; debt security; tax-exempt security.**

municipal bond fund   (a) name used for unit investment trusts, funds consisting of a fixed portfolio of tax-free bonds, passing interest and liquidated proceeds to investors.

(b) an open-end fund which operates as a limited partnership investing in tax-free bonds. Holdings of municipal securities are freely traded as other types of specialized mutual funds trade in specified classes of securities. See **limited partnership; mutual fund; tax-exempt security; unit investment trust.**

Municipal Bond Insurance Association (MBIA)   an insurance association made up of several insurance companies, whose purpose is to insure payment of interest and repayment of principal on municipal securities. See **bond; interest; principal; tax-exempt security.**

municipal investment trust (MIT)   a type of unit investment trust whose portfolio consists strictly of municipal securities. See **tax-exempt security; unit investment trust.**

municipal note   a municipal security with maturity of two years or less. Notes are distinguished from bonds by the time to maturity, and otherwise may contain provisions identical to bonds. See **debt security; maturity date; note.**

Municipal Securities Rulemaking Board (MSRB)   an organization formed in 1975 by amendment to the Securities Exchange Act of 1934. The MSRB sets rules and guidelines and provides arbitration within the municipal securities industry. See **Maloney Act; Securities and Exchange Commission (SEC); Securities Exchange Act of 1934.**

mutilation   the act of partially destroying a certificate to the point it is not negotiable, due to certain items being missing: serial number, amount or date payable, for example. See **bond; certificate; negotiability.**

mutual fund   an open-end management company (or investment company) which is designed to meet specific investing goals or specializes in a particular class of products. Popular objectives of mutual funds include current income, long-term growth, and preservation of capital. Specialized funds may invest only in high-yielding stocks and bonds, gold, options, or tax-free debt instruments.

Valuation is expressed in net asset value per share of mutual fund owned. Daily increases and decreases are listed in financial pages.

Mutual funds may charge a load (sales charge), or may be no-load. Whether or not a load is charged is not an indicator of possible performance in the future, and past performance cannot be used reliably. One of the most dependable ways to choose a mutual fund is to compare performance during poor markets, looking for consistent returns better than the market.

The primary advantages of investing in mutual funds are: diversification among a large number of issues, professional management, and a low periodic minimum investment for most funds. See **diversification; investment company; Investment Company Act of 1940; investment objective; load mutual fund; net asset value per share (NAV); no-load (NL); open-end management company; plan company.**

mutual fund custodian   a trustee, often a commercial bank, acting in behalf of mutual funds and providing safekeeping services for cash and securities. See **commercial bank; custodian; open-end management company; trust.**

mutual savings bank   a type of bank owned by its depositors. Each has an equal share of ownership and net profits are distributed on a pro rata basis. Mutual savings banks do not have capital stock. See **savings bank.**

N

naked option   an option sold by an investor who does not own the underlying security or another option to offset the position and reduce contingent losses.

A naked call has unlimited liability, as the stock may increase indefinitely. Writers of these options undertake a high level of risk along with their potential for greater profits. The risk is that the writer will be forced to sell stock at the exercise price, which may be substantially lower than current market value.

A put, when sold, is always uncovered unless a form of offsetting position covers or partially covers the risk. Put sellers have a contingent liability that is limited, because a stock's value may decrease only so far. The risk is that a depressed stock will be assigned to the writer at the then-higher strike price, and will be forced to purchase those shares because the put had been sold. See **call; covered option; put; short; uncovered option; underlying security; write.**

naked position   a term describing the status of an option writer's account when uncovered calls are held, also called a short position in the option. See **short; short sale; uncovered option.**

NASD Form FR-1   a form filed by foreign broker-dealers interested in participating in a hot issue, but who do not belong to the syndicate. This is a blanket

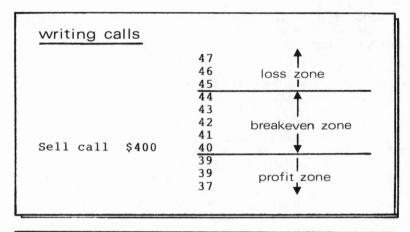

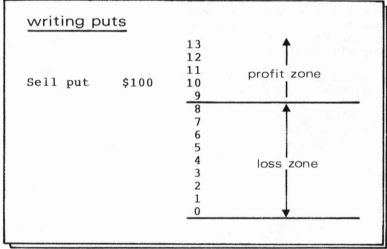

naked option

certification form on which the filing broker-dealer agrees to abide by the terms established by the NASD for participation in the issue. See **blanket certification form; broker-dealer; hot issue; National Association of Securities Dealers (NASD); syndicate.**

NASD manual a perpetually updated book of rules, policies and procedures published by the National Association of Securities Dealers (NASD) for broker-dealers and registered representatives under their jurisdiction. Each office selling or offering securities is required to maintain an updated NASD manual on the premises. See **broker-dealer; compliance; jurisdiction; National Association of Securities Dealers (NASD); registered representative.**

National Annual Report Service (NARS) a service formed by the New York Stock Exchange for professional investors, enabling them to obtain financial information on listed corporations. See **annual report; New York Stock Exchange (NYSE); financial statement; fundamental analysis.**

National Association of Investors Corporation (NAIC) a non-profit organization serving investment clubs in the United States, and the largest association of its kind. The club provides investors manuals, information, guidelines and sample contracts. See **investment club.**

National Association of Real Estate Investment Trusts (NAREIT) an organization located in Washington, D.C. that provides information to the public on the real estate investment trust industry. See **real estate investment trust (REIT).**

National Association of Securities Dealers (NASD) a self-regulatory agency for the securities industry, founded under the Maloney Act, a 1938 amendment to the Securities Exchange Act of 1934. The NASD is registered with the Securities and Exchange Commission and has a membership restricted to broker-dealers and securities underwriters.

The policies, procedures and rules of the NASD are guidelines for conduct and standards for the industry covering over-the-counter (OTC) securities and broker-dealer practices. These are collectively referred to as the rules of fair practice.

Broad powers of the NASD entitle it to examine and even expel members who do not abide by its rules. See **broker-dealer; full disclosure; Maloney Act; over-the-counter (OTC); rules of fair practice; Securities and Exchange Commission (SEC); Securities Exchange Act of 1934; underwriter.**

National Association of Securities Dealers Automated Quotations (NASDAQ) an automated system providing current quotations on over-the-counter securities and identification of market makers. See **broker-dealer; Level I service; Level II service; Level III service; market maker; over-the-counter (OTC); quotation; shopping the street.**

National Association of Securities Dealers Automated Quotations Over-the-Counter Price Index an automated index updated throughout the trading day and showing broad movement and activity in the over-the-counter (OTC) market. See **index; over-the-counter (OTC).**

National Bureau of Economic Research (NBER) a private, non-profit organization founded in 1920, which performs research on business cycles, the financial markets and economic conditions domestically and overseas. See **business cycle; financial institution; index.**

National Clearing Corporation (NCC) an organization associated with the National Association of Securities Dealers (NASD) which provides continuous net settlement (CNS) for clearance of transactions over the major exchanges. See **clearance; continuous net settlement (CNS); National Association of Securities Dealers (NASD).**

national commodity futures license the title of an individual who has passed the Series 3 examination, also called a commodity broker. The broker is licensed to trade in futures contracts. See **commodity broker; futures contract; Series 3.**

National Futures Association (NFA) a self-regulatory agency of the commodities industry, founded in 1982 in anticipation of increased federal regulations. The NFA is financed by member firms, over whom the agency has broad disciplinary powers. See **commodity; Commodity Futures Trading Commission (CFTC); futures contract; self-regulatory organization (SRO).**

National Market Advisory Board (NMAB) a board created by the Securities Reform Act of 1975, appointed by the Securities and Exchange Commission. The board consists primarily of individuals in the securities business, and advises the SEC on operations and regulations of the national markets. See **Securities and Exchange Commission (SEC); Securities Reform Act of 1975.**

National Market System (NMS) a system mandated by the Securities Reform Act of 1975, intended to ensure a national trading structure efficient for the transaction of securities. See **Securities Reform Act of 1975.**

National Quotation Bureau (NQB) an organization that publishes daily listings of bids and offers on the over-the-counter (OTC) market, and identifies market makers involved. See **market maker; over-the-counter (OTC); pink sheets; quotation; yellow sheets.**

National Quotations Committee (NQC) a committee of the National Association of Securities Dealers (NASD) that establishes criteria for the publication of quotations. See **National Association of Securities Dealers (NASD); quotation.**

National Securities Clearing Committee (NSCC) a committee formed from the consolidation of clearing operations of the New York Stock Exchange and the American Stock Exchange, to facilitate receipt and delivery in securities transactions. See **American Stock Exchange (AMEX); clearance; facilitation; New York Stock Exchange (NYSE).**

National Security Trading Association (NSTA) a New York-based membership association for securities traders. See **trader.**

National Security Trading System (NSTS) an automated system designed for dealer trading over the Cincinnati Stock Exchange (CSE). See **Cincinnati Stock Exchange (CSE); dealer; trader.**

National Stock Exchange (NSE) a New York exchange formed in 1962 that does not list issues carried by other exchanges as do the regional exchanges. See **regional exchanges; stock exchange.**

negative amortization condition in an adjustable rate mortgage (ARM) contract when a payment cap is in effect. Interest rates are high enough that the maximum payment is not sufficient to pay monthly interest. As a result, the loan balance grows each month, rather than declining. See **adjustable rate mortgage (ARM); mortgage; real estate.**

negative pickup transaction a form of investment in which a completed movie or film is purchased by the investor or the partnership. The transaction may provide a limited investment tax credit, assuming the investors are at risk and that the film is produced for viewing by the public or as an educational venture. Depreciation benefits are also allowed on the basis of the purchase. See **at risk; depreciation; investment tax credit (ITC); limited partnership; nonrecourse loan; recourse loan; syndicate; tax shelter.**

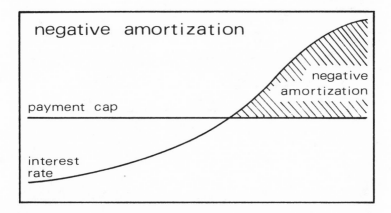

negative amortization

payment cap

negative amortization

interest rate

negotiability the transferability of assets. The term applies to forms of registration of securities making their sale as easy as possible. See **delivery; good delivery; transfer.**

negotiable instrument a readily transferable asset, such as cash or a registered and correctly signed certificate. See **assignment; certificate; registered form.**

negotiable-order-of-withdrawal (NOW) a type of investment combining the convenience of a checking account and the interest income from passbook savings. See **commercial bank; interest; savings account; savings and loan association; savings bank.**

negotiated marketplace a type of market in which the price in a transaction is agreed between the buyer and the seller, as in the over-the-counter market; the opposite of an auction marketplace. See **auction marketplace; over-the-counter (OTC).**

negotiated offering the form of offering most common in revenue bond issues, in which prospective investors are given an official statement. This serves the same purpose as a prospectus in other offerings. See **municipal bond; official statement; prospectus; revenue bond.**

net asset value per share (NAV) a ratio involving the division of net assets (tangible assets less liabilities) by the number of shares outstanding.
NAV is a calculation used to place current value on shares of open-end mutual funds. See **assets; investment company; liabilities; mutual fund; offering price; open-end management company; tangible value.**

net book value per share (NBV) a ratio for determining book value, computed by dividing net book value by the number of outstanding shares of a corporation. Book value represents the total net worth or, difference between tangible assets and liabilities. See **book value; corporation; fundamental analysis; net worth.**

net capital requirement a rule of the Securities and Exchange Commission, known as Rule 15c3-1. It states that the aggregate indebtedness of a broker-dealer may not exceed defined net capital by a certain percentage, generally 1,500 percent.
Within this definition, net capital is the equity of the broker-dealer, less assets

$$\frac{\text{tangible assets} \quad - \quad \text{liabilities}}{\text{outstanding shares}} = \text{NAV}$$

$$\frac{\$2,406,000 \quad - \quad \$1,007,900}{1,000,000} = \$1.40$$

net asset value per share (NAV)

net book value per share (NBV)

$$\frac{\text{total net worth}}{\text{outstanding shares}} = \text{NBV}$$

$$\frac{\$1,448,100}{1,000,000} = \$1.45$$

Net Change

net change	decimal	dollars per 100 shares
1/16	.0625	$ 6.25
1/8	.1250	12.50
3/16	.1875	18.75
1/4	.2500	25.00
5/16	.3125	31.25
3/8	.3750	37.50
7/16	.4375	43.75
1/2	.5000	50.00
9/16	.5625	56.25
5/8	.6250	62.50
11/16	.6875	68.75
3/4	.7500	75.00
13/16	.8125	81.25
7/8	.8750	87.50
15/16	.9375	93.75
1	1.0000	100.00

disallowed. Only those assets readily convertible to cash may be included. See **aggregate indebtedness; broker-dealer; SEC Rule 15c3-1.**

net change   the difference in market value of a security from one day to the next. In financial papers, the last column of an issue's summary is the net change for that day.

Net change is expressed in per-share amounts, with partial dollars represented by fractions. On the listed exchanges, this may be broken down as far as eighths of a dollar (one-eighth is twelve cents); on the over-the-counter market, net change is broken down as far as sixteenths. See **listed stock; over-the-counter (OTC); price.**

net current assets   the difference between current assets and current liabilities, also called working capital. See **balance sheet; current ratio; fundamental analysis; working capital.**

net income   the profits realized from operations of a company, which may mean actual income either before or after providing for federal income taxes. See **income; income statement; profit.**

net income ratio   the percentage of total sales represented by net income. This ratio may be expressed on a pre-tax or on an after-tax basis. See **fundamental analysis; income statement; profit.**

```
              INCOME STATEMENT

    Total Sales              $21,400,000
    Cost of Goods Sold        12,804,000

    Gross Profit             $ 8,596,000
    Administrative Expenses    6,040,000

    Net Income Before Taxes  $ 2,556,000
    Income Taxes                 803,400

    Net Income After Taxes   $ 1,752,600
```

Pre-Tax Ratio:

$$\frac{\$2,556,000}{\$21,400,000} = 11.94\%$$

After-Tax Ratio

$$\frac{\$1,752,600}{\$21,400,000} = 8.19\%$$

net income ratio

net tangible assets per share

Balance Sheet

Current Assets	$ 9,400,800	
Long-Term Assets	43,000,100	
Prepaid Assets	37,000	
Intangible Assets	150,000	
Total Assets		$52,587,900
Current Liabilities	$ 3,904,500	
Long-Term Liabilities	41,300,000	
Total Liabilities		$45,204,500
Common Stock, 1,000,000 shares outstanding	$ 6,000,000	
Preferred Stock, 3,000 shares outstanding	300,000	
Retained Earnings	1,083,400	
Total Shareholders' Equity		$ 7,383,400
Total Liabilities and Shareholders' Equity		$52,587,900

$$\frac{\text{Assets} \quad \text{less} \quad \text{Intangible Assets} \quad \text{less} \quad \text{Total Liabilities} \quad \text{less} \quad \text{Preferred Stock}}{\text{Common Stock Outstanding}} = \text{net per share}$$

$$\frac{\$52,587,900 - (\$150,000 + \$45,204,500 + \$300,000)}{1,000,000} = \$ 6.93$$

net interest cost (NIC) the total cost of an offering to the issuer, which includes both coupon rate and premium or discount; it may also be expressed as the total cost to maturity of the entire issue. See **bond; discount; issuer; premium; underwriter.**

net proceeds (1) the actual amount credited to a customer's account or paid in cash from sale of securities. It is the gross proceeds less transaction costs and any adjustments.
(2) on the sale of any asset, the amount realized after deducting all costs related to the sale. See **basis; capital gain; capital loss.**

net profit interest a form of sharing arrangement in an oil and gas partnership, in which the sponsor shares in the profits realized from productive wells. See **oil and gas; sponsor.**

net tangible assets per share a valuation for common shareholders, consisting of book value without preferred shareholder ownership.
The calculation involves reducing total assets by intangibles, total liabilities, and the book value of preferred stock. This sum is divided by the total number of common shares outstanding. See **book value; net book value per share (NBV); tangible value.**

net transaction a form of securities transaction in which the quoted amount includes any sales commission. Thus, the price quoted is also the actual amount a buyer will pay. See **commission; trade.**

net worth total stockholder's equity in a corporation, or the net value of ownership in a partnership or sole proprietorship. See **assets; balance sheet; equity; liabilities; stockholders' equity.**

net yield the return on a bond that takes into account the price — premium or discount, coupon rate and years until maturity. Some instruments, such as Treasury bills and municipal bonds, are quoted by net yield instead of simple coupon rate, because varying maturities will change the total return; also called yield to maturity. See **debt security; discount; municipal bond; premium; return on equity; Treasury bill; yield to maturity.**

network A the consolidated tape system's round-lot transaction reporting, available by subscription. Transactions are reported from the NYSE as well as other exchanges in the third and fourth markets, for all NYSE-listed securities. See **consolidated tape system (CTS); fourth market; New York Stock Exchange (NYSE); round lot; third market.**

network B the consolidated tape system's round-lot transaction reporting for the American Stock Exchange. Transactions on the AMEX and other markets in AMEX-listed stocks are reported through this service. See **American Stock Exchange (AMEX); consolidated tape system (CTS); fourth market; round lot; third market.**

new account form a form that must be completed and maintained by broker-dealers for each customer, and updated as necessary. It records the customer's experience and background as an investor, financial status, and investment objectives. See **broker-dealer; customer; investment objective.**

Discount bond:

net yield

$$\frac{\text{annual interest} + \text{allocated annual discount}}{(\text{redemption price} + \text{acquisition price}) \ / \ 2}$$

$$= \quad \text{net yield}$$

price 96, 7% for 10 years:

$$\frac{\$70.00 + \$4.00}{(\$1,000 + \$960) \ / \ 2} = 7.55\%$$

Premium bond:

$$\frac{\text{annual interest} + \text{amortized annual premium}}{(\text{redemption price} + \text{acquisition price}) \ / \ 2}$$

$$= \quad \text{net yield}$$

price 102, 8% for 8 years:

$$\frac{\$80.00 - \$2.00}{(\$1,000 + \$1,020) \ / \ 2} = 7.72\%$$

---

new basis   the adjusted basis of real estate after adjusting the cost of both new and old properties for improvements, depreciation and the cost of transaction. For tax purposes, gain on the sale of a residential property is deferred by adjusting property to the new basis, as long as the purchase price of the new residence exceeded the sale price of the old. See **deferral; real estate; tax basis.**

new issue   the offering of shares by a corporation in a class that has not been offered previously. See **authorized shares; issued and outstanding; outstanding stock; stock.**

New York Futures Clearing Corporation (NYFCC)   an organization that processes post-trading for futures contracts, founded by the New York Futures Exchange (NYFE). See **commodity; futures contract; trade.**

New York Futures Exchange (NYFE)   20 Broad Street, New York NY 10005; an exchange specializing in financial futures — Treasury securities and GNMA deben-

new basis

Cost of new property		$183,950
Plus: closing costs		4,430
Gross cost		$188,380
Less: Sale of old property		
Sales price	$160,000	
Less: Closing costs	(14,300)	
Less: Depreciation	(12,800)	
Plus: Improvements	12,000	
Less: Original net cost	(34,950)	
Net gain on old property		$109,950
New basis		$ 78,430

---

tures — founded by the New York Stock Exchange. See **financial futures; futures contract; New York Stock Exchange (NYSE).**

New York Mercantile Exchange (NYMEX) 4 World Trade Center, New York NY 10048; an exchange where trading in certain futures contracts takes place, including currency, agricultural, metals and petroleum. See **commodity; futures contract.**

New York plan name of a procedure for the transacting of equipment financed by an equipment trust bond, in which title is passed according to the schedule of repayment. See **equipment trust bond; Philadelphia plan.**

New York Stock Exchange (NYSE) 11 Wall Street, New York NY 10005; the oldest U.S. stock exchange, founded in 1792. The NYSE is a marketplace for the purchase and sale of securities at prices determined by the auction marketplace. Most of the largest corporations in the country are listed on the NYSE, which has high standards for acceptance of a new listing. See **auction marketplace; listed company; member organization; stock exchange; voluntary association.**

New York Stock Exchange Index a composite index weighted by the number of shares outstanding on each issue. Its four categories are industrials, transportations, utilities, and finance. The periodic changes in the index reflect overall increases or decreases in average value of all listed companies. See **composite index;** NYSE **Composite Index; value.**

nine-bond rule common name for SEC Rule 396, which states that bonds traded in lots fewer than 10 must be left at the trading floor for best effort at transacting at the indicated price. The rule may be waived by obtaining prior permission from the New York Stock Exchange. See **bond; New York Stock Exchange (NYSE);** SEC **Rule 396.**

90-day branch a category of branch office accepted for membership by a broker-dealer, when none of the individuals holds a general securities principal license (Series 24). It is agreed that, within 90 days, at least one of the new branch members will pass the NASD examination and will then be appointed as branch manager. See **branch office manager; broker-dealer; general securities principal; National Association of Securities Dealers (NASD); Series 24.**

no-action letter a letter from the Securities and Exchange Commission (SEC), sent upon request by a broker-dealer, stating that no civil or criminal actions will be taken in the event that the broker-dealer pursues a course of action previously described. The purpose of the inquiry is to receive a ruling that a contemplated action does not violate securities laws. See **broker-dealer; Securities and Exchange Commission (SEC).**

no-load a type of mutual fund that does not reduce an investor's capital by a sales charge. Load funds do deduct a charge, primarily to pay a representative's commission for the transaction. Because no sales commission is taken in a no-load fund, these must be purchased directly. See **load mutual fund; mutual fund; net asset value per share (NAV); open-end management company; sales load.**

no-par value a form of issue of capital stock in which a par value is not assigned. The number of shares and par value are not significant measures of a corporation's solvency. But the tangible value of shares at the time of issue and as adjusted by earnings will affect market value. As there is no dollar value assigned per share, a value is assigned arbitrarily when certificates are issued. See **corporation; financial statement; par value.**

nominal yield the simple expression of the amount yielded on a bond, determined by dividing the total interest payments per year, by the par value of the bond. See **bond; coupon rate; par value; simple interest.**

$$\frac{\text{annual payments}}{\text{par value}} = \text{nominal yield}$$

$$\frac{\$83.50}{\$1000.00} = 8.35\%$$

nominal yield

noncallable (1) a type of bond that cannot be converted by its issuer to an equity position.

(2) preferred stock that the issuing corporation cannot convert to common stock as long as it is held by the investor.

(3) bonds or preferred stock that cannot be called for a specified period of time. Following this period, it becomes callable. See **call feature; maturity date; redemption.**

nonclearing member a member organization that does not clear directly with the exchange, or does not maintain an operating facility. Rather, the nonclearing member subcontracts clearing processes to another member. See **clearing member;**

member organization; National Association of Securities Dealers (NASD); New York Stock Exchange (NYSE); Stock Clearing Corporation (SCC).

noncompetitive bid   a type of bid placed for U.S. Treasury securities that will be granted without the requirement of competing with other bidders. The price is agreed in advance to be the average of all other accepted bids for the same period. See **competitive trader; Treasury bill; Treasury bond; Treasury note.**

noncumulative preferred   a class of stock for which passed dividends cannot be recaptured later. See **cumulative preferred; dividend; passed dividend; preferred stock.**

nondiversified management company   a form of management company not subject to the rules of a diversified firm (that 75 percent of total assets must be in cash or receivables; government securities; the shares of another investment firm; in stock representing 10 percent or less of voting stock; or in other issues representing five percent or less of total assets of the company). See **diversified management company; management company.**

nonexclusive rule   a rule requiring compliance in order to achieve a certain status (such as exemption from registration), but that otherwise does not require compliance. See **compliance; exempt security; Securities and Exchange Commission (SEC).**

nonguaranteed municipal bond   revenue bonds issued upon the full faith and credit of a municipality, and not tied to a tax increase. These are used to finance public construction projects that should be self-supporting and capable of repayment of the bond issue from its own revenues. See **municipal bond; revenue bond.**

nonmarketable securities   securities traded only in a prescribed manner, but not available for trading in the public exchanges. See **registered form; retirement plan bond; Series E bond; Series H bond.**

nonqualifying annuity   a type of annuity that is not appropriate for purchase within a qualified retirement plan. Taxation of annuity appreciation is sheltered until annuitization, in accordance with the terms and conditions of annuities generally. See **fixed annuity; qualifying annuity; tax shelter; variable annuity.**

nonqualifying stock option   a form of option given as a benefit or incentive, often to key employees of a corporation. Upon exercise, the difference between the option price and current market value is taxed. See **fixed charge; option; qualified stock option; tax basis.**

nonrecourse loan   loans granted within a direct participation program. Investors leverage their capital by signing a nonrecourse note. They are not at risk for the amount of the loan. In real estate programs, nonrecourse loans may be included in total basis when partnership units are pledged for the loan. In other types of programs, no nonrecourse financing may be included in the investor's basis for tax purposes. See **at risk; collateral; direct participation program; leverage; limited partner; tax basis.**

normal investment practices   a guideline used by the NASD board of governors related to the acceptable practices of broker-dealers. See **board of governors; broker-dealer; customer; National Association of Securities Dealers (NASD).**

normal trading unit   a round lot. For stocks, the normal trading unit is 100 shares or blocks divisible by 100. Many institutional traders transact in units divisible by 500 shares. For inactive stocks, trading units as low as 10 shares are considered normal. For bonds, the normal trading unit is 10 bonds with par value of $1,000 each. See **round lot; odd lot.**

North American Securities Administrators' Association (NASAA)   an association of the state securities agencies, also including membership from some Canadian provinces. See **state securities agency.**

not held (NH)   a provision attached to an order, allowing the floor broker the discretion to try and obtain a better price than indicated on the order, if, in the broker's opinion, a better price can be obtained. If the opportunity to buy or sell at the preferred price is lost, the broker will not be held responsible. See **floor broker; order ticket.**

note   a debt security with a maturity that is generally shorter than that for a bond, under 10 years. See **debt security; short-term debt.**

notification   a disclosure statement that may be used in lieu of registration of a security. The Securites Act of 1933 allows notification, and the SEC sets limits for the size of offerings that may be offered without a registration statement. See **registration statement; Regulation A; Securities Act of 1933.**

novation   a form of substitution, in which one debt security is replaced by another. The buyer or seller pays the difference in market value to equalize the exchange. See **market value; substitution.**

now account   a type of bank account combining checking and saving privileges. See **negotiable-order-of-withdrawal (NOW).**

NYSE composite index   a composite index of all stocks listed on the New York Stock Exchange, weighted by the number of outstanding shares and reporting the change in value, assigning a dollar value to that change to communicate relative movements. See **New York Stock Exchange Index.**

O

odd lot   a stock trade of less than 100 shares. Round lots are traded in groups of 100 or multiples of 100 shares. See **normal trading unit; round lot.**

odd lot differential   an adjustment in the price of shares when odd lots are traded, usually one-eighth of one point. See **differential; price; round lot.**

odd lot theory   the belief that small investors, especially those trading in odd lots, predict market movements accurately. For example, as a bull market peaks, the odd lot traders would begin to sell, under the theory. See **bear; bull; technical analysis.**

off-board   a secondary distribution of securities or trades occurring over-the-counter or outside of a national exchange; a trade occurring between member organizations. See **over-the-counter (OTC); secondary distribution; unlisted security.**

offer wanted (OW)   a listing in the pink sheets or the yellow sheets, when a dealer is inviting other dealers to make an offer on a security. See **bid wanted (BW); pink sheets; yellow sheets.**

offeree representative   an individual who is allowed to receive a fee for referring customers to a registered representative. Usually a registered investment advisor (RIA) or other recognized professional, the representative's fee must be disclosed to the investor. See **full disclosure; registered investment advisor (RIA); registered representative.**

offering   a term to describe an issue of securities, in which shares or units are available to investors. See **issue; new issue.**

offering circular   a document similar to a prospectus, used for private placements. The circular spells out pertinent details and assumptions underlying the program, and discloses conflicts of interest, management, and planned acquisitions. See **private placement; prospectus; SEC Rule 254.**

offering date   the first date on which securities are available for sale to the public. See **dated date; offering.**

offering price   the asked price; the price of securities at which a holder is willing to sell. See **asked price; market value; price.**

offering scale   the current price of a serial bond, expressed in dollars and cents, and representing actual yield to maturity. A bond offered at 10.50 is being offered at a discount that will yield 10.5% to maturity. See **underwriter; serial bond; yield to maturity.**

Office of Supervisory Jurisdiction (OSJ)   a branch office of a broker-dealer recognized by the National Association of Securities Dealers (NASD) as the entity responsible for supervision of the activities of representatives in that branch. Some broker-dealers have one OSJ for the entire firm, while others establish a number of OSJs, each with its own branch manager.
   The OSJ is required to maintain and comply with a written procedures manual, and to ensure procedures for the direct supervision of registered representatives. See **branch office; broker-dealer; National Association of Securities Dealers (NASD); rules of fair practice; supervision.**

office ticket   an order report completed by every active office of a member organization. See **floor ticket; order ticket.**

official statement   a document prepared for revenue bond issues that serves the same purpose as a prospectus for a registered program or an offering circular for a private placement. The report is prepared by the underwriter and given to each investor. See **municipal bond; negotiated offering; prospectus; revenue bond; underwriter.**

offshore   a financial institution that is domiciled outside of the United States and its jurisdiction. Offshore companies selling securities are subject to the regulations of the U.S. if those securities are sold in the jurisdiction. See **financial institution; regulation; securities.**

oil and gas a type of investment program involved in the development and marketing of energy products, often designed to offer substantial tax benefits to investors. Common types of oil and gas programs include:

Income — the operation and development of working interests in producing fields.

Development — drilling for oil or gas in proven reserve fields.

Exploratory — seeking as-yet-undiscovered reservoirs in new oil or gas fields, or expanding known reservoirs to new limits or depths.

Balanced — programs engaged in exploratory and development activities.

Completion — programs that fund the costs of drilling and completing productive wells. See **exploratory program; investment program; tax shelter; working interest.**

on-the-quotation an order specifying that a purchase or sell of an odd lot is to take place at the current bid or offer price. Odd lots normally are traded at the price of the next round lot transaction. See **odd lot; order ticket; round lot.**

open (1) status of programs not yet approved for offer or sale, when indications of interest are invited.

(2) an investment program that is approved for offer and sale, in which shares or units are available.

(3) Orders, such as good til cancelled (GTC) orders as yet unfilled. See **closed position; good til cancelled (GTC); indication of interest; offering.**

open box the location in a brokerage house where collateral securities are kept. See **active box; brokerage house; collateral.**

open interest the total count of option or commodity contracts that are open at any specific time that have not expired or been exercised. See **clearing member; futures contract; option series.**

open market operation the transactions that are managed by the Federal Open Market Committee for the Federal Reserve Board, in which federal securities are brought to the secondary market. See **Federal Open Market Committee (FOMC); Federal Reserve Board (FRB); secondary market.**

open order an order that has been given but is not yet placed. It can be eliminated in any one of three ways: by cancellation, execution or expiration. See **good til cancelled (GTC).**

open-end management company a company without a set capitalization. It will sell shares to investors whenever they desire to buy, and will redeem those shares upon request. This type of organization is commonly known as a mutual fund. See **capitalization; management company; mutual fund; redemption.**

open-end mortgage a form of financing property in which additional bonding may be issued. All such open-end issues would have equal claim against the property in case of default. See **lien; mortgage bond.**

Opening Automated Report Service (OARS) a system in use by the New York Stock Exchange, organizing orders received before the opening of trading. Orders are matched and tabulated, and the specialist for each security is informed of the status of buy and sell orders. See **New York Stock Exchange (NYSE); specialist.**

opening price   the price of a security in effect as of the opening of trading. See **auction marketplace; closing price; market value.**

opening purchase/sale   a transaction that either opens or increases a long or short position in an option contract or series. When an investor buys an option contract, it creates (opens) a long position. When selling a contract, it opens a short position. See **closing purchase transaction; closing sale transaction; long; option series; short.**

operating cost ratio   a ratio showing the percentage of cost of goods sold to total sales. It is the inverse of gross margin. See **fundamental analysis; gross margin ratio; income account ratios; ratios.**

INCOME STATEMENT		
	Amount	%
Gross Sales	$12,840,400	100.0
Cost of Goods Sold	8,004,800	62.3
Gross Profit	4,835,600	37.7
Operating Expenses	3,770,100	29.4
Net Income	1,065,500	8.3

$$\frac{\$8,004,800}{\$12,840,400} = 62.3\%$$

operating cost ratio

operating lease   a gross or net lease lasting for a short term (commonly less than half the useful life of equipment), in which total of payments is lower than the leased equipment's purchase price. See **equipment leasing; investment program; short-term.**

operating leaseback   a form of agreement for a lessee who intends to sub-lease to other tenants. See **master lease; real estate; sale-leaseback.**

operating profit   net profits before income taxes are provided for or paid. See **fundamental analysis; net income; profit; tax basis.**

operating profit margin   the percentage of net profit to gross sales, before provision for or payment of income taxes. See **fundamental analysis; income account ratios; net income; profit; ratios.**

```
                    Income Statement

   Gross Sales                        $84,790,000

   Cost of Goods Sold                  51,103,600

   Gross Profit                        33,686,400

   Operating Expenses                  26,945,100

   Operating Profit                     6,741,300

   Provision for Income Taxes           2,450,000

   Net Profit                           4,291,300
```

operating profit

$$\frac{\$6,741,300}{\$84,790,000} = 7.95\%$$

operating profit margin

operating ratios   ratios involving the relationship between an item of cost or expense, and gross sales. The most common operating ratios are the gross margin ratio (gross profit divided by sales) and the net income ratio (net income divided by sales). See **expense control ratio; fundamental analysis; gross margin ratio; income account ratios; net income ratio; operating profit margin; ratios.**

operating ratios

Gross Margin
$$\frac{\$33,686,400}{\$84,790,000} = 39.7\%$$

Net Income
$$\frac{\$4,291,300}{\$84,790,000} = 5.1\%$$

operations   a term broadly applied to the back office departments of a broker-dealer. See **back office; broker-dealer; clearance; customer; execution.**

operations manual   the procedures, rules and policies book that is maintained in every office of a broker-dealer. Each Office of Supervisory Jurisdiction (OSJ) is required by the NASD rules of fair practice to keep an updated compliance (or operations) manual at its location. See **branch office; compliance manual; Office of Supervisory Jurisdiction (OSJ); National Association of Securities Dealers (NASD); rules of fair practice.**

option   a contract allowing the holder (buyer) to purchase or sell 100 shares of a security. Unlike stocks, options have a finite life, and become worthless following an expiration date.

Calls are options to purchase 100 shares of the underlying security, and may be bought for speculation or as a hedge against other stock positions. They may also be written (sold). An uncovered, or naked option is one sold when the seller does not own 100 shares of the underlying security. Uncovered calls are high risks, as the stock might rise, presenting an unlimited liability. A covered call is one written when the writer owns 100 shares of the underlying security.

Puts are options to sell 100 shares of the underlying security. A put buyer is either speculating that the underlying security will decline in value (and the put will then increase) or is hedging another security position. A put seller cannot actually cover the position, but liability is limited to the value of the underlying security below the strike price of the option.

Strike price is the identified value of the underlying security against which the option contract is written. Both strike price and expiration month are identified in every option contract. The January 50 call expires on the Saturday following the third Friday in January, and has a strike price of $50 per share. See **call; expiration; intrinsic value; put; strike price; tangible value; underlying security.**

option agreement   an information form completed by a customer prior to trading in options with a broker-dealer. The customer discloses financial condition and agrees to comply with the stated limits of trading and exercise of options. A prospectus from the Options Clearing Corporation (OCC) is given to the customer, and the broker-dealer is responsible for determining that the customer understands options well enough to engage in trading. See **broker-dealer; customer; Options Clearing Corporation (OCC).**

option fund   a type of mutual fund specializing in option investments, either through writing of covered stock options or of financial futures or stock index options. See **covered option; mutual fund; open-end management company.**

option premium   the price of an option contract. To the buyer, it is the amount that must be paid for the option (before commissions are added in). To the seller, it is the gross amount that will be received or credited for selling the option contract.

Option premium has two components: intrinsic value and time value. Intrinsic (tangible) value consists of one point (dollar) for each point that the underlying stock is in the money. If the strike price of a call is 50 (fifty dollars per share) and current market value is $53, the option will have three dollars of intrinsic value. When the security is out-of-the-money, there is no intrinsic value.

The remaining premium is time value only. The longer an option has to go until its expiration date, the higher the time value premium. As expiration nears, time

option spread

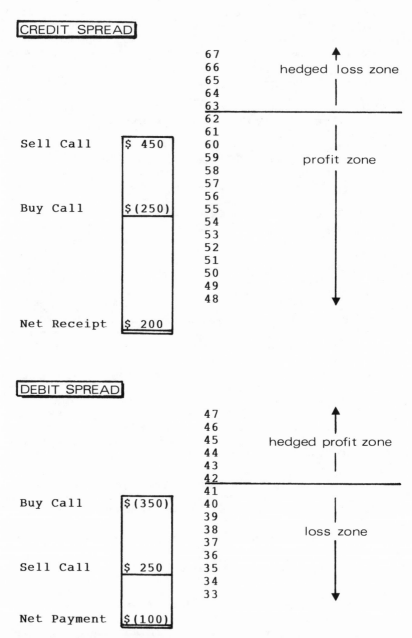

CREDIT SPREAD

Sell Call	$ 450	67 66 hedged loss zone 65 64 63 62 61 60 59 profit zone 58
Buy Call	$(250)	
Net Receipt	$ 200	

DEBIT SPREAD

Buy Call	$(350)
Sell Call	$ 250
Net Payment	$(100)

value premium evaporates rapidly, until there is none left on the day of expiration. See **expiration; intrinsic value; tangible value; time value premium.**

option series   a reference to the characteristics of option contracts that distinguish them from one another. Every option is identified by four components, which make up an individual series: the identified underlying security; the type of contract (put or call); the expiration date; and the strike price. See **expiration; strike price; underlying security.**

option spread   a strategy in which an investor takes a long and a short position in related options. The strategy may involve calls or puts, and may be a debit spread (net cost) or a credit spread (net receipt). See **bear spread; bull spread; credit spread; debit spread; hedge.**

Options Clearing Corporation (OCC)   the organization that handles option transactions: the trade clearance, guarantees, and regulations. The OCC also publishes a prospectus describing the rules and risks of option trading. The company acts as seller to all option buyers, and as buyer to all option sellers, and assigns exercised contracts. The OCC is owned jointly by the exchanges carrying listed options. See **assignment; buyer's option; prospectus; seller's option.**

Options Price Reporting Authority (OPRA)   a service for option traders, providing a quotation service by subscription, transmitted electronically. See **price; quotation.**

or better   terminology for limit orders, in which the execution price desired is the minimum the seller will accept or the maximum a buyer will accept for the trade. All limit orders are understood to be "or better," that the best bid or offer is desired, given the limit indicated. See **limit order; order ticket.**

orchards   investment in which the assets — trees — are considered to be personal property, subject to depreciation and investment tax credits. This makes orchard investments through limited partnerships attractive for those investors seeking tax shelters. See **direct participation program; investment objective; limited partnership; tax shelter.**

order book official (OBO)   an employee of an exchange engaged in option trading, who accepts option trade orders that cannot be executed immediately. OBO's perform the same functions as board brokers. See **board broker; option.**

order ticket   a form for the buy or sell of securities. It is completed by the registered representative upon receiving a specific request for a transaction from a customer, and is then maintained as a record by the brokerage. Information on the order ticket is transmitted to the exchange for execution. See **brokerage house; buy; good til cancelled (GTC); limit order; registered representative; sell order.**

original issue discount (OID)   a type of bond issue sold at discount, for which the I.R.S. requires special tax treatment. A portion of the discount is recognized as income each year the bond is held, adjusting the basis upward so that it will reach par as of maturity. See **bond; capital gain; discount; maturity date.**

original maturity   the period of time between the issue date of a bond and the maturity date. Once a bond is traded subsequent to its original maturity, reference is made only to the current time until maturity. See **bond; maturity date.**

BUY	□ solicited □ unsolicited	□ day □ open	entered date
		limit	entered time
□ op □ cl □ short □ long	trader	execution	trade date
			reported time
	special instructions		reg. representative
cage: □ hold □ transfer □ remit			osj principal
quantity	security		symbol

account type		a.e. type	officer approval
□ new account			

customer name	commission
social security or tax i.d. no.	

order ticket

Discount $150

Year	Recognized	Bond Value
1	$15.00	$ 865.00
2	15.00	880.00
3	15.00	895.00
4	15.00	910.00
5	15.00	925.00
6	15.00	940.00
7	15.00	955.00
8	15.00	970.00
9	15.00	985.00
10	15.00	1,000.00

original issue discount

OSJ manager   the branch office manager, responsible for the supervision of registered representatives in the Office of Supervisory Jurisdiction (OSJ). This person generally must have a general securities principal license from the National Association of Securities Dealers. See **branch office manager; broker-dealer; general securities principal; National Association of Securities Dealers (NASD).**

OTC option   also called a conventional option, a contracted option for which the premium and expiration are negotiated between the buyer and the seller. See **conventional option; Options Clearing Corporation (OCC); over-the-counter (OTC); unlisted security.**

out-of-the-money   term describing an option when the market value of the underlying security is lower (for calls) or higher (for puts) than the strike price. An option consists of intrinsic value and time value. For an out-of-the-money option, there can be no intrinsic value. See **intrinsic value; option; in the money; strike price.**

out of the money

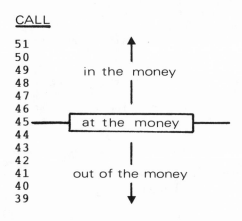

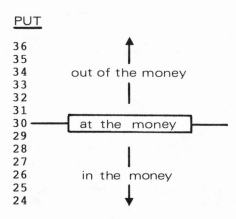

outstanding stock   all issued shares of a corporation, less any treasury stock (stock repurchased by the company). See **authorized shares; common stock; corporation; issued and outstanding; preferred stock; stock; treasury stock.**

over-the-counter (OTC)   reference to securities traded among broker-dealers and not through listings on an exchange. Such securities include those of corporations not meeting listing criteria of the exchanges; government and municipal debt securities; and the securities of many financial service companies (banks, insurance companies). See **broker-dealer; debt security; stock exchange.**

overbought/oversold   the status of a security that, in the opinion of a technical analyst, has experienced a distorted movement in its market value. Overbought issues are those whose price have moved upward too quickly, in the opinion of the analyst. Oversold issues are the opposite, issues whose prices have declined more rapidly than justified by present conditions. See **buying climax; selling climax; technical analysis.**

override   the split of a registered representative's commission or fee, usually with a branch office manager or with the broker-dealer, as part of a contracted arrangement.

Reasons for override agreements may include: payment for administrative expenses paid by the branch office manager; incentive to attain a higher level of sales volume; or a temporary withholding of commissions pending the representative's obtaining a higher securities license. See **branch office manager; broker-dealer; commission; registered representative.**

overriding royalty interest   rights given to the sponsors of an oil and gas limited partnership, in which profits from operation accrue even though none of the program costs are paid by the sponsor. See **direct participation program; limited partnership; oil and gas; sponsor.**

Overseas Private Investment Corporation (OPIC)   an agency formed in 1971 to aid developing nations in private investment enterprise. An independent agency of the U.S. Government, OPIC offers consultation services and shares the cost of new ventures. See **investment market; joint venture; risk.**

overtrading   a practice not allowed by the National Association of Securities Dealers (NASD), in which a broker or a broker-dealer offers a customer a price above fair value for securities. In exchange, the customer accepts a position in a new issue for which the broker-dealer is an underwriter. This position is subscribed at a higher basis than is offered otherwise. The spread in positions results in a small profit for the underwriter. See **broker-dealer; customer; new issue; underwriter.**

P

Pacific Stock Exchange (PSE)   301 Pine Street, San Francisco CA 94014; a regional exchange with offices in San Francisco and Los Angeles, both offices connected by an electronic link. The PSE trades its own listed securities as well as the securities of other regional exchanges and listed options. See **listed option; listed stock; regional exchanges.**

paid-in capital   the capital surplus of a corporation, or the difference between par value and the sales price of shares. Paid-in capital is adjusted negatively when a corporation repurchases its own shares (treasury stock). See **balance sheet; capital surplus; fundamental analysis; par value; shareholder's equity; treasury stock.**

paper   term applied broadly to short-term debt instruments, including banker's acceptances, certificates of deposit, commercial paper, and mortgages carried by a property's seller. See **banker's acceptance; certificate of deposit (CD); commercial paper; debt security; mortgage; short-term debt.**

paper profit/loss   a profit or loss that would be realized if a security position were to be closed. However, as long as the position is left open, the loss is not realized or treated as a profit or loss for tax purposes.

A paper profit or loss may remain so until one of several events takes place: a closing of the position (selling against a long position or buying or covering against a short position); expiration of the outstanding position; or exercise in the case of an option or warrant. Any one of these events eliminates the paper profit/loss and makes it a realized one. See **long; losses; profit; short; tax basis.**

par bond   a bond currently valued at its redemption value. See **bond; discount; market value; premium; redemption.**

par value   (1) the face value of a bond at maturity. Bonds may be sold below par (at a discount) or above par (at a premium). Upon maturity, the par value will be redeemed. Face value of bonds is commonly $1,000.

(2) the value of a share of stock, reflecting the value of dollars actually placed with the corporation to purchase those shares. But tangible value of stock is a factor of operations and the amount of capitalization. Many shares of stock are issued with no par value. For preferred stock, the par value is used to compute the rate of return for dividends. See **bond; common stock; discount; face value; maturity date; preferred stock; premium; redemption.**

parity   (1) the equality in market values between a convertible security and the underlying common stock.

(2) a relationship between an option's price and the current intrinsic value. When the option is trading exactly for intrinsic value, it is at parity. See **common stock; convertible security; futures contract; in-the-money; intrinsic value; market value; option; underlying security.**

parity (bond)

Convertible To:	Bond Value	Stock Value
20 shares	$ 800	$40 per share
30 shares	900	$30 per share
40 shares	1,000	$25 per share
50 shares	800	$16 per share

part-paid stock   stock sold to investors for less than its subscription or par value, disallowed in most states. See **issued and outstanding; par value; stock.**

partial delivery   a form of delivery when the full contracted amount of a security is not delivered. See **delivery.**

participate but do not initiate (PNI)   an order used by institutional investors to buy or sell securities at current prices, but not to create price movement in the security. See **auction marketplace; institutional investor; price.**

participating preferred   a form of preferred stock promising its holders dividends of a specified amount, plus extra dividends in some cases. The extras often are shared between participating preferred and common shareholders. See **common stock; dividend; preferred stock.**

participating trust   a plan company, a form of unit investment trust that invests in the shares of mutual funds. See **mutual fund; plan company; unit investment trust.**

participation certificate   a document of ownership in a mortgage pool. See **mortgage pool.**

partitioning   the right of an investor to force other partners in a venture to divide ownership among holders. In a limited partnership, partitioning is disallowed for practical reasons. The investor owns shares or units of the partnership, and cannot claim properties directly. See **joint venture; limited partnership.**

partnership   a form of business organization consisting of two or more other entities — individuals, partnerships, or corporations — engaged in a common enterprise. Partnerships do not pay taxes directly, but pass through profits and losses to the partners. See **general partnership; limited partnership; Uniform Partnership Act (UPA).**

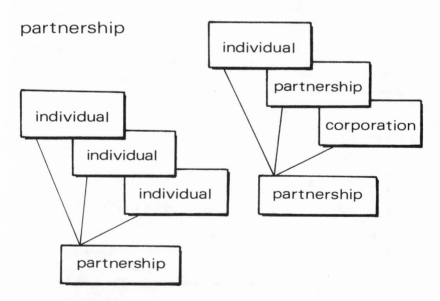

partnership

pass-through security a form of investment in which repayments on debt securities are made up of a combination of interest, principal, or return of capital. See **debt security; mortgage pool.**

passed dividend (1) an omitted dividend, especially when not declared although investors expected the board of directors to do so.
(2) a dividend that was not paid on cumulative preferred shares. The corporation is obligated to pay these before subsequent dividends can be made to other classes of shareholders. See **arrearage; cumulative preferred; dividend.**

payback a measure of return on investment that takes into consideration the period of time required to achieve the return. See **limited partnership; return; tax shelter; yield.**

payback

Investment	$5,000	$5,000	$5,000	$5,000
1st yr-cash returned	$ -0-	$ 625	$1,000	$ 350
-tax savings	4,000	-0-	1,000	500
2nd yr-cash returned	$ 500	$ 625	$1,000	$ 350
-tax savings	-0-	-0-	500	500
3rd yr-cash returned	$ 500	$ 625	$1,000	$ 450
-tax savings	-0-	-0-	500	500
4th yr-cash returned	$ 500	$ 625	$ 800	$ 450
-tax savings	-0-	-0-	250	500
5th yr-cash returned	$ 500	$ 625	$ 800	$ 450
-tax savings	-0-	-0-	250	500
6th yr-cash returned	$ 500	$ 625	$ 400	$ 450
-tax savings	-0-	-0-	-0-	-0-
7th yr-cash returned	$ 300	$ 625	$ 400	$ 450
-tax savings	-0-	-0-	-0-	-0-
8th yr-cash returned	$ 300	$ 625	$ 400	$ 450
-tax savings	-0-	-0-	-0-	-0-
Payback	3 years	8 years	3 years	6 years

paydown a method of replacing one bond issue with another, when the replacement bond has a lower total issue face amount than the original. See **debt service; Ginnie-Mae pass-through.**

paying agent the individual or organization responsible for actually making principal and interest payments to bondholders. See **bond; commercial bank; fiduciary.**

payment date   the indicated or promised date on which principal, interest and dividend payments, or total payments on a note, will be made. See **dividend; interest.**

payout ratio   a ratio showing the percentage of net income paid in common stock dividends, after discounting the value of dividends paid on preferred stock. See **common stock; dividend; fundamental analysis; preferred stock; ratios.**

pay-through bond   a form of debt security in which the issue is guaranteed by a mortgage pool owned by the issuer. Unlike a pass-through security treatment, bonds are shown as liabilities on the balance sheet of the issuing corporation, even when portions of the mortgage pool are sold. See **debt security; mortgage bond; mortgage pool.**

penalty plan   a description of a contractual plan mutual fund, assessing penalties in cases when the plan is terminated early. See **contractual plan; load; mutual fund; sales charge.**

penalty syndicate bid   a form of underwriting that assesses penalties to underwriters not following guidelines for distribution of securities. See **syndicate; underwriter.**

penny stock   a security selling for less than one dollar per share and considered to be very speculative. See **market value; price; speculation.**

pension plan   a retirement plan providing employees with specified benefits based upon the level of compensation and years of service. See **defined benefit pension plan; money purchase plan; retirement plans; target benefit pension plan.**

Pension Reform Act of 1974   legislation commonly called the Employee Retirement Income Security Act of 1974 (ERISA). This law was enacted to safeguard Americans' retirement assets, define the qualifications for inclusion in plans, and develop fair standards for vesting and funding. See **Employee Retirement Income Security Act (ERISA); retirement plans; vesting methods.**

per capita debt   a measurement of the level of debt of a municipality. Total debt is divided by the population. See **debt security; general obligation bond (GO); municipal bond.**

$$\frac{\text{Dividends on Common Stock}}{\text{Net Income} - \text{Dividends on Preferred Stock}} = \text{Payout Ratio}$$

$$\frac{\$325,000}{(\$4,085,600 - \$100,000)} = 8.15\%$$

payout ratio

percentage defined pension plan   a type of plan designed to pay each employee a retirement benefit based upon level of compensation. The calculation of contributions is based upon both current pay and the years of service. See **pension plan; retirement plans.**

percentage depletion   a deduction allowed for some mineral rights and in some circumstances. It is considered a tax preference deduction and is one of the tax-oriented attractions of several limited partnerships. See **cost depletion; depletion; oil and gas; tax preference.**

percentage order   a type of limit price order specifying that a transaction is to take place only after a number of shares of the security have been traded. See **limit price; order ticket; volume.**

performance stock   an alternate name for growth stock, an issue that is expected to appreciate in value over time, as opposed to an income stock that will provide high yield from dividends. See **capital appreciation; growth stock; market value.**

permanent mortgage REIT   a real estate investment trust that engages in the financing of property developments, frequently issued by insurance companies and other financial institutions. See **financing; mortgage REIT; real estate investment trust (REIT).**

perpetual warrant   a type of warrant — a contract allowing the purchase of shares in a corporation at a fixed price — that is distinguished from other warrants in that there is no expiration date. See **expiration date; warrant.**

personal holding company   a corporation in which five or less shareholders own 50 percent or more of the outstanding stock. Other criteria apply in defining a personal holding company, relating specifically to the nature of income earned by the corporation. A penalty tax is imposed on undistributed personal holding company income that meets those criteria. See **corporation; holding company; outstanding stock; shareholder.**

personal property   assets not defined as real estate, including furniture and fixtures that can be depreciated, but that have a shorter class life than the structure itself. See **depreciation; real estate.**

personal trust   a trust established by one individual for a specified purpose, for the benefit of one or more beneficiaries. A trust is established to transfer assets from one owner to another, but holds those assets and produces income until title passes at a later date. See **inter vivos trust; life insurance trust; living trust; testamentary trust; trust.**

phantom income   forms of income without a cash flow, commonly occurring when deductions run out but debt service must continue in a tax shelter. The investor has to report and pay taxes on income, but has received no cash during the same period. See **debt service; tax basis; tax shelter.**

phantom stock   reference to agreements between a corporation and key officers. Future bonus payments are tied to increases in the market value of stock. They are paid as though they owned shares in the corporation. See **common stock; corporation; underlying security.**

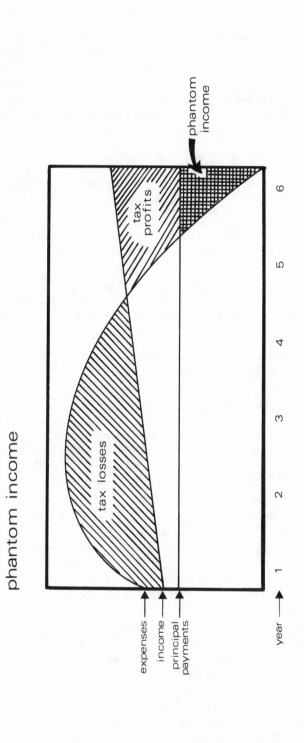

phantom income

Philadelphia plan a form of equipment trust bond in which title to the property remains with an independent trustee until the entire bond issue has been retired. See **equipment trust bond; New York plan.**

Philadelphia Stock Exchange (PHLX) 1900 Market Street, Philadelphia PA 10103; a stock exchange founded in 1790 engaging in listed security and options trading. See **regional exchanges; security exchanges.**

pickup bond a callable bond with the potential for a higher-than-expected return. If interest rates fall and the bond is called at a premium, the investor receives a greater return than if interest rates rise and they are not called. See **bond; callable bond; coupon rate.**

piggyback a type of primary-secondary distribution of securities, allowing investors who previously purchased shares to include and offer their holdings in a new offering. See **primary distribution; secondary distribution; underwriter.**

pink sheets a listing of over-the-counter securities activities, published by the National Quotation Bureau (NQB). Supplied are the bid and asked prices as well as identification of market makers. See **National Quotation Bureau (NQB); over-the-counter (OTC); white sheets; yellow sheets.**

pipeline theory (1) reference to the practice of passing tax liabilities and capital gains directly to investors in a large pool such as a mutual fund. The organization itself pays no income tax, as all taxable income is passed to investors through the pipeline.
(2) pipeline: mortgage agreements that have been agreed upon but not closed (in the pipeline).
(3) pipeline: unsold securities in an underwriting that are pending placement. See **mortgage; mutual fund; public offering; real estate; underwriter.**

plan company unit investment trusts managing interests in mutual funds for underwriters. See **mutual fund; participating trust; underwriter; unit investment trust.**

plus tick reference to a trade at a higher price than the previous trade. See **price; regular way; zero-plus tick.**

plus tick rule an SEC restriction on the price of round lot short sales. It states that such a transaction must be made at a price higher than the last regular way round lot trade on the security's primary exchange. A zero-plus tick — a transaction at the same price as the previous price — may be allowed when the previous trade itself represented a plus tick in the security's price. See **regular way; round lot; SEC Rule 10a-1; Securities and Exchange Commission (SEC); short sale; zero-plus tick.**

point (1) a point of reference for relative value in several different markets. A point represents the following values: $1.00 — stock market; 1% of par — bond market; 1/100 cent — foreign exchange; 1/100 cent per pound — commodity market; 1% of total balance — mortgages. See **bond; commodity; mortgage; stock.**

point and figure chart a type of chart used by technical analysts, using the letter "x" or a combination of "x" and "o" to show price increases and decreases. There is no allowance for the time factor. The chart trend changes direction each time the price does, establishing a trading pattern. See **price; technical analysis.**

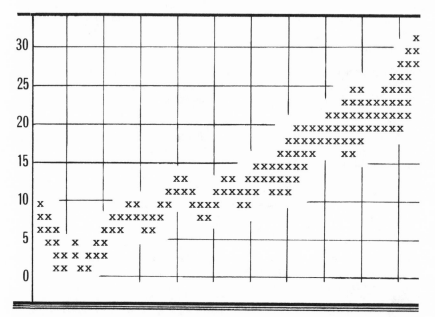

point and figure chart

portfolio   reference to the securities held by an investor, with the most common usage not including commodity futures or intangible assets. See **investment; primary market; secondary market.**

portfolio manager   an investment manager, one who has been given fiduciary responsibility to handle the assets of another. See **fiduciary; investment manager.**

position   (1) the status of an investor's or a dealer's holdings. A position may be long (when securities are owned) or short (when they are open sold positions). An open position is one in which the status requires resolution through a subsequent transaction, expiration, or exercise of an option.

(2) establishment of a long or short position in a security, to buy or sell in order to create, or take a position. See **facilitation; long; short; strategy.**

position limit   the highest allowed open positions one investor is allowed to hold on the same side of the market. Especially applicable to option trading, an example of the same side of the market is long calls and short puts. See **long; option; short; underlying security.**

positive carry   the advantage held when borrowed money is used to invest. If the investment yields a return higher than the cost of borrowing money, the net difference is the positive carry. See **yield.**

positive yield curve   a description of the different yields that can be earned on the same or a similar class of securities by agreeing to a longer holding period. The positive yield curve is seen frequently in interest rates offered on certificates of deposit. More yield is offered to depositors agreeing to leave their cash for a longer period. See **interest; time value of money; yield.**

positive yield curve

%	4-yr. 6-yr. 8-yr.
12	
11	
10	
9	
8	
7	
6	
5	
4	
3	
2	
1	
0	

post one of the locations in a securities exchange where specialists give quotations and transact trades in a security or class of securities. See **auction marketplace; quotation; securities; specialist; stock exchange.**

power of attorney document allowing discretionary powers to an individual in behalf of another in the handling of financial matters. The document may provide full or limited discretion, and is granted to a custodian, trustee or other representative acting as a fiduciary. A limited discretionary power would allow a broker to make investment decisions, but not to withdraw funds. A full, or unlimited discretionary account does not set limits on the management of funds. See **custodian; discretionary account; fiduciary; limited discretion; trustee.**

precedence the right of one broker to execute a trade before other brokers. This is determined by the time of a bid and the size of the transaction and the number of shares to be traded. Precedence may also refer to an order that will satisfy the greatest portion of a contra order when several trades are pending execution. See **execution; floor trader.**

precious gemstones an investment in stones such as rubies, sapphires or emeralds that, due to their quality and rarity, are thought to have a potential for increasing in value. Gemstones are generally not considered to be securities as defined by the Securities and Exchange Commission. See **gemstones; investment; securities; Securities and Exchange Commission (SEC).**

precious metals investments in tangible rare metals, such as gold or silver, that may increase in value due to increased demand. Precious metals are generally not considered to be securities as defined by the Securities and Exchange Commission. See **investment; securities; Securities and Exchange Commission (SEC).**

preemptive rights privilege of current holders of stock in a corporation, to purchase a proportionate amount of a new issue. The purpose of these rights is to

new issue, 20,000 shares:

Current Shares	%	New Shares
1,000	1%	200
5,000	5%	1,000
10,000	10%	2,000

preemptive rights

provide the opportunity to stockholders to maintain their relative portion of total ownership of the corporation's stock. See **current market value (CMV); new issue; subscription privilege.**

preference   the right of a broker to execute a trade before another broker, when they are on parity (both brokers have available trades to fulfill a contra order). Preference is given to the broker who first arrived in the trading crowd (the brokers interested in executing transactions in the security). See **auction marketplace; execution; floor; parity.**

preference income   forms of compensation identified as providing special favored tax treatment to the individual, and that is accordingly subject to a minimum tax under the Internal Revenue Code. See **alternative minimum tax; minimum tax; tax preference.**

preferred dividend coverage   a ratio showing the relationship between income net of taxes and the dollar amount of preferred stock dividends. It is derived by dividing net income by the preferred dividend payments. See **corporation; dividend; senior security.**

$$\frac{\text{Net Income}}{\text{Preferred Dividends}} = \text{Preferred Dividend Coverage}$$

$$\frac{\$18,014,000}{\$1,500,000} = 12 \text{ to } 1$$

preferred dividend coverage

preferred stock   a form of equity security that has specific features distinguishing it from common stock. Preferred stock has priority of claim on the assets of a corporation in the case of dissolution, over common stock. Priority is also granted over common stock in the payment of dividends. Preferred has a set dividend

and a call price (it may be converted to common stock). Finally, the holders of preferred stock have no voting rights, as do common stockholders. See **common stock;
corporation; cumulative preferred; dividend; equity security; noncumulative preferred; par value; priority; senior security; voting rights.**

preferred stock ratio a ratio showing the relationship between preferred stock
at its par value and total capitalization of a corporation, expressed as a percentage.
See **capitalization; corporation; outstanding stock; par value; ratios; total
capitalization.**

$$\frac{\text{Preferred Par Value}}{\text{Total Capitalization}} = \text{Preferred Stock Ratio}$$

$$\frac{\$1,500,000}{\$22,303,000} = 6.73\%$$

preferred stock ratio

preliminary agreement an agreement between a corporation issuing a security
and an underwriter, which is entered before the effective date. The contract gives the
underwriter an opportunity to judge the marketability of the securities prior to a final
agreement. See **effective date; indication of interest; new issue; underwriter.**

preliminary prospectus also called a "red herring" because of the red ink on the
cover page, this is a document filed with the Securities and Exchange Commission
before an issue can be offered to the public, an advance copy of the proposed final
prospectus. See **new issue; red herring; Securities and Exchange Commission (SEC).**

premature distribution the payment of funds from a qualified plan (IRA or
Keogh, for example) prior to the allowed age of the individual. Distributions are
taxed immediately and subjected to a penalty, and income averaging is not allowed.
See **individual retirement account (IRA); Keogh plan; qualified plan; retirement
plans.**

premium (1) the amount over par value of a bond or of preferred stock,
reflected in current market value.
(2) the total market price of an option contract.
(3) a fee to the lender in a short sale transaction. See **bond; call premium; discount; face value; market price; option; par value; preferred stock; redemption;
short sale.**

premium bond a bond with current market value greater than the actual par
value. See **bond; discount bond; face value; par value.**

premium over investment value a ratio used to express in percentage form the
difference between a security's investment value and market price. See **conversion
value; investment value; market price.**

prepaid expenses

	Prepaid Assets	Insurance Expense
Payment, 3-year Premium	$360.00	
Current Year	$100.00	$100.00
Second Year	120.00	120.00
Third Year	120.00	120.00
Fourth Year	20.00	20.00

$$\frac{\text{Market Price} - \text{Investment Value}}{\text{Investment Value}} = \text{Premium}$$

$$\frac{100 - 85}{85} = 17.6\%$$

premium over investment value

pre-offering questionnaire   a document that must be completed by an investor in a private placement prior to approval of the transaction by a broker-dealer. The form should be completed by the investor in his or her own handwriting, with signatures required on every page. The purpose is to make certain the investor understands the special risks of the program. See **broker-dealer; customer; investment objective; private placement; SEC Rule 146; tax shelter.**

pre-opening costs   a distinction of costs and expenses in a construction project, new business or project. Pre-opening costs, or organizational expenses in a new business, must be capitalized and amortized over a period of years. See **amortization; capital expenditure; syndicate.**

prepaid assets   purchases of an organization applying to periods beyond the current year. Prepaid assets is a balance sheet account title in which costs and expenses are posted, to be amortized over two or more years. See **amortization; assets; balance sheet.**

prepaid expenses   those expenses posted to a prepaid assets account, because all or part of the total applies to future accounting periods. The portion of prepaid expenses applying to each period is charged off to an expense account in the appropriate period. See **amortization; balance sheet; income statement.**

prepaid interest   interest paid in advance of the applicable period. Such interest may not be accrued for federal tax purposes. See **balance sheet; income statement; interest.**

pre-payment penalty   a charge included in a mortgage contract, to be assessed if more than the annual allowed amount of a debt's balance is paid before an allowed time. See **interest; mortgage; real estate.**

prerefunding   the offering of one bond issue to be used to refund a prior bond issue before its call date. Proceeds commonly are invested in Treasury securities, and receive the highest rating. See **bond; refunding.**

present value   the value of a future sum of money, assuming a rate of interest in today's terms. The present value is used in the computation of exact return in analysis of investments, because it precisely compares different investments with similar yields, but that require different holding periods. See **compound interest; rate of return; interest; simple interest; time value of money.**

Present Value

5% Table		present value of $100	present value of $200	present value of $500
Year	Value of 1			
1	.952381	$ 95.24	$190.48	$476.19
2	.907029	90.70	181.41	453.51
3	.863838	86.38	172.77	431.92
4	.822702	82.27	164.54	411.35
5	.783526	78.35	156.71	391.76
6	.746215	74.62	149.24	373.11
7	.710681	71.07	142.14	355.34
8	.676839	67.68	135.37	338.42
9	.644609	64.46	128.92	322.30
10	.613913	61.39	122.78	306.96

pretax margin   the ratio of profit of an organization before payment or accrual of income taxes, also called operating profit margin. See **operating profit margin; ratios.**

pretax profit   the net income of an organization before payment or accrual of income taxes, also called operating profit. See **income statement; operating profit.**

price   the amount of money or exchange that is to be paid to acquire a security, right, option or other asset. See **assets; market value; value.**

price-earnings ratio (P/E)   a ratio used as a standard for measuring the risk and market demand of common stocks. It is derived by dividing the market value by the earnings per common share for the latest available twelve-month period. The P/E ratio is expressed as "x to y" (10 to 1, for example), or simply as "x" (10). A low P/E ratio is considered relatively safe, but less likely to increase in value in a bull market. A high P/E ratio denotes greater risk, popularity, and volatility. See **common stock; earnings; market value; ratios; technical analysis.**

price/equity ratio   a ratio showing the relationship between current market value and book value per common share. See **book value; common stock; market price; ratios; technical analysis.**

price gap   term describing price movement in a security with a chart gap. The situation is seen when an issue opens at a price higher than the previous day's high or lower than the previous day's low. See **break-away gap; overbought/oversold; technical analysis.**

primary distribution the first sale of a stock or bond issue, or of a class of security not previously offered. See **new issue; offering; secondary distribution; treasury stock.**

primary earnings per share a calculation of earnings that includes an allowance for all convertible shares, if conversion were to occur; also known as fully diluted earnings per share. See **fully diluted earnings per share.**

primary market a broad term describing the method of placing securities on the market. Primary includes new issues, opening sales of option and futures contracts, government security auctions and other activities occurring through recognized stock exchanges. See **auction marketplace; issuer; new issue; over-the-counter (OTC); secondary market; stock exchange; underwriter.**

primary movement technical term for a market trend lasting more than one year, also called a major trend. See **Dow Theory; major trend; technical analysis.**

prime paper a rating of commercial paper, indicating investment quality. See **commercial paper; investment grade.**

prime rate the lowest interest rate a commercial bank will charge to its preferred customers, for short-term unsecured debt. The prime also is referred to as an indicator of interest rate trends. See **commercial bank; interest; short-term debt; unsecured debt.**

principal (1) an individual trading for his or her own account or who acts as underwriter and purchases securities for resale to other investors.
(2) an investor's capital before earnings are added.
(3) a general securities principal, licensed by the NASD upon passing the Series 24 examination. See **agent; as principal; capital; general securities principal; interest; Series 24; underwriter.**

principal registration an NASD designation for an individual licensed to perform all regulated functions in a broker-dealer except those requiring a financial and operations principal license. See **financial and operations principal; general securities principal; National Association of Securities Dealers (NASD); Series 24.**

principal stockholder a holder of a substantial portion of a corporation's voting stock, generally 10 percent or more. If the corporation is registered with the SEC, the qualification includes long calls on the organization. See **affiliated person; control person; corporation; Securities and Exchange Act of 1934.**

prior lien bond a type of secured bond that is issued with the permission of bondholders of previous issues. The prior lien bond is a senior lien over other bonds of the corporation. See **debt security; secured debt; senior lien.**

prior preferred a class of preferred stock that has seniority of claim on assets and earnings. In the event of dissolution, prior preferred shareholders have a senior lien on assets. And when a dividend is declared, they have a senior claim on earnings and receive payment before other preferred stockholders. See **dividend; liquidation; preferred stock; senior lien.**

priority (1) the right of a broker in the auction marketplace to have his or her order executed before others seeking the same price, if the broker is the first to place a bid or offer.

$$\frac{\text{Market Value}}{\text{Earnings Per Common Share}} \quad = \quad \text{P/E}$$

$$\frac{\$23}{\$3.10} \quad = \quad 7.4 \text{ to } 1$$

price-earnings ratio (P/E)

$$\frac{\text{Market Value}}{\text{Book Value Per Common Share}} \quad = \quad \text{Price/Equity}$$

$$\frac{\$23}{\$17} \quad = \quad 1.35 \text{ to } 1$$

price/equity ratio

price gap

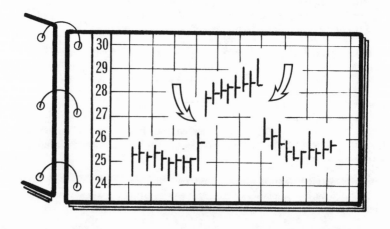

(2) the privilege of a limited partner in a direct participation program to receive a specified level of return before the general partner is given a subordinated payment. See **auction marketplace; direct participation program; execution; precedence; subordination.**

private placement   the distribution or offering of a security involving a limited number of investors, usually 35 or less. Private placements were exempt from registration with the Securities and Exchange Commission (SEC) under provisions of the Securities Act of 1933. The Deficit Reduction Act of 1984 (DEFRA) modifies the law, requiring registration of all tax shelter programs.

Private placement offering circulars may not be shown to a potential investor until a pre-offering questionnaire has been completed. See **accredited investor; Deficit Reduction Act of 1984 (DEFRA); limited partnership; offering circular; pre-offering questionnaire; SEC Rule 146; Securities Act of 1933; Securities and Exchange Commission (SEC).**

pro forma   descriptive of a form of financial statement presented in a particular way: a projection of a future condition; a statement which reflects fairly the current conditions of the business but that has not been audited; or information presented in anticipation of an action that is pending, which will affect the way that a report is to be prepared. See **due diligence; financial statement.**

proceeds sale   a type of securities transaction in which the proceeds of a closing transaction are used specifically to open another. The National Association of Securities Dealers limits the percentage of commission that can be charged on the total value of this transaction in the secondary market. See **commission; contingent order; five percent rule; mark down; mark up; National Association of Securities Dealers (NASD); secondary market; swap order.**

Producer Price Index (PPI)   an index of inflationary trends, based upon the changes in price for finished goods (processed and ready to be moved to the marketplace). Full name: Producer Price Index for Finished Goods. See **index; inflation.**

production payment   payments to obtain drilling rights in an oil and gas program, based upon a percentage of production. Production payments are considered mineral acquisition costs in drilling programs. See **cost depletion; mineral acquisition costs; oil and gas.**

production purchase program   also called an income program, this is a form of oil and gas investment in which reserves in the ground are purchased. Investors seek income as a primary objective. See **income; oil and gas.**

production rate   in Ginnie Mae pass-through securities, the current coupon rate. It is set according to the current mortgage rate on FHA mortgages. See **coupon rate; Ginnie Mae pass-through; Government National Mortgage Association (GNMA); residential mortgage.**

professional corporation   an organization owned by shareholders in professions, including physicians, attorneys, or accountants, for example. Since 1969, professionals have been allowed to incorporate to take advantage of corporate privileges for retirement planning and taxes. However, many of the retirement planning advantages were removed by new legislation in 1982, TEFRA. See **corporation; retirement plans; Tax Equity and Fiscal Responsibility Act of 1982 (TEFRA).**

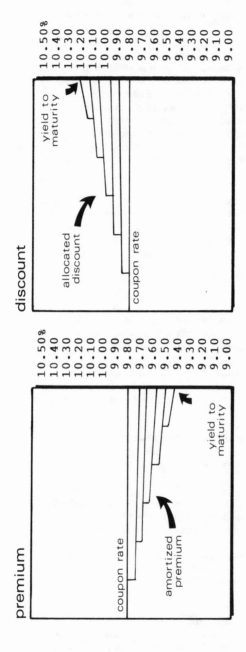

premium

discount

10.50%
10.40
10.30
10.20
10.10
10.00
9.90
9.80
9.70
9.60
9.50
9.40
9.30
9.20
9.10
9.00

yield to
maturity

allocated
discount

coupon rate

10.50%
10.40
10.30
10.20
10.10
10.00
9.90
9.80
9.70
9.60
9.50
9.40
9.30
9.20
9.10
9.00

coupon rate

amortized
premium

yield to
maturity

professional method

professional method   an accurate method of computing yield to maturity on a bond. It assumes that capital gains or losses should be calculated over the holding period of the security, including their periodic effect on overall gain or loss. See **bond; coupon rate; current yield; discount; interpolation; premium; yield to maturity.**

profit   (1) accounting term referring to the amount by which gross revenues exceed costs (gross profit) or costs and expenses (net profit).

(2) the gain on a security transaction, when the adjusted sales price exceeds the adjusted cost. See **basis; capital gain; fundamental analysis; income statement; market value; tax basis.**

profit and loss statement   an alternate term for the income statement, that financial statement showing a period's operating results. See **financial statement; fundamental analysis; income statement.**

profit margin   the percentage of return on sales, which may be reviewed on three levels:

a) gross profit margin, the profit after direct costs are deducted from sales;

b) operating margin, when costs and operating expenses are deducted from sales; or

c) net profit margin; when all costs, expenses and income taxes are deducted from sales. See **financial statement; fundamental analysis; income statement.**

INCOME STATEMENT

Gross Sales	$42,314,000	100.00%	
Cost of Goods Sold	29,016,000	68.57	gross
Gross Profit	$13,298,000	31.43% ◄	margin
Operating Expenses	9,446,000	22.33	
Operating Profit	$ 3,852,000	9.10% ◄	operating margin
Income Taxes	2,416,000	5.71	
Net Profit	$ 1,436,000	3.39% ◄	net margin

profit margin

---

profit range   a term describing a zone of profitability on a transaction, also known as the profit zone. See **break-even point; position; profit zone; strategy.**

profit-sharing plan   a form of retirement plan in which employees of an organization share in the company's profits based upon a set formula. Provisions may include contributions based upon the number of years of service, the employee's age, and allowance for voluntary contributions. See **Employee Retirement Income Security Act (ERISA); pension plan; retirement plans.**

profit taking   the closing of positions to realize profits following a rise in prices, often the cause of an adjusting drop in market values over the short term. See **market price; short-term capital gain; technical analysis.**

profit zone   a price range in which profits will be realized in a security transaction. See **break-even point; position; profit range; strategy.**

---

profit zone

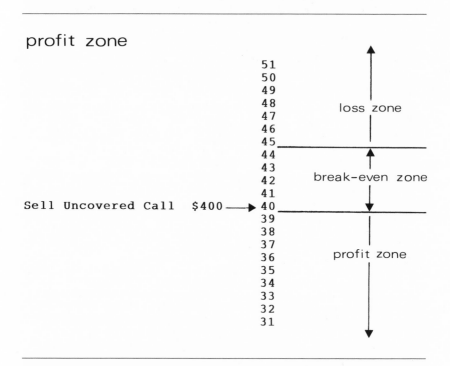

---

program   (1) term applied to an investment, especially a direct participation program organized as a limited partnership. The term may also apply to mutual funds, variable annuities and other contracts, but not generally to stocks, bonds, or commodities.

(2) an investment program organized to reach identified investment objectives, as part of a financial plan. See **direct participation program; financial plan; investment objective; limited partnership; private placement; public offering.**

project note (PN)   temporary financing for public housing projects, issued as short-term municipal notes and to be redeemed from the long-term debt issue. See **bond; financing; municipal note; short-term debt.**

projected benefits   the value of benefits to be paid from a pension plan in the future, based upon current and expected yield, the mix of ages of participating employees, and future compensation estimates. See **pension plan; present value; retirement plans.**

promotional interest   the income committed to the promoter of a direct participation program. If unsubordinated, the promoter will receive a percentage of profits or cash values regardless of the success of the program. Subordinated interests allow a level of priority to investors before promotional interests will be paid. See **direct participation program; priority; subordination; syndicate.**

property manager   the individual or organization retained by the management of a direct participation program to manage properties. Property management may involve on-site and live-in management, or remote management of the property. See **direct participation program; investment program; real estate.**

proprietorship   a form of business organization involving one owner. The business is not incorporated, and the self-employed individual is qualified to participate in a Keogh plan. See **corporation; Keogh plan; partnership; self-employment.**

prospectus   a document required to be given to investors before the offer of sale can be made. It is a shorter version of the registration statement that must be filed with the Securities and Exchange Commission before a public program may be marketed.
The prospectus includes information about the program, the sponsor, economic, legal and tax assumptions, and use of proceeds. See **direct participation program; mutual fund; public offering; red herring; registration statement; SEC Rule 430; Securities and Exchange Commission (SEC).**

protected strategy   a strategy reducing or limiting risks, such as a long position combined with a long put option, or a short position protected by a long call. See **arbitrage; combination; risk arbitrage; straddle; strategy.**

protective covenant   promises made to investors in municipal bonds that the issuer will ensure its ability to repay the debt. The covenant may include discussion of fees charged by completed facilities, insurance coverage, maintenance and upkeep of the facility, and other provisions. See **debt security; municipal bond.**

proxy   a transfer authorization given by a shareholder, allowing another shareholder to use his or her vote in a shareholder's meeting. See **corporation; shareholder; voting rights.**

proxy contest   also called a proxy fight; an attempt by one group of shareholders to collect enough shareholder votes to either replace a corporation's management or force a vote on one or more business decisions. See **corporation; proxy fight; shareholder; voting rights.**

proxy department   a brokerage department responsible for handling and mailing of proxies and related authorizations. See **beneficial owner; brokerage house; voting rights.**

proxy fight   the attempt of a group of shareholders to gather enough votes to replace the corporation's management or overrule it on specific decisions. See **corporation; proxy contest; shareholder; voting rights.**

proxy statement   a disclosure of material information that must be given to shareholders when proxies are being solicited. The statement is a requirement of the Securities and Exchange Commission. See **corporation; Securities and Exchange Commission (SEC); Securities Exchange Act of 1934; shareholder; voting rights.**

prudent man rule a general rule requiring that anyone recommending an investment or acting in a fiduciary capacity should use the same level of care and diligence that would be used in his or her own account. See **fiduciary; legal investment.**

public book orders entered for securities by public investors. The book is maintained by the specialist or board broker. See **board broker; market maker; specialist.**

public housing authority bond a long-term municipal bond used to finance construction of public housing. See **bond; long-term debt; municipal bond.**

public offering the offer and sale of securities to the general public. The issue refers as well to direct participation programs offered publicly. See **direct participation program; issue; offering; private placement;** SEC **Rule 10b-6.**

public offering price the asked price of a primary distribution. See **asked price; investment banker; primary distribution; underwriter.**

Public Utility Holding Company Act of 1935 legislation that sets jurisdiction of gas and electric holding companies and their subsidiaries under the Securities and Exchange Commission. It establishes the SEC's right to review and approve offerings of securities by such holding companies, to control intercompany transactions, and review attempts to alter the priority of shareholder voting rights. See **holding company; jurisdiction; Securities and Exchange Commission (SEC); voting rights.**

publicly held corporation a corporation with substantial ownership among the public, and subject to the rules and regulations of the Securities and Exchange Commission and the exchange on which shares are traded. See **allied member; closely-held corporation; corporation; New York Stock Exchange (NYSE); Securities and Exchange Commission (SEC).**

purchase and sales department (P-S) part of the back office system of a broker-dealer operation from which security confirmations are issued, orders executed, and receivable and payable balances computed for customers and other brokers. See **back office; broker-dealer; confirmation.**

purchaser's representative an individual responsible for determining the risks associated with an investment in behalf of another individual who does not have the expertise to make such evaluations. See **fiduciary; investment objective; risk.**

purchasing power the amount of equity a customer possesses directly or with the available credit in a margin account. See **buying power; excess margin; margin account; Regulation T; special miscellaneous account (SMA).**

purpose loan a loan using securities as collateral to purchase additional securities in a margin account. See **collateral; margin security.**

put an option with a finite life that gives the owner (buyer) the right to sell a specified number of shares in the underlying security (100 shares per option contract), at a specified price and within the space of time until expiration date. Upon expiration the unexercised put option becomes worthless.

A put may be used in speculative trading. A put is bought in the hope that the underlying security will decrease in value. If it does so, a corresponding increase will result in the put's value. Puts may be sold naked (uncovered), producing premium — income — and also a level of risk that is limited to the strike price of the underlying security. Puts cannot be covered as call options can. See **call; naked option; option; uncovered option; write.**

put to seller the exercise of a put option, when the buyer exercises and thus forces the seller to purchase 100 shares per put contract. See **exercise; option; underlying security.**

pyramiding (1) of paper profits to make additional security investments on margin.

(2) a condition in which the owner of real estate reduces the principal balance on a mortgage while the property appreciates, so that equity can be used to make other real estate investments. See **appreciation; leverage; margin; paper profit/loss; principal; real estate.**

Q

qualified plan a retirement plan set up under guidelines qualifying for tax-deferred treatment of contributions and earnings, including corporate, Keogh and IRA accounts. See **corporate retirement plan; individual retirement account (IRA); Keogh plan; retirement plans; tax deferral.**

qualified stock option a type of stock option granted prior to May, 1981, in which a long-term capital gain could be claimed if the stock was held for three years or longer. See **exercise; fair market value (FMV); long-term capital gain.**

qualifying annuity an annuity structured to be included in a qualified retirement plan, with its premiums and earnings deferred for tax purposes according to provisions of the plan. See **retirement plans; tax deferral.**

qualifying coupon rate the rate below production rate of a Ginnie Mae pass-through security, requiring an adjustment in the aggregate exercise price. See **aggregate exercise price (AEP); coupon rate; Ginnie Mae pass-through; Government National Mortgage Association (GNMA); production rate; residential mortgage.**

qualitative analysis a form of risk and value assessment based on non-financial information, including the management, operations environment, litigation, and union relations. See **risk; value.**

quantitative analysis a form of risk and value assessment based upon financial information as well as non-financial. This may include balance sheet as well as qualitative information. See **fundamental analysis; risk; value.**

quick asset ratio a ratio measuring the liquidity of a company, the availability of cash and assets convertible to cash, against bills that are due in a short period of time. The ratio involves taking total current assets without inventory, and dividing the net by current liabilities. In most industries, a quick asset ratio of one to one is considered the minimum acceptable. See **acid test ratio; balance sheet ratios; fundamental analysis; ratios.**

$$\frac{\text{Current Assets} \quad - \quad \text{Inventory}}{\text{Current Liabilities}} \quad = \quad \text{Ratio}$$

$$\frac{\$427,500 \quad - \quad \$250,600}{\$156,300} \quad = \quad 1.13 \text{ to } 1$$

quick asset ratio

quotation a stated price representing the lowest offer to sell or highest bid to buy shares of a security. See **asked price; bid; price; SEC Rule 15c2-11.**

R

raid the attempt by a person or group to acquire or control enough stock of a corporation to pick its own management, or to sell enough stock in a security with the intention of buying it later at a lower price. See **bear raid; control person; outstanding stock.**

rally a sudden and unexpected increase in market values, most often applied to the market as a whole, but also applicable to single securities or the securities of a single industry. See **bull; price.**

random walk a theory of market values that states the price of securities cannot be determined, but is entirely random. See **market value; technical analysis.**

range the description of a day's activity in one issue, consisting of opening price, the day's high and low, and the closing price. See **market value; price.**

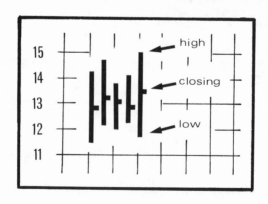

range

rally

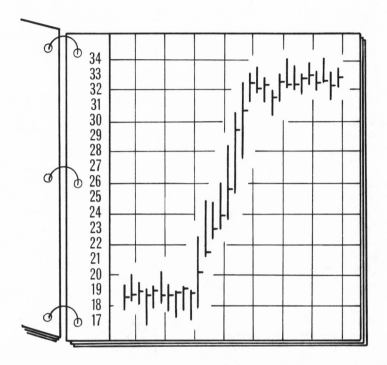

rate covenant   provisions included in a municipal bond resolution that ensures adequate returns from developed facilities to repay principal and interest. See **bond; municipal bond; protective covenant; revenue bond.**

rate of return   the current yield, computed by dividing cash flow from an investment by the basis, also known as return on invested capital. See **basis; cash flow; current yield; net income; ratios; return on invested capital.**

$$\frac{\text{Cash Flow}}{\text{Basis}} = \text{Return}$$

$$\frac{\$800}{\$10,000} = 8\%$$

rate of return

rating systems   services publishing judgement ratings of security issues, particularly of bonds, so that investors may decide the level of risk they are willing to undertake in selection. See **Fitch Investors Service; Moody's Investors Service; Standard and Poor's Corporation.**

ratio calendar combination a complex option strategy that combines two ratio calendar spreads.

As an example, assume the following transactions:

buy 1 August 40 call	$(300)
sell 2 May 40 calls	350
buy 1 November 35 put	(75)
sell 2 August 35 puts	125
net receipt	$ 100

Note the two ratio calendar spreads, one involving calls and the other involving puts. In this example, the ideal price movement of stock would be for the price to remain below 40 until the May call expirations, so that the short call positions would not be exercised and create a loss; then to surge above 40 before the August call expiration, so that the long call can be sold at a profit; finally, to fall below 33 dollars per share before the November put expiration date, so that long puts can be sold at a profit. See **calendar spread; call; combination; option; put; strategy.**

ratio calendar spread an option strategy involving the selling of near-term options at a net premium greater than the cost of longer-term options in long positions. All involved options have the identical strike price. See **calendar spread; option; put; risk; strategy.**

ratio spread an option strategy involving the simultaneous buying and selling of contracts on the same underlying security. The strike price is different but expiration dates will normally be the same. The net receipt from sold options will exceed the cost of a lower number of purchased contracts, and the strategy may be designed to profit in an up market or to profit in a down market. See **option; spread; strategy.**

ratio strategy the practice of purchasing and selling option contracts on the same security, when the degree of risk increases with the size of the ratio. Thus, a one-to-two ratio is more risky than a four-to-three or five-to-four strategy. See **combination; option; spread; straddle.**

Rating Systems

	Highest Quality	Speculative	Poorest Quality	Questionable Value
Fitch Investors Service	AAA AA A	BBB BB B	CCC CC C	DDD DD D
Moody's Investors Service	Aaa Aa A	Bbb Bb B	Ccc Cc C	
Standard and Poor's	AAA AA A	BBB BB B	CCC CC C	DDD DD D

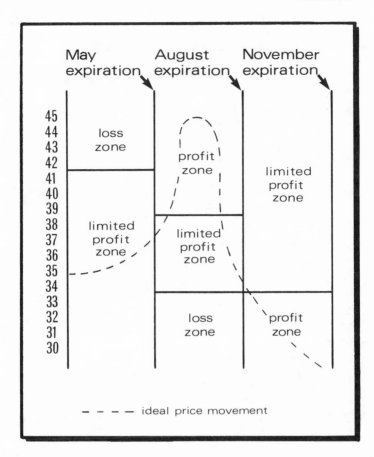

May expiration
August expiration
November expiration

45
44   loss
43   zone
42   profit
41   zone   limited
40   profit
39   zone
38   limited
37   profit   limited
36   zone   profit
35   zone
34
33
32   loss   profit
31   zone   zone
30

– – – – ideal price movement

ratio calendar combination

ratio write a strategy of writing calls against a long position in the underlying security, but when the number of options exceeds the 100 lot shares held. An investor holding 200 shares, who writes 3 options effectively has a ratio write of three to two (two are covered and one is not; or, the entire position is 67% covered). It is also a ratio write to sell one call when fewer than 100 shares are held in the security. See **covered option; option; uncovered option; write.**

ratios comparisons of two related factors, showing the relationship and its significance. Ratios are used in fundamental analysis, with the results expressed in percentage form, a count of the times an event occurs (such as turnover of inventory), or fractionally (x to y). See **balance sheet ratios; combined ratios; fundamental analysis; income account ratios.**

real estate investments in land and structures, emphasizing growth in value for capital gains; potential high returns from leverage of equity; positive cash flow from rental income that is sheltered partially or wholly by depreciation deductions; and relative safety when compared to other investments. Risks include the requirement that capital remain committed for several years in a program; the chance that high

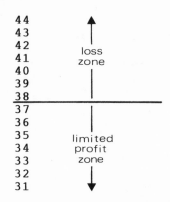

```
Buy 2 calls 40        $(300)
Sell 4 calls 35         500

   Net receipt        $ 200
```

```
44          ↑
43
42        loss
41        zone
40
39          |
38 ─────────────────────────
37
36
35        limited
34        profit
33        zone
32
31          ↓
```

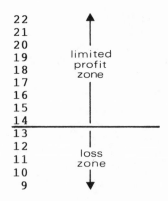

```
Buy 1 put 15          $( 75)
Sell 2 puts 20          175

   Net receipt        $ 100
```

```
22          ↑
21
20
19        limited
18        profit
17        zone
16
15          |
14 ─────────────────────────
13
12
11        loss
10        zone
 9          ↓
```

ratio spread

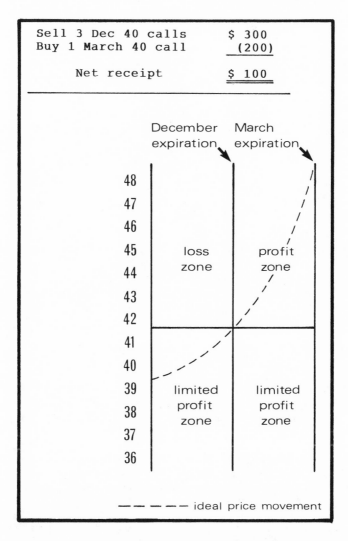

```
Sell 3 Dec 40 calls        $ 300
Buy 1 March 40 call         (200)

      Net receipt           $ 100
```

ratio calendar spread

vacancy rates will adversely affect cash flow and profits; and the deteriorating value caused by local or national economic conditions and interest rates. See **capital gain; depreciation; investment objective; leverage; liquidity; tax shelter.**

Real Estate Investment Act of 1961 federal legislation setting criteria and controls for real estate investment trust (REIT) investing and other forms of real estate investment ventures. See **investment; regulation.**

real estate investment trust (REIT) a form of real estate company that is, in effect, a closed-end pool. Investors buy units in the trust, and may trade publicly. Losses may not be passed through to investors, so tax shelter is not a primary objective of the REIT. Principal types are equity REITs — those in which the trust actually

ratios

Percentage form:

$$\frac{\$523,600}{\$745,100} = 70.27\%$$

Count form:

$$\frac{\$835,000}{\$217,800} = 3.83 \text{ times}$$

Fractional form:

$$\frac{\$594,200}{\$291,500} = 2.04 \text{ to } 1$$

---

purchases properties—and mortgage REITs—where financing is provided for development of properties. See **closed-end; equity REIT; investment company; mortgage REIT.**

Real Estate Securities and Syndication Institution (RESSI) an organization formed in 1972 by the National Association of Realtors. RESSI's purpose is to create and maintain standards of performance in the real estate syndication industry. See **direct participation program; investment program; syndicate.**

real estate stock corporation corporations engaged primarily in real estate, through direct purchase, financing or management. Investors may purchase stock in the corporation and, indirectly, become involved in real estate, with higher liquidity and diversification than is available through syndication. See **corporation; investment program; stock.**

real property property with tangible and identifiable value, subject to depreciation if used in a trade or business, or as part of an investment program. It is distinguished from real estate for purposes of depreciation. See **assets; depreciation; real estate; tangible value.**

real turnover the comparison of the cost of goods sold to inventory, for the purpose of computing turnover. Because both inventory and costs are reflected on a cost basis, real turnover is more accurate than the traditional comparison between sales and inventory. See **fundamental analysis; inventory; ratios; turnover.**

$$\frac{\text{Cost of Goods Sold}}{\text{Inventory}} = \text{Ratio}$$

$$\frac{\$1,124,600}{\$286,100} = 3.9 \text{ times}$$

real turnover ratio

reallowance an additional level of sales concession that is paid by an underwriter in a corporate issue, when NASD members participate in marketing the underwriting by offering shares of the issue to their customers. See **concession; underwriter.**

recapture treatment for tax purposes of a portion of accelerated depreciation upon sale. The excess amount of depreciation over what has been allowed under straight-line rates is recaptured and treated as ordinary gain, at less favorable rates. See **accelerated depreciation; capital gain; tax basis; tax preference.**

receiver's certificate debt security issued for a corporation in bankruptcy proceedings solely to provide funds during the three-to-four-month period of inquiry. These have priority over all other forms of debt. See **debt security; priority; short-term debt.**

reclamation the right of either side of a security sale to cancel the transaction if irregularities are discovered. The seller may reclaim securities or the buyer may reclaim cash in this event. See **rejection.**

recognized gain the amount of gain subject to income tax. See **profit; tax basis.**

recognized net loan relief the net excess of acquired loans over ceded loans in an exchange transaction. See **debt security; exchange.**

record date the day on which a shareholder is recognized as owner of securities, usually for the purpose of accruing dividends or to participate in the voting of corporate matters. See **corporation; dividend; exdividend date; stockholder; voting rights.**

recourse loan a form of loan in an investment program recognized as part of the investor's basis and, accordingly, at risk. See **basis; direct participation program; nonrecourse loan; partnership; tax shelter.**

recovery period the class life of an asset under provisions of the Economic Recovery Tax Act of 1981 (ERTA). See **class life; depreciation; Economic Recovery Tax Act of 1981 (ERTA).**

red herring the preliminary prospectus of an offering of securities, required under provisions of the Securities Act of 1933. It is so called due to the red-ink caveat

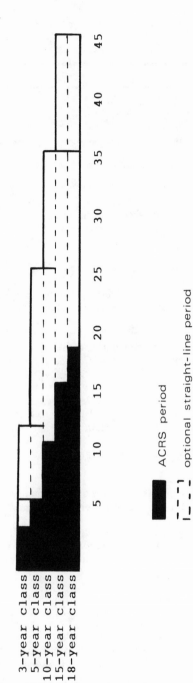

recovery period

3-year class
5-year class
10-year class
15-year class
18-year class

5   10   15   20   25   30   35   40   45

■ ACRS period

⌐ ⌐ optional straight-line period

that information contained in the document is not necessarily in final form. See **prospectus; SEC Rule 430; Securities Act of 1933.**

redeemable bond   a form of bond that may be redeemed at the issuer's choice during a period prior to maturity date. See **callable bond.**

redeemable preferred stock   a form of preferred stock that may be retired at the issuer's choice at a specified price. See **callable preferred stock.**

redemption   (1) repayment of a bond issue's principal, or the price paid to call preferred stock.
(2) the right of a mutual fund investor to cash in shares for the current net asset value. See **bond; callable bond; callable preferred stock; mutual fund; net asset value per share (NAV); preferred stock.**

rediscount   the process by which commercial banks use pledged collateral funds of borrowers to obtain additional borrowings from the Federal Reserve. See **collateral; commercial bank; Federal Reserve bank.**

refinancing   (1) revision of mortgage agreements by consolidation of two or more existing loans, or replacing one mortgage with another.
(2) a term meaning the same as refunding. See **mortgage; real estate.**

refunding   replacement of one outstanding bond issue by the issuance of another, undertaken to create more favorable rates and conditions. See **bond; debt security; redemption.**

refunding bond   a bond identified as a refinance or refunding of a prior issue. See **bond; debt security; interest; new issue.**

Reg T call   a notification to a customer that the current equity in a margin account does not meet the minimum standards of the Federal Reserve, demanding that more equity be deposited by a deadline. See **broker-dealer; Federal Reserve Board (FRB); margin requirement; Regulation T.**

Reg T excess   identification of the amount of equity in a margin account above minimum requirements of the Federal Reserve, also called excess margin. See **excess margin; Federal Reserve Board (FRB); margin account; Regulation T.**

regional exchanges   stock exchanges serving distinct regions or trading securities nationally or with emphasis on a particular region. The stock exchanges in the U.S. are: New York, American, Philadelphia, Pacific, Boston, Midwest, Intermountain, Spokane, Honolulu, Cincinnati, Detroit, and National. See **Securities Exchange Act of 1934; stock exchange.**

registered as to principal only   a type of bond registration in which the registered owner alone may redeem at maturity, but for which interest payments are made to the coupon bearer. See **bond; coupon.**

registered as to interest only   a type of bond registration in which the registered owner is identified for receipt of interest, but which may be redeemed at maturity by its bearer. See **bearer bond; bond.**

registered bond a bond whose owner is registered by the issuing corporation, and may be redeemed only by that owner or transferred with proper endorsement. See **bearer bond; coupon bond.**

registered company a corporation required to file a registration statement and periodic reports with the Securities and Exchange Commission, due to the scope of publicly held outstanding stock. See **corporation; registration statement; Securities and Exchange Commission (SEC).**

registered competitive market maker an NYSE member who, in addition to transacting for his or her own account, may be required to undertake trades to stabilize the market in a particular security or group of securities. See **auction marketplace; competitive market maker; market maker; New York Stock Exchange (NYSE).**

registered equity market maker a member of the American Stock Exchange acting in the same capacity as an NYSE registered competitive market maker, who is additionally subject to restrictive rules for option trading. See **American Stock Exchange (AMEX); competitive market maker; market maker.**

registered form a type of ownership in which the owner's name is printed on a certificate and a record is maintained by the issuing corporation. See **bond; bearer bond.**

registered investment advisor (RIA) an individual allowed to charge a fee for investment advice, or to act as an offeree representative for a fee. The RIA is registered with his or her state securities agency and is subject to provisions of the Investment Advisors Act of 1940. A primary requirement is that the advisor fully disclose to clients the activities, sources and amounts of compensation, and other pertinent facts. See **full disclosure; investment advisor; Investment Advisors Act of 1940; offeree representative; state securities agency.**

registered options principal (ROP) an individual associated with a broker-dealer who holds an NASD Series 4 license, who is responsible for supervision over registered representatives' trading activities in listed options. See **broker-dealer; National Association of Securities Dealers (NASD); option; Series 4.**

registered options representative a licensed employee of a broker-dealer authorized to handle option transactions for customers, under the supervision of a registered options principal. The representative generally will be required to hold an NASD Series 7 or Series 24 license, or a Series 5 if interest rate options will be traded. See **National Association of Securities Dealers (NASD); option; Series 5; Series 7; Series 24.**

registered options trader a specialist of the American Stock Exchange (AMEX) responsible for maintaining the trading market in listed options. See **American Stock Exchange (AMEX); option; specialist.**

registered representative a licensed employee of a broker-dealer (full title: general securities registered representative) who holds a Series 7 license from the National Association of Securities Dealers. The registered representative is allowed to trade in stocks and bonds, direct participation programs, and investment company securities. See **broker-dealer; general securities registered representative; National Association of Securities Dealers (NASD); Series 7.**

registered secondary   a "shelf" distribution of securities held by affiliated or control persons, or a combined primary and secondary offering (requiring the filing of a registration statement). See **affiliated person; control person; primary distribution; registration statement; secondary distribution; Securities and Exchange Commision (SEC); shelf distribution.**

registered security   (1) a security whose public offering was made under registration with the SEC and under SEC Rules 144 or 145.
(2) a security issued in registered form, when the owner's identification is recorded by the issuing corporation and a certificate issued with the owner's name. See **public offering; registered form; SEC Rule 144; Securities and Exchange Commission (SEC).**

registered trader   a New York Stock Exchange member engaged in transactions for his or her own account. See **New York Stock Exchange (NYSE); trader.**

registrar   a commercial bank or trust company that keeps records of issued stock for a corporation; ensures that issued stock does not exceed authorized; and verifies ownership transfers. See **authorized shares; commercial bank; transfer agent; trustee.**

registration fee   a fee assessed by the Securities and Exchange Commission upon the making of a public offer. See **public offering; Securities and Exchange Commission (SEC); transfer.**

registration statement   a document required under provisions of the Securities Act of 1933. It is filed with the SEC by the organization making an offer of securities publicly. It contains all information pertaining to a new offering, including management, description of securities, legal and financial disclosures and use of proceeds. The statement is also filed with the appropriate exchange or blue-sky commission. See **blue-sky laws; public offering; Securities Act of 1933; Securities and Exchange Commission (SEC).**

regular specialist   at the New York Stock Exchange, an individual responsible for handling buy and sell orders in a group of securities, who will also trade for his or her own account in maintaining an orderly market. See **associate specialist; New York Stock Exchange (NYSE); relief specialist; specialist.**

regular way   for stocks, corporate bonds and municipal bonds, the term for delivery and payment of a transaction. Securities are deliverable by the seller and payment is due from the buyer on the fifth business day following the trade date. See **SEC Rule 10a-1; secondary market; settlement date; trade date.**

regulated investment company   an organization that has met IRS qualifications not to pay income taxes directly, but to pass gains through to investors (including mutual funds and unit investment trusts, for example). See **investment company; mutual fund; unit investment trust; real estate investment trust (REIT).**

regulation   a rule or policy of an agency having jurisdiction, either governmentally (such as the Securities and Exchange Commission or a state securities agency) or through a self-regulatory organization (SRO) like the National Association of Securities Dealers (NASD). A regulation is established by the organization itself, and is distinguished from a law, which is established by a legislature. See **jurisdiction; self-regulatory organization (SRO).**

regular way

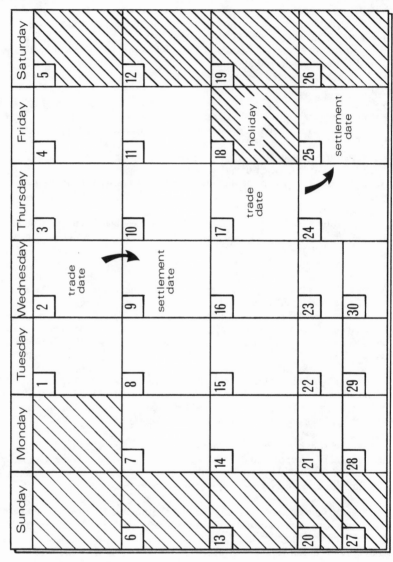

Regulation A   a provision of the Securities Act of 1933, specifying the limits under which an offer of securities may be made publicly without being required to undergo the registration process. See **notification; offering; public offering; registration statement; SEC Rule 254; Securities Act of 1933; Securities and Exchange Commission (SEC).**

Regulation G   a Federal Reserve Board rule specifying the terms under which a person or organization other than a bank or broker-dealer may extend margin credit. See **Federal Reserve Board (FRB); margin security.**

Regulation Q   a Federal Reserve Board rule controlling the rate of interest a commercial bank may pay to holders of time deposits. See **commercial bank; Federal Reserve Board (FRB); time deposit.**

Regulation T   a Federal Reserve Board rule specifying terms for broker-dealers when dealing with margin account customers. It specifies the level and amount of margin that will be allowed, and contains provisions for enforcement of those rules. See **broker-dealer; Federal Reserve Board (FRB); margin account.**

Regulation U   a Federal Reserve Board rule specifying terms for banks advancing credit to customers. See **collateral; Federal Reserve Board (FRB); purpose loan.**

Regulation W   a Federal Reserve Board rule specifying terms for commercial credit, particularly relating to consumer installment loans. See **debt service; Federal Reserve Board (FRB).**

Regulation X   a Federal Reserve Board rule setting equal responsibility for compliance on lenders and borrowers under Regulations G, T and U. See **compliance; Federal Reserve Board (FRB).**

rehypothecation   the pledging of margin securities with an outside source, as a means of financing that account's debit balance. See **collateral; customer; debit balance; hypothecation; margin account.**

reinvestment rate   (1) the calculated rate of growth of an organization, computed by multiplying the return on equity by the rate of retention.

(2) the prevailing rate at which current income or sale proceeds from an investment can be reinvested.

(3) for the purpose of comparing total yields, the calculated rate an investor can obtain from future income yielded, assuming the future rate will be the same as that rate available now. See **cash flow; rate of return; retention rate; return on equity.**

rehypothecation

bank

rehypothecation

broker-dealer

hypothecation

customer

rejection the act of reclamation, the right to refuse payment or delivery when the transaction cannot be fully closed, certificates are not negotiable, or improper form is present. See **reclamation.**

relative value a comparison between two securities, taking into account several factors: price history and potential, level of risk, liquidity, call features, and ratings. See **investment objective; risk; yield.**

release letter a document explaining the procedures to be used in a competitive bid offering, sent by the syndicate manager to those active in making the offering. See **offering; syndicate.**

relief specialist a New York Stock Exchange affiliate who may substitute for a regular specialist and has the same level of responsibility. See **New York Stock Exchange (NYSE); regular specialist; specialist.**

renegotiable rate mortgage a rollover mortgage, with interest rate and monthly payment constant for a period of time, with periodic adjustments. See **rollover mortgage.**

rental pool the structure for collection of rental income and subsequent distribution to individual limited partners. See **direct participation program; income; real estate.**

reorganization department a back office function connected with the cashiering department, where conversions and tender offers are handled, with the exchange of certificates and cash included. See **back office; brokerage house; cashiering; conversion; exchange.**

replacement cost an estimate of the lowest cost for replacement of improvements and assets in an operating property. See **real estate; real property.**

repurchase agreement also referred to as a "repo," a contract to close a position at a specified time in the future, and at an agreed price. As a Federal Open Market Committee transaction, a repo involves a government security with provisions for resale; for other exempt securities, a repo may be used for government and municipal securities to reduce carrying costs. See **Federal Open Market Committee (FOMC); government bond; interest; municipal bond.**

research and development a form of tax shelter investment designed to allow investors to deduct costs

$$\frac{\text{Net Income}}{\text{Shareholders' Equity}} \times \frac{\text{Retained Income}}{\text{Net Income Before Dividends}} = \text{Rate}$$

$$\frac{\$800,000}{\$6,007,400} \times \frac{\$225,600}{\$1,025,600} = 2.93\%$$

reinvestment rate

in the program's early years, and report profits at capital gains rates in later years, and to qualify for tax credits. See **capital gain; direct participation program; limited partnership; tax shelter.**

reserve city bank   a commercial bank located in a city where a central bank of the Federal Reserve is also located, having demand deposits of $400 million or more. See **central bank; commercial bank; demand deposit; district bank; Federal Reserve Bank.**

reserve requirement   the amount of tangible assets that a commercial bank must set aside and may not lend out, representing security for demand and time deposits. See **commercial bank; demand deposit; district bank; Federal Reserve Bank; time deposit.**

reserves   (1) a commercial bank's required assets, kept available to meet obligations to depositors, as required by the Federal Reserve. Primary reserves consist of cash on hand and in collection process, and outstanding balances due from other banks.
(2) an insurance company's computed liability representing the present value of future claims of policyholders.
(3) funds set aside by companies for future contingencies, the amount of which cannot be known precisely. Example: the reserve for bad debts that reduces the balance of outstanding accounts receivable in anticipation that a portion of those accounts will not be collectible. See **balance sheet; commercial bank; Federal Reserve Bank; financial statement; life insurance.**

resident manager   an individual residing on site at a rental property. See **direct participation program; limited partnership; property manager; real estate.**

residential mortgage   the debt instrument on a single-family or multi-family property, represented by FHA-insured mortgages under Title II of the National Housing Act of 1934; VA-guaranteed mortgages as legislated under the Serviceman's Readjustment Act of 1944; conventional issues of the Federal National Mortgage Association (FNMA); issues of the Federal Home Loan Mortgage Corporation (FHLMC); or mortgages issued by savings and loans and banking institutions. See **Federal Home Loan Mortgage Corporation (FHLMC); Federal National Mortgage Association (FNMA); mortgage; real estate; second mortgage.**

resistance level   a term used by technical analysts to describe the top price a security may reach under present conditions. Investor resistance is met at this point, and the price is likely to fall back upon reaching it. See **price; support level; technical analysis.**

restricted account   (1) a margin account that fails to meet current minimum requirements under Regulation T, and is therefore restricted from any additional trading.
(2) a cash account in which the customer has not paid for securities by delivery date. Under Regulation T, additional trading is forbidden for 90 days. See **Federal Reserve Board (FRB); margin account; Regulation T.**

restricted category   individuals subject to National Association of Securities Dealers limitations regarding participation in hot issues. See **board of governors; hot issue; National Association of Securities Dealers (NASD).**

resistance level

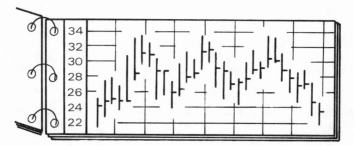

restricted list a listing of securities that are registered or pending registration with the SEC, published by broker-dealers for their registered representatives. The list contains names of issues and issuers whose securities may not be traded, or which may be traded on an unsolicited basis only. See **broker-dealer; public offering; Securities and Exchange Commission (SEC).**

retail investor a general description of investors not generating the volume of investment dollars and commissions seen from institutional investors. See **commission; institutional investor.**

retained earnings also called earned surplus, the total amount of cumulative net profits reinvested in the corporation after payment of dividends. See **balance sheet; corporation; earned surplus; equity.**

retained earnings statement a type of specialized financial statement seen in annual reports of detailed financial presentations. It shows the annual sources and applications of surplus, including in many cases annual dividend payment comparisons. See **annual report; balance sheet; financial statement.**

retention (1) the portion of a total underwriting kept available for sale to customers. The balance of the issue is kept available for other members of the selling group and institutional investors.
(2) the withholding of a portion of loan proceeds upon withdrawal of a portion of its collateral. See **collateral; institutional investor; syndicate; underwriter.**

retention rate the opposite of payout ratio, representing the percentage of net earnings reinvested in the company. It is computed by dividing retained income by the net income before dividend payments. See **dividend; net income; payout ratio.**

retirement (bond) the total repayment or conversion of a debt security, through early payment at face value, calling of the issue according to the conversion terms, or replacement with a new issue. See **bond; debt security; face value; redemption.**

retirement fund assets placed in qualified, tax-deferred plans established specifically to provide a retirement income. See **individual retirement account (IRA); Keogh plan; pension plan; profit-sharing plan; qualified plan; tax deferral.**

retirement plan bond bonds designed for purchase within a qualified plan, issued in denominations of $50 to $1,000 each. See **Keogh plan; nonmarketable**

$$\frac{\text{Retained Income}}{\text{Net Income Before Dividends}} = \text{Retention Rate}$$

$$\frac{\$425,800}{\$1,225,800} = 34.7\%$$

retention rate

securities; pension plan; profit-sharing plan; qualified plan; Self-Employed Individual's Tax Retirement Act of 1962.

retirement plans   investments built on a tax-deferred basis, to provide retirement assets to investors. See **corporate retirement plan; individual retirement account (IRA); Keogh plan; pension plan; profit-sharing plan.**

return   in its most common usage, return is synonymous with yield or rate of return, the annual percentage of interest, dividends or capital gains received or credited, compared to the total amount of investment. See **rate of return; yield.**

return if exercised   the calculated yield an investor will earn in the event of exercise against a covered option. See **covered option; exercise; option; underlying security.**

return if exercised

Basis $43:

```
a) sell call $45                          $300
   gain on stock ($45 - $43)               200

   return if exercised                    $500    (11.6%)


b) sell call $40                          $650
   loss on stock ($40 - $43)             (300)

   return if exercised                    $350    ( 8.1%)
```

return if unchanged   the calculated yield an investor will earn in the event a covered call expires without any change in the value of the underlying security. See **covered option; expiration; option; underlying security.**

return if unchanged

Basis $43:

a)	sell call $45, gain	$300	(7.0%)
b)	sell call $50, gain	$ 50	(1.2%)

---

return on equity a calculation of the percentage of return on stockholders' equity that is represented by net profits during one year. Net profits are divided by shareholders' equity at the beginning of the year to arrive at yield on beginning equity. Another calculation involves using as a denominator the average equity (beginning plus ending equity, divided by two). See **equity; fundamental analysis; net income; shareholders' equity; yield.**

$$\frac{\text{Net Income}}{\text{Shareholders' Equity}} = \text{Return on Equity}$$

$$\frac{\$418,300}{\$8,007,400} = 5.2\%$$

return on equity

return on invested capital a calculation of the yield represented by net profits during one year, including total capitalization (shareholders' equity and the par value of long-term bonds). Because payment on bonds is a form of return on equity, total interest expense on those bonds is added to net income in the calculation. See **capitalization; fundamental analysis; long-term debt; net income; shareholders' equity; total capitalization; yield.**

Revenue Act of 1971 legislation creating the investment tax credit (ITC) as an incentive for business investment in capital assets. A tax credit effectively discounts the purchase price of eligible assets. However, the ITC provision includes recapture rules for assets disposed within a recapture period. See **assets; investment tax credit (ITC).**

Revenue Act of 1980 tax law setting rules for valuation of a deceased limited partner's assets. Upon death, assets are valued at current market value, so that heirs are relieved from inheritance tax on gains from greatly appreciated properties and securities. See **inheritance tax; limited partner; tax basis.**

revenue anticipation note (RAN) a discounted short-term municipal debt secured by future revenues. See **municipal note; short-term debt.**

return on invested capital

$$\frac{\text{Net Income} + \text{Interest Expense}}{\text{Shareholders' Equity} + \text{Par Value of Long-Term Bonds}} = \text{Return}$$

$$\frac{\$418,300 + \$250,800}{\$8,007,400 + \$2,752,000} = 6.2\%$$

revenue bond a municipal bond issued on the premise that principal and interest will be repaid from the revenues created from facilities to be constructed with proceeds of the issue. See **bond; municipal bond.**

reversal arbitrage a transaction involving writing a put, buying a call, and selling short the underlying security, often called a "riskless" transaction. See **arbitrage; conversion arbitrage; riskless transaction; short sale.**

reverse annuity mortgage a device allowing homeowners (usually restricted to those older than 62) to obtain the equity in their homes without risking loss of the home from too-high mortgage payments. A monthly annuity payment is made to the homeowner, which accrues as a loan to be repaid upon sale of the home or death of the owners. See **annuity; equity; real estate.**

reverse conversion (1) the short sale of a security when an open option is held, converting the status of the option by creation of an offsetting short position.

(2) term describing the recognition of taxable income when no cash flow is being generated, also known as phantom income. See **cash flow; phantom income; short sale; tax-advantaged investment.**

reverse hedge (1) the purchase of a number of calls exceeding lots of the underlying security in a short position, also called a synthetic straddle.

(2) a tactic employed by investors holding common stock. A convertible security on the same company is sold short, on speculation that parity will decline enough so that a net profit will result from the transaction. See **common stock; convertible security; ratio write; short sale; straddle; underlying security; write.**

reverse repurchase agreement the provision of funds by a broker-dealer to a customer, represented by securities purchased under an agreement that the security will be resold at a later date, and at the same price adjusted by interest. See **broker-dealer; customer.**

reverse split the reduction of the total shares outstanding, achieved by reissuing shares at a higher par value. A corporation may enact a reverse split of "one for two," in which half the original number of shares are reissued, each for twice the original value. Other adjustments can be put into effect, depending upon the price level the corporation desires to create. See **split; split down; outstanding stock.**

reverse strategy   any strategy employed that goes against traditional investor practices. See **ratio strategy; strategy.**

reversionary interest   a condition written into some direct participation programs, especially oil and gas partnerships. It provides for an interest in profits that is the right of the sponsor on a cost-free basis. See **direct participation program; oil and gas; sponsor.**

revocable trust   a form of trust that can be discontinued at the discretion of the grantor. At that point, assets in the trust become the grantor's property. See **grantor trust; living trust; trust.**

right of accumulation   a privilege allowed by some open-end mutual funds, allowing investors to pay a lower rate of sales charge if additional funds are deposited within a specified time. The lower rate is calculated at a breakpoint as though the entire investment were made at one time. See **breakpoint; commission; load mutual fund; open-end management company; sales charge.**

right of rejection   the right of a buyer to refuse completion of a transaction because the certificate is in a condition not constituting good delivery. See **certificate; good delivery; reclamation; rejection.**

right of rescission   the right to cancel a contract because terms, conditions or actions of the other side in the transaction were conducted in conflict with laws or regulations. See **cancellation.**

rights   the privilege of buying additional stock in a company, based upon proportionate ownership. Rights commonly are offered below the market value of securities, and may be traded in a fashion similar to options and warrants. Failure to exercise rights within a specified period of time may result in expiration. See **option; subscription right; warrant.**

Rights		
Shares Held	Percentage	Rights
1,000	2%	10
6,000	12	60
4,000	8	40
22,000	44	220
17,000	34	170
50,000	100	500

rights offering   a subscription offering to the purchase of securities in a corporation, made available to existing stockholders. See **offering; subscription right; warrant.**

risk the danger in all investments that, in one way or another, an adverse condition will prevail. There is the risk of loss of capital, the most common association between investments and risk. There is the risk of inflation outpacing the yield from an investment; the risk of illiquidity; the effects of interest rate movement; market risks, such as a changing demand for securities; and the risk of tax consequences, audit, or disallowance of deductions. See **inflation; interest; investment objective; liquidity.**

risk arbitrage a form of arbitrage involving the purchase of shares in one company and the short sale of shares in another. Typically, the strategy will be applied in expectation of a pending announcement of a take-over. By selling short the shares of the acquiring company (in anticipation of the market value decreasing) and buying the shares in the company to be taken over (in anticipation that the market value will increase), the investor hopes to gain from both sides of the transaction. See **arbitrage; bona fide arbitrage; dividend arbitrage; merger; speculation; take-over.**

risk factor (1) a general term describing the element of risk that may influence an investor in deciding whether or not to choose a particular security.
(2) a part of the prospectus or offering circular that discloses the risks associated with an offering. See **investment objective; offering; offering circular; prospectus.**

riskless transaction a type of transaction undertaken by a broker-dealer who has a firm order for the securities, also called a simultaneous transaction. See **broker-dealer; firm order; simultaneous transaction.**

roll down an option transaction involving the closing of one position, and opening of another at a lower strike price. See **expiration date; option; strike price.**

```
long roll down
      Purchase October 55              $ 300

      Roll Down:
                Sell October 55        ( 50)
                Buy October 50          200

                Adjusted Basis         $ 450

   short roll down
      Sell March 35                    $(250)

      Roll Down:
                Buy March 35             25
                Sell March 30          (200)

                Adjusted Basis         $(425)
```

roll down

roll forward an option transaction involving the closing of a near-expiration position, and opening of a longer-term position. This strategy may be undertaken to avoid an unfavorable exercise or to defer a current loss in the hope of an overall gain at a later date. If the new position is for a higher strike price, it is a roll up and forward; if for a lower strike price, it is a roll down and forward. See **expiration date; option; strike price.**

roll up (1) an option transaction involving the closing of one position, and opening of another at a higher strike price.

(2) an exchange of units or shares in a partnership for shares in a corporation. Under certain guidelines, this would qualify as a tax-free exchange. See **corporation; exchange; expiration date; limited partnership; option; partnership; strike price.**

```
long roll up
    Purchase October 55              $ 300

    Roll Up:
              Sell October 55         (600)
              Buy October 60           800

              Adjusted Basis         $ 500

short roll up
    Sell March 35                    $(250)

    Roll Up:
              Buy March 35             600
              Sell March 40           (900)

              Adjusted Basis         $(550)
```

roll up

rollover (1) the reinvestment upon maturity of a bond in another debt security.

(2) movement of funds in a qualified retirement fund, such as an IRA, from one account to another. The term describes a situation in which there is no tax assessed.

(3) the repurchase of a security following the closing of a previous position in the same security, at a net gain. See **bond; capital gain; debt security; individual retirement account (IRA); IRA rollover; maturity date; qualified plan; retirement plans; tax-free rollover.**

rollover mortgage a type of mortgage agreement similar to an adjustable rate mortgage, but generally with a longer fixed interest rate term provision. The rate may be adjusted each 36 months, with some terms as long as 60 months. See **adjustable rate mortgage (ARM); floating rate note (FRN); mortgage; variable rate mortgage.**

rollover option the right of an investor to reinvest funds from one investment into a related one, often with a deferral of taxes on profits. See **individual retirement account (IRA); IRA rollover; qualified plan.**

rotation   a procedure used by option exchanges, calling for the sequential bidding and offering of option contracts, month by month and strike price by strike price. Rotation is used whether or not trades actually occur at those prices. See **option; option series; underlying security.**

round lot   a standard unit of trade, as dictated by common practice. Round lots are 100 shares for active stocks, 10 shares for some inactive stocks, and $1,000 par value units for listed bonds. See **bond; inactive stock; institutional investor; normal trading unit; retail investor; odd lot; par value; stock.**

royalty interest   a landowner's right to future production profits in an oil and gas program, the other side being called working interest. See **exploratory program; oil and gas; working interest.**

rule of 45   a vesting method in pension and profit-sharing plans, in which vestation is based upon a combination of the employee's age and years of service. When these factors add up to 45, vesting begins. See **pension plan; profit-sharing plan; retirement plans; vesting methods.**

rules of fair practice   a series of specific rules established by the National Association of Securities Dealers (NASD), concerning the proper conduct of registered representatives and member organizations. The principles of fair treatment and full disclosure are central to the theme of these rules, and the NASD has the power to censure, fine or suspend violators. See **fair treatment; full disclosure; National Association of Securities Dealers (NASD); registered representative; Uniform Practice Code (UPC).**

run   (1) term describing the continued movement of a security's market price in the same direction.
(2) a panic in a particular market, in which investors or depositors move to close positions in order to avoid further losses or the threat of losses.
(3) the range of prices — bid and asked — for a particular security or group of securities. See **bid; offering price; par value.**

run on the bank   a situation in which a significant number of depositors in a bank demand immediate withdrawal of their funds. See **commercial bank.**

S

S Corporation   previously referred to as a Subchapter S Corporation, the S Corporation is a small business corporation enjoying the protection of stockholders via limited liability. The S Corporation's stockholders have elected to be taxed as a partnership. The organization must contain a limited number of shareholders to qualify, all of whom must agree to the election. All earned net profits, capital gains, and interest and dividend income is passed through to the stockholders each year instead of being taxed at the corporate level. See **corporation; small business corporation; Subchapter S.**

safe harbor   a condition under which certain acts avoid tax legally. Equipment leasing transactions particularly were granted safe harbor provisions under the

Rule of 45

Years of Service	Employee Age	Percent Vestation	Total Contributions	Vested Contributions
1	36	0%	$ 5,000	$ 0
2	37	0	10,000	0
3	38	0	15,000	0
4	39	0	20,000	0
5	40	50	25,000	12,500
6	41	60	30,000	18,000
7	42	70	35,000	24,500
8	43	80	40,000	32,000
9	44	90	45,000	40,500
10	45	100	50,000	50,000

Economic Recovery Tax Act of 1981 (ERTA), with later modifications to those rules. See **Economic Recovery Tax Act of 1981 (ERTA); equipment leasing; tax basis.**

safekeeping   a fiduciary responsibility undertaken by broker-dealers in holding customers' securities. Rules for proper safekeeping include procedures for identification of securities, policies against commingling of funds, and definition of conditions under which securities under safekeeping may be repledged. See **broker-dealer; commingled funds; fiduciary; SEC Rule 15c2-1.**

safety   a qualifying test and objective applied when considering an investment. The level of safety reflects the degree of risk an investor is willing to take. A higher level of safety corresponds with a lower potential yield in most cases. Safety is also a reflection of the quality of an investment and its risk of loss, sensitivity to economic conditions, and the investor's own diversification. See **diversification; investment objective; qualitative analysis; quantitatitve analysis; risk; yield.**

sale-leaseback   the act of selling real property to someone else, and then leasing it from that party. The purpose of this action is to liquidate an asset and recognize a long-term capital gain at a favored tax rate, often in a year most beneficial to the seller. The seller can continue to claim annual deductions, from lease payments rather than from depreciation expenses. A sale-leaseback may be employed when an asset has been depreciated fully, as a tax-planning strategy. See **operating leaseback; real property; user leaseback.**

sale – leaseback

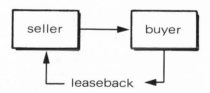

sales   the gross amount received by a business in exchange for placing its product or services on the market. Sales are the first item reported on an income statement, and are used as the basis for measurement of operating results on gross or net levels. See **financial statement; fundamental analysis; income statement.**

sales charge   the amount charged by a mutual fund or other investment company, and deducted from the gross amount of capital deposited. The charge is applied to compensating the underwriter, sponsor and selling representative. See **front-end load; letter of intent; load mutual fund; mutual fund; open-end management company; right of accumulation; sales load.**

sales literature   a broad term applied to any correspondence or printed material sent from a broker-dealer to customers, falling under the rules and guidelines applied to advertising in general under the NASD rules of fair practice. See **advertising; National Association of Securities Dealers (NASD); rules of fair practice.**

sales load   the sales charge deducted from each investor's contribution in a mutual fund or other investment program. See **front-end load; sales charge.**

Sallie Mae   shortened name for securities issued by the government-sponsored Student Loan Marketing Association (SLMA), which backs loans to students and educational institutions. See **Student Loan Marketing Association (SLMA).**

salvage value   the estimated worth of an asset after it has been fully depreciated. The concept of salvage value was required under depreciation rules prior to the accelerated cost recovery system (ACRS) method, in which no salvage values are assumed. See **accelerated cost recovery system (ACRS); depreciation.**

same-day substitution   an action taken in a margin account, in which a purchase and sale are transacted at the same time, but there is no change in value. Accordingly, no additional margin requirement takes effect. Regulation T allows for same-day substitution as long as values of each side of the transaction are equal. See **initial margin; Regulation T; special miscellaneous account (SMA).**

savings account   an account without a maturity date that bears interest at a set rate. See **commercial bank; Regulation Q.**

savings and loan association   a company that operates much like a commercial bank, but offers less service and facilities. Savings from depositors are invested in mortgages, secured notes and other financial instruments. See **mortgage; thrift institution.**

savings bank   a type of bank allowing time and demand deposits and investing its assets in mortgages, notes and other financial instruments. See **demand deposit; thrift institution; time deposit.**

savings deposit   an account in a commercial bank that bears interest and is not subject to a maturity date. See **commercial bank.**

scale order   a combination order containing a series of related limit orders. Multiple round lots are specified on the order, scaled to buy down from a specified level, or to sell up from a specified level. The purpose is to obtain a favorable average price on the collective trade. See **limit order; order ticket; round lot.**

scalping   an action by an investment advisor, recommending that customers buy a security in which he or she has taken a position, in the hope that those subsequent purchases will cause the price to increase. See **investment advisor; manipulation.**

Schedule C   (1) a National Association of Securities Dealers by-law specifying the standards by which a licensed principal or representative may be associated with a broker-dealer.
(2) a financial planning term used to describe broadly the market for self-employed individuals, so called because sole proprietorships file a Schedule C with their federal income tax returns. See **broker-dealer; financial and operations principal; financial planning; general securities principal; general securities registered representative; National Association of Securities Dealers (NASD); self-employment.**

Schedule K-1   an attachment to Form 1065, supplied to each member of a partnership. It summarizes what must be reported for federal tax purposes in net income, capital gains, self-employment income, and other reportable operating and capital results. See **Form 1065; partnership; tax basis.**

Schedule 13D   a filing requirement under the Securities Exchange Act of 1934. Any person who purchases or acquires five percent or more of the securities in a corporation registered with the SEC must, within 10 days, file this schedule. It reports the purchaser's intentions for control and management of the company, in anticipation of the investor's becoming a control person (a holder of 10 percent or more stock of the company). See **control person; Securities and Exchange Commission (SEC); Securities Exchange Act of 1934.**

Schedule 13G   a version of Schedule 13D, to be filed by any person or organization who, as of the end of a calendar year, holds or controls five percent or more of a registered corporation's securities. See **Securities and Exchange Commission (SEC); Securities Exchange Act of 1934.**

scrip   a partial share of stock issued by a corporation to an investor upon spin-off, dividend, or stock split. The investor may sell the scrip, redeem it for the partial share, or submit it with a cash balance to purchase a full share. See **dividend; spin-off; stock split.**

seasoned issue   descriptive of a new issue that has been distributed with a high level of liquidity in the secondary market. See **liquidity; new issue; secondary market.**

seat   a membership in a national stock exchange. Subject to the approval of the exchange board of directors, a purchaser must be over 21 and a United States citizen. Seats may be leased, bought and sold at auction, or traded for other consideration. See **allied member; stock exchange.**

SEC fee   a fee paid by the seller of a security, assessed by the Securities Exchange Commission (SEC) against the seller of the security. See **Securities and Exchange Commission (SEC).**

SEC Rule 10a-1   a rule, also known as the plus tick rule, requiring that short sales are to be made for a price higher than the last regular way transaction in the same security. See **plus tick rule; regular way; short sale; zero-plus tick.**

SEC Rule 10b-4   a rule stating that a short sale cannot be made due to a tender offer. See **short sale; tender offer.**

SEC Rule 10b-6   rule governing the activities of underwriters in offering securities for sale prior to a public offering, including prohibitions against manipulation and deceptive devices. See **indication of interest; manipulation; public offering; underwriter.**

SEC Rule 10b-10   the rule governing the preparation, mailing and disclosures on confirmations. See **broker-dealer; confirmation.**

SEC Rule 10b-16   the specific guidelines for disclosure of financial information—rates, terms and conditions—for lending money to customers in margin accounts. See **broker-dealer; financing; margin account.**

SEC Rule 11a   the guidelines and rules for exchange members who trade on their own account. See **trader.**

SEC Rule 15c2-1   the rule for safekeeping of customer securities by a broker-dealer, prohibiting commingling or excess hypothecation. See **hypothecation; margin account; safekeeping.**

SEC Rule 15c2-11   the rule for giving of quotations on securities without a determinable value. See **quotation.**

SEC Rule 15c3-1   the rule setting specific guidelines for broker-dealers in calculating aggregate indebtedness and net capital. See **aggregate indebtedness; net capital requirement.**

SEC Rule 15c3-3   guidelines for handling of fully-paid customer securities held by a broker-dealer in a segregated account. See **segregated account.**

SEC Rule 144   a rule permitting the sale of restricted or letter securities, without SEC registration. See **letter security.**

SEC Rule 146   regulation stating that private placement offerings must be negotiated between the issuer and the buyer's investment advisor. Financial information must be made available to the buyer and the issuer is responsible for determining that the buyer has the understanding of the investment to make an informed decision. See **investment advisor; pre-offering questionnaire; private placement.**

SEC Rule 147   the intrastate exemption rule, stating that there is an exception to SEC registration requirements when an offering is made within one state only. See **intrastate exemption.**

SEC Rule 237   an allowance made to the holders of letter securities, stating that they may be sold publicly under some circumstances. The rule was rescinded in October, 1983. See **letter security.**

SEC Rule 254   a rule setting a limit on the amount of sales that are permissible under the terms of Regulation A, allowing a non-registered offering and requiring the publication of an offering circular. See **offering circular; Regulation A.**

SEC Rule 396   a regulation also known as the "nine-bond rule," stating that a best efforts attempt must be made on the exchange floor to obtain a price for bonds sold in lots of nine or less. See **nine-bond rule.**

SEC Rule 405   the "know your customer" rule that specifies an investment advisor or broker must be aware of a customer's financial condition and investment knowledge prior to and during an investing transaction. See **know your customer.**

SEC Rule 430   a rule setting down the conditions under which a preliminary prospectus (red herring) may be given to customers. This was SEC Rule 433 prior to March, 1982. See **prospectus; red herring.**

SECO license   also called the Series 2, this is the license for a Securities Exchange Commission Organization (SECO), a broker-dealer not registered with the National Association of Securities Dealers (NASD). The license permits interstate selling activity of those broker-dealers and its representatives. See **broker-dealer; registered representative; Securities and Exchange Commission Organization (SECO); Series 2.**

SECO member a broker-dealer registered with the Securities and Exchange Commission (SEC), but not with the NASD or a major exchange. See **broker-dealer; Securities and Exchange Commission Organization (SECO).**

second mortgage a mortgage pledged by real estate when a required down payment is not available in cash, or when an existing owner desires cash representing equity in the property. A second generally is written for a short term, between five and 15 years. See **financing; mortgage; real estate; short-term debt.**

secondary distribution a public redistribution of stock. An organization purchases a large block from current stockholders and subsequently offers smaller blocks at a fixed price, reflecting the current market for the security. See **exchange distribution; primary distribution; special offering.**

secondary distribution

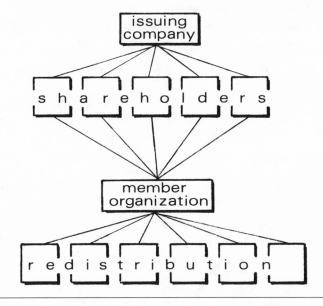

secondary market a market in which securities can be bought and sold by the public, following an initial offering. This includes the public exchange market and the over-the-counter market. See **exchange; over-the-counter (OTC); primary market.**

secondary movement a term in technical analysis, describing the way a security's price moves counter to a primary movement. Secondary shifts are interim adjustments in value within an overall trend. See **Dow Theory; primary movement; technical analysis.**

secondary movement

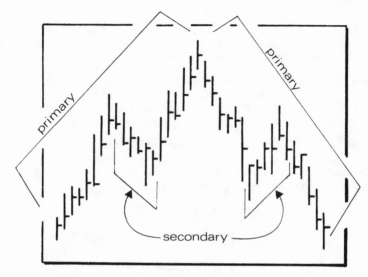

sector   description of bonds with certain similarities. Factors used to group bonds into sectors include price, yield and rating. See **bond; price; yield.**

secured bond   a highly rated bond for which a specific asset is pledged as security against interest and principal payments. In the event of default, holders of secured bonds have a claim on the pledged asset. See **bond; collateral.**

secured debt   a debt with tangible collateral pledged, to protect the lender or investor. A mortgage is a type of debt secured by the real estate itself. A secured bond has specific assets set aside as collateral for the bondholders. See **collateral; debt security; unsecured debt.**

securities   instruments representing either tangible interests in organizations or agencies, or the intangible future claim from an option, warrant, right or futures contract. Securities are classified in two broad categories: debt and equity. A debt security (bond, mortgage, or note) is a loan to the issuer. An equity security (stock, mutual fund shares or partnership interest) is partial ownership, directly or indirectly, in a corporation or other organization and its net assets. See **debt security; equity security; investment.**

Securities Act of 1933   major securities legislation making issuers responsible for full and fair disclosure. The act also sets forth rules for the preparation and filing of registration statements and prospectuses, and dictates the disclosure in those documents of material information. Under this law, certain investment programs meeting qualifications are exempt from registration. These exemptions include intrastate offerings (Rule 147) and private placements (Rule 146). See **accredited investor; full disclosure; intrastate exemption; private placement; prospectus; public offering; registration statement; SEC Rule 146; SEC Rule 147.**

Securities and Exchange Commission (SEC)   a federal agency created under terms of the Securities Exchange Act of 1934, originally to administer the terms of the Securities Act of 1933. The SEC today has the authority to interpret and enforce federal securities laws and to exact civil penalties or recommend criminal prosecution in cases of violation. See **broker-dealer; investment company; registered representative; Securities Exchange Act of 1934.**

Securities and Exchange Commission Organization (SECO) a broker-dealer coming under SEC jurisdiction, who is not a member of the National Association of Securities Dealers (NASD), the industry's self-regulating agency, or of a national securities exchange. See **jurisdiction; National Association of Securities Dealers (NASD); SECO member; stock exchange.**

securities blotter a broker-dealer's principal record of all investment transactions by clients of its registered representatives. One blotter is maintained for each security. The customer's name, investment date and the amount invested are recorded.

The blotter serves as the source of internal audit trail and volume analysis in a security, and is required as a basic record, to be available for examination by agencies having jurisdiction, notably the state securities agency, the SEC and the NASD. See **broker-dealer; customer; National Association of Securities Dealers (NASD); registered representative; Securities and Exchange Commission (SEC); state securities agency.**

Securities Exchange Act of 1934 legislation requiring individuals marketing securities to hold proper licenses.

Among its major provisions, licensed individuals are required to submit signed disclosure statements upon registration with a securities broker-dealer. They must also submit fingerprints to the U.S. Attorney General. Strict rules are set forth in this law concerning fraudulent devices.

The SEC has the power to fine, censure, suspend or revoke the license of broker-dealers not complying with the terms of the '34 act. See **broker-dealer; registered representative; Regulation T.**

Securities Industry Association (SIA) a lobbying association for member securities firms, founded in 1972. Most members are NASD broker-dealers and exchange firm members. See **broker-dealer; member organization.**

Securities Industry Automation Corporation (SIAC) a subsidiary jointly owned by the New York Stock Exchange and the American Stock Exchange to communicate trade information. SIAC, in addition to sharing of information between the two exchanges, also provides data to other industry quotation and trading services. See **balance order; continuous net settlement (CNS); quotation; trade.**

Securities Investors Protection Act of 1970 legislation providing insurance to customers of securities companies, through creation of the SIPC. In the event of insolvency of a member securities company, the customer's cash and securities are protected up to a specified limit. See **broker-dealer; customer; securities.**

Securities Investors Protection Corporation (SIPC) a government-sponsored, non-profit organization that insures customer cash and securities on deposit with a member securities firm. SIPC was formed under provisions of the Securities Investors Protection Act of 1970. See **broker-dealer; customer; securities.**

securities log a document maintained in an Office of Supervisory Jurisdiction (OSJ), on which all customer transactions are recorded. It provides an audit trail and must be kept available for review by the broker-dealer, the state securities agency, or the Securities and Exchange Commission. See **broker-dealer; branch office manager; customer; Office of Supervisory Jurisdiction (OSJ).**

Securities Reform Act of 1975 legislation amending the Securities Exchange Act of 1934. It established rules for the control of securities of states and municipalities. The amendment also defined the scope and authority of the Municipal Securities Rulemaking Board (MSRB). See **Municipal Securities Rulemaking Board (MSRB); Securities Exchange Act of 1934.**

security (1) the investment objective sought by those desiring to maintain maximum protection of capital while minimizing the risk of loss.
(2) the tangible ownership in a security position, by way of either equity (stock) or debt (bond), evidenced by an instrument that is negotiable upon endorsement.
(3) the collateral for a loan, pledged for the repayment of principal. In the event of default, pledged assets can be seized by the lender. See **capital preservation; collateral; debt security; equity security; investment objective; negotiable instrument; tangible value.**

security dealer an individual who engages in transactions for his own account or for the account of his organization, specifically in investment securities. See **broker-dealer; dealer; trade.**

security districts geographic jurisdictions established by the National Association of Securities Dealers. Each of 13 districts is controlled by a committee in the district and by the NASD board of governors. See **board of governors; district business conduct committee (DBCC); National Association of Securities Dealers (NASD).**

security exchanges auction marketplace for the trading activities between buyers and sellers, through their brokers. A continuous trading market is maintained by the exchange system, consisting of 12 outlets: New York, American, Pacific, Midwest, Boston, Philadelphia, Detroit, Cincinnati, Spokane, National, Intermountain, and Honolulu. See **auction marketplace; broker; stock exchange.**

segmentation a financial planning term describing the analysis of a client's income and cash flow, each in separate segments. The purpose of segmentation is to structure the planning process in terms of both positioning and future cash flow. Each component of a segment is defined as to its purpose, risk level and objectives. See **assets; cash flow; financial planning; income; investment objective.**

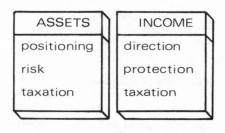

ASSETS	INCOME
positioning	direction
risk	protection
taxation	taxation

segmentation

segregated account a customer's fully paid securities in a cash account or excess margin in a margin account, which cannot be used by the broker-dealer in its business, or otherwise commingled with other funds. See **broker-dealer; commingled funds; customer; excess margin; SEC Rule 15c3-3.**

self-directed plan a qualified retirement plan such as a Keogh or individual retirement account (IRA), in which the owner is able to make a variety of investment decisions. Within the bounds set by the trustee, most self-directed plans may include as investments mutual funds, stocks, bonds, covered call options, and public syndications. Excluded are commodity futures contracts, naked options, and investments in tangibles. In retirement plans other than self-directed accounts, the owner cannot exercise control, as investment choices are limited to one product. See **Keogh plan; individual retirement account (IRA); qualified plan; retirement plans; trustee.**

Self-Employed Individual's Tax Retirement Act of 1962 known as bill HR-10, this legislation created provisions under which sole proprietors and individual general partners are allowed to establish and fund retirement plans. Named after the bill's originator, these are known as "Keogh" plans. See **general partner; Keogh plan; retirement plans; self-employment.**

self-employed retirement account a Keogh plan, established by an individual operating an active and profit-generating sole proprietorship or a general partnership. See **Keogh plan.**

self-employment the establishment and operation of one's own business, operated for profit. The self-employed individual is responsible for payment of income taxes, social security, insurance and all other benefits. As an employee, all or some of these benefits are provided by employers. The self-employed individual has the independence to earn an income at a level set by the market and personal effort, but does not enjoy benefits as do employees. See **proprietorship; tax basis.**

self-liquidating program an investment program intentionally designed for automatic return of capital at a known date in the future. A unit investment trust, for example, contains a finite portfolio of bonds with known maturity dates. A direct participation program can be structured with a definite date in the future when full liquidation of assets is promised. See **direct participation program; maturity date; unit investment trust.**

self-regulatory organization (SRO) an agency or organization whose purpose is to regulate an industry from within. The National Association of Securities Dealers (NASD) is an SRO for the members of the securities industry. See **Municipal Securities Rulemaking Board (MSRB); National Association of Securities Dealers (NASD).**

sell at best a market order instruction to obtain the highest available selling price in an over-the-counter transaction. See **market order; order ticket; over-the-counter (OTC).**

sell order an order given by a customer to a broker-dealer to liquidate a security on the market. See **customer; broker; day order; good til cancelled (GTC); limit order; month order; order ticket.**

sell-out procedures a seller's right to dispose of securities without notification to the purchaser, if the purchaser fails to accept delivery without good cause. See **good delivery; regular way; rejection.**

sell-plus   an instruction given as part of a limit or market order, to sell securities at a price higher than the last price transacted in the same security. See **limit order; market order; order ticket.**

sell stop order   a type of order that becomes a market order when a round lot is traded at or below a specified price. The order instructs the broker to sell as a market order at that time. See **at the market; market order; order ticket; round lot.**

sell the book   an instruction to sell as many shares as possible in a security, at the best available price. This type of order is used by institutional investors with substantial holdings in a security, or with margin credit adequate to meet requirements for significant volume in a short sale. See **institutional investor; short sale.**

seller take-back   an arrangement in the sale of a residence where the seller provides all or part of the buyer's financing, through first or second mortgages. See **mortgage; real estate.**

seller's option   a provision built into some contracts for the transaction of securities, allowing the seller to defer delivery for a specified number of days beyond regular way delivery. The option allows a delay between six and 60 days from the date of the transaction. See **delivery; regular way; settlement date.**

selling climax   description of a sudden and substantial drop in a security's market price, with a corresponding increase in volume. It is often characterized by break-away gaps in day-to-day market value. See **break-away gap; buying climax; technical analysis; volume.**

selling concession   that portion of the underwriting spread allowed to a selling group as compensation for placing shares or units of an offering with investors. See **commission; concession; offering; selling group; underwriting spread.**

selling dividends   the practice of soliciting orders for the purchase of mutual fund shares based upon an upcoming dividend payment or similar distribution. It is considered an unethical practice. See **dividend; mutual fund.**

selling group   one or more broker-dealers who have entered into an agreement with an underwriter to place all or part of an offering. The selling group acts in an agency capacity and does not assume any of the underwriter's liabilities in connection with the offering. See **broker-dealer; concession; underwriter.**

senior lien   a classification of mortgage, implying priority of claim against assets over junior liens. The term also is used in reference to bonds and, in some cases, to classes of preferred stock. See **bond; junior lien; mortgage; preferred stock; priority.**

senior preferred   also called prior preferred, a class of preferred stock, when more than one class is issued. The senior preferred class has a priority of claim over junior preferred classes. See **junior preferred; preferred stock; prior preferred.**

senior registered options principal (SROP)   an officer of a broker-dealer responsible for supervision and compliance of all option-trading activities. See **option; registered options principal (ROP).**

selling climax

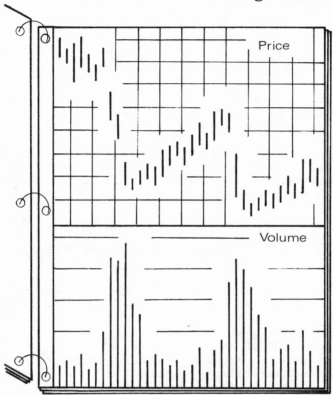

senior security   term applied to all debt and equity securities having priority of claim over common stock, including bonds and all classes of preferred stock. See **bond; common stock; preferred stock.**

separate account   arrangement established by contract in a variable annuity. A separate account may include the assets of other investors with similar variable annuity contracts, but may not be commingled with other funds of the issuer. See **commingled funds; variable annuity.**

serial bond   a type of bond issue with periodic, specified maturities of a portion of the total, rather than a single maturity date. See **bond; maturity date; municipal bond.**

series   a grouping of options of a single underlying security, identified by four characteristics: type of contract (call or put); expiration date; striking price; and underlying security. Also called an option series. See **expiration; strike price; option series; underlying security.**

Series 2   an exam administered by the NASD for the Securities and Exchange Commission (SEC), for those who are not NASD members, classified as SECO (Securities and Exchange Commission Organization) investment advisors. See **investment advisor; SECO member; Securities and Exchange Commission Organization (SECO).**

Series 3 the national commodity futures exam, administered by the NASD. It is a requirement of all commodity brokers. See **commodity broker; futures contract; national commodity futures license.**

Series 4 the registered options principal license, required for individuals supervising representatives trading in security options. The exam is administered by the NASD. See **option; registered options principal (ROP).**

Series 5 the interest rate options license administered by the NASD. It is a requirement for anyone marketing interest rate options in GNMA securities and other interest markets. See **Government National Mortgage Association (GNMA); interest.**

Series 6 the NASD license required of anyone engaging in the marketing of investment company products and variable contracts. See **investment company products/variable contracts limited representative; limited representative; mutual fund; unit investment trust; variable annuity.**

Series 7 the NASD license required of any individual selling stocks, bonds, direct participation programs or mutual funds. Not covered under the Series 7 license are commodities or interest rate options. See **general securities registered representative; registered representative.**

Series 8 the NASD license for branch office supervisors, who are not involved directly in sales of securities. See **limited principal general securities sales supervisor; supervision.**

Series 12 the branch office manager license, administered by the NASD, for individuals supervising an Office of Supervisory Jurisdiction (OSJ). See **branch office manager license; Office of Supervisory Jurisdiction (OSJ).**

Series 22 the direct participation programs registered representative license, allowing an individual (limited representative) to sell direct participation programs. The license is administered by the NASD. See **direct participation programs registered representative; limited representative; tax shelter.**

Series 24 an NASD license qualifying an individual to act as a general securities principal. This includes direct supervision of registered representatives in an Office of Supervisory Jurisdiction (OSJ). See **general securities principal; Office of Supervisory Jurisdiction (OSJ); registered representative.**

Series 26 an NASD license for individuals supervising limited representatives (Series 6), involved in the marketing of mutual funds, unit investment trusts and variable annuities. See **investment company products/variable contracts principal; mutual fund; unit investment trust; variable annuity.**

Series 27 an NASD license for the financial and operations principal. This individual is responsible for calculating a firm's net capital and filing of financial reports. See **financial and operations principal; net capital requirement.**

Series 39 the NASD license for a limited principal, allowing the holder to supervise Series 22 licensees in the marketing of direct participation programs. See **direct participation program.**

Series 52   a license of the Municipal Securities Rulemaking Board (MSRB), allowing the sale of municipal bonds. See **MSRB registered representative; Municipal Securities Rulemaking Board (MSRB).**

Series 53   license for the MSRB supervisory principal, the holder of which oversees selling activities of MSRB registered representatives. See **MSRB supervisory principal; Municipal Securities Rulemaking Board (MSRB).**

Series 54   a license allowing the computation of net capital and preparation of other financial reports concerning municipal bond business. See **MSRB financial principal; Municipal Securities Rulemaking Board (MSRB).**

Series 63   a license administered by the NASD for individuals selling securities in multiple states. Also known as the Uniform Securities Agent State Law Examination (USASLE), it does not take the place of a state's approval and permission to conduct business. See **blue-sky laws; Uniform Securities Agent State Law Examination (USASLE).**

series bond   a sequential issue of open-end mortgage bonds, with varying call prices, interest rates and maturities. See **bond; mortgage bond.**

Series E bond   savings bond issued by the U.S. Government between the 1940's and the end of 1979, offered at a discount and redeemable at face value after five years. See **bond; government bond; nonmarketable securities.**

Series EE bond   U.S. Government bonds issued at 50 percent discount. Interest rates vary with the rate of other government securities, and the holder has the option of paying tax on gains each year or upon redemption. See **bond; government bond.**

Series H bond   a face value government security that pays interest twice per year and is redeemable after 10 years. See **bond; government bond.**

Series HH bond   a government bond available only by exchange of a Series EE bond. Interest is taxed as earned, although tax on interest earned on a traded Series EE bond is deferred until sale of the HH bond. See **bond; government bond.**

settlement date   the date that securities are to be delivered to the purchaser, normally five working days from the transaction date. See **regular way; secondary market.**

severally and jointly   responsibility of each party to an agreement for the performance of all other parties. In an "eastern," or united type of underwriting, each syndicate member agrees to be collectively liable in the event one or more of the other members fails to place an allocated share of the offering. See **eastern account; syndicate; underwriter; united account.**

severally but not jointly   also referred to as a divided account, a form of underwriting in which each syndicate member agrees to be responsible for sale of a portion of the total offering. However, no one member will be held responsible for the failure of other members to sell their allocations. See **syndicate; underwriter; western account.**

share a portion of ownership in a corporation's equity, purchased by investors for dividend income and the expectation of an increase in market value. In publicly held corporations, the value of a company's share is set by market demand. See **authorized shares; corporation; equity.**

shared appreciation mortgage a home mortgage offering a below-market interest rate and low monthly payments. In exchange, the lender receives a portion of profits upon sale of the home at a later date. See **mortgage.**

shares outstanding the authorized shares of a corporation that are owned by investors and not held by the corporation itself. See **authorized shares; corporation; equity security.**

shareholder the holder of an equity interest in a corporation, with ownership via stock or units of equity. See **common stock; corporation; equity; preferred stock; stockholder.**

shareholders' equity that portion of total capitalization represented by equity ownership; the value of total shares issued and outstanding. See **capitalization; equity; issued and outstanding.**

shelf distribution the sale of securities by an affiliated person, who accumulated those securities under a provision of the original registration statement for resale to other investors. See **affiliated person; effective date; registration statement.**

shopping the street the practice of inquiring with market makers in the over-the-counter market to obtain price ranges. This establishes a negotiating range in a security. See **firm market; market maker; over-the-counter (OTC); quotation; subject market.**

short the status of owing money or securities to another. A short position in a security occurs when an investor has sold, with the obligation to close the position by buying the same security at a later date. See **closed position; long; open.**

short		
	Short	Long
open position	SELL	BUY
closing transaction	BUY	SELL

short against the box a strategy in which the investor holds a long and a short position at the same time and in the same security, without effecting a close of either position. A short sale is made while long in the same security. This strategy is used to defer a gain until the following tax year, or until it will qualify as a long-term capital gain. At the same time, being short against the box eliminates the chance of loss in a position, as the long and short offset one another. See **closed position; long; long-term capital gain; tax basis.**

short bond (1) a bond with a short period of time to go until maturity. The term may be relative to the entire duration of the issue, or may mean there is one year or less remaining in the bond's issue life.

(2) the status of a short sale involving a bond. See **bond; maturity date.**

short coupon (1) an initial coupon due date on a bond that is less than six months from the issue date. In this case, the first interest payment will be prorated for the short period.

(2) reference to a bond that will mature in one year or less, or in a period of time relatively short in terms of the issue's total duration (short bond). See **bond; coupon; issued date; maturity date.**

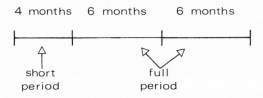

4 months   6 months   6 months

short
period

full
period

short coupon

short exempt an exemption to the rule requiring a short sale to be made at a price higher than the previous regular way transaction in the same security. Bona fide arbitrage transactions and those trades made to correct prior errors are executed under short exempt status. See **bona fide arbitrage; plus tick rule; regular way.**

short hedge a strategy that reduces or eliminates the risk of loss in a long position. It may involve establishing an offsetting short position, the purchase of put options, or the sale of call options. See **downside protection; hedge; option.**

short interest the collective open short positions in the stock market at a specified time. See **long; open; short.**

short interest theory the belief that changes in short interest are market indicators. The theory states that increases in short positions signal an upcoming demand for the security, as positions eventually must be purchased to close the shorts. Conversely, a decline in short positions in a security is considered a bearish signal. See **technical analysis.**

short market value (SMV) the current market value of security positions in a margin account in short status (sold short against equity of the account). See **long market value (LMV); margin account.**

short sale the sale of securities that creates an open position (as opposed to the sale of a long holding, which closes the position). In a short sale, there is a requirement that the same security be purchased at a later date to close the position. Short sellers believe that the price will decline and that they will be able to purchase (close) at a lower price. Short sales against the box are made to defer tax consequences of a profit, without the chance of price deterioration. See **closed position; open;** SEC **Rule 10a-1;** SEC **Rule 10b-4.**

short selling power the limit on securities that may be sold in a margin account under Regulation T of the Federal Reserve. See **initial margin; margin requirement; Regulation T.**

short straddle an option strategy involving the sale of a call and a put option with the same strike price and expiration date. This is a high-risk strategy in which the writer assumes the total premium income will exceed the potential losses from expiration. See **exercise; expiration date; option; straddle; writer.**

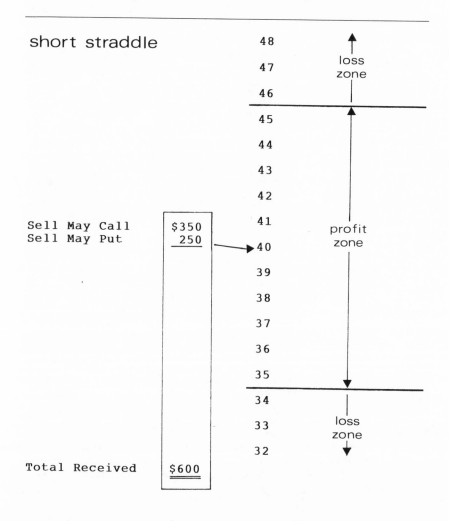

short-term (1) for capital assets, a holding period of six months or less. Assets bought and sold within the short-term period are subject to full taxation (of gains) or deduction (of losses).

(2) in debt financing, notes that are repayable in one year or less.

(3) accounting term for cash or assets convertible to cash (current assets), or liabilities due and payable (current liabilities) in one year or less. See **capital gain; capital loss; current assets; current liabilities; holding period; tax basis.**

short-term capital gain the profit resulting from a transaction involving a purchase and a sale of a capital asset within six months or less, or involving a short sale followed by a closing purchase, regardless of the time span. See **long-term capital gain.**

short-term capital loss the loss resulting from the purchase and sale of a capital asset, when the holding period is less than six months. See **long-term capital loss.**

short-term debt (1) liabilities or securities with one year or less until maturity or payment date.

(2) debt securities with a pending maturity that will arrive in a short period of time, relative to the total life of the issue. See **current liabilities; debt security; long-term debt; maturity date.**

silent partner an investor in a direct participation program who places capital with the general partners but has no rights to manage the business. See **direct participation program; limited partner; partnership.**

simple interest interest computed without compounding. Annual simple interest is computed as a one-time benefit based on the starting principal balance only. Compound interest is computed quarterly, monthly or daily and includes "interest on interest" over time, resulting in a higher actual yield rate. See **compound interest; interest; yield.**

---

simple interest

	8% interest	
	simple	compounded quarterly
Balance January 1	$ 100.00	$ 100.00
Interest:		
March 31	-0-	2.00
June 30	-0-	2.04
September 30	-0-	2.08
December 31	8.00	2.12
Balance December 31	$ 108.00	$ 108.24
Annual Interest Rate	8.00%	8.24%

simplified employee pension plan (SEP)   a form of retirement plan in which employers contribute in behalf of employees with three years or more service and aged 25 or older. The contributions may be based on the employer's net profits or on the employee's compensation. Upon termination, vested interests may be rolled over to an IRA, with continuing deferral of taxation. See **pension plan; profit-sharing plan; retirement plans.**

simultaneous transaction   a position taken in a security by a broker-dealer, after a customer has placed an identical order for the security. See **broker-dealer; riskless transaction.**

single purchase contract   an annuity contract in which the customer's obligation is satisfied by a lump-sum payment. In return, immediate or future periodic payments are made to the annuitant. A single purchase contract may be arranged for a fixed or a variable annuity. See **annuity; fixed annuity; variable annuity.**

sinking fund   a fund to which payments are made over a period of time, to accumulate a predetermined amount of money by a known date in the future.
Sinking funds are used as capital reserve accounts by corporations to redeem bonds to maturity in some cases, protecting investors against the risk of default and as an alternative to other means of retirement (such as payment from current earnings; refunding; or conversion).
The computation for sinking fund deposits is used also in the process of financial planning, when an investor desires a known sum of money at a future date, assuming a given rate of return. An amount of money is deposited at regular intervals to achieve the accumulation value of the fund by the established deadline. See **Moody's Investors Service; retirement (bond); Standard and Poor's Corporation.**

Small Business Administration (SBA)   a federal government agency supporting small businesses through counseling services and financial aid. The SBA issues bonds that are exempt from state and local tax to fund its lending programs. See **bond; debt security; financing.**

small business corporation   an S Corporation (previously known as a Subchapter S Corporation), a form of organization enjoying the limited liability of a corporation but taxed like a partnership. See **corporation; partnership; S Corporation; Subchapter S.**

social security   a federal government program designed to provide retirement, disability and health benefits to American workers and their families. The system has four major components:
a) retirement benefits—monthly income based upon earnings history, payable for life after reaching retirement age.
b) survivor's benefits—payable to dependents of workers who die.
c) disability benefits—for workers unable to work due to a long-term disability.
d) health benefits—also called Medicare, for retired or disabled workers. See **retirement plans.**

Society for Worldwide Interbank Finance Telecommunications (SWIFT)   a computer network coordinating international currency transfers and transmittal of financial data. See **financing.**

special arbitrage account   a margin account through which an investor buys and sells shares of the same security, taking advantage of price spreads in other markets. Margin requirements for this form of trading are different than for other margin accounts. See **arbitrage; margin account; Regulation T.**

special assessment bond   a type of bond for which the payment of principal and interest will be made from a special tax, assessed upon the beneficiaries of the facility to be constructed. This is popular for development of public utility and service programs. See **bond; debt service; municipal bond; special tax bond.**

special bid   a form of bid used by institutional investors, in which the potential buyer pays a special commission to the broker handling the bid. The seller will not be assessed a commission, and the bid must be made at a fixed price that is not lower than the latest sale or the current bid on the security. The special bid is used for transaction of large blocks. See **bid; block; commission; institutional investor; round lot; special offering.**

special bond account   a margin account providing favorable credit terms for the purchase of U.S. Government-sponsored bonds, municipal issues and selected corporate bonds. See **bond; exempt security; initial margin; margin account; Regulation T.**

special cash account   a customer trading account requiring settlement of trades within five working days from trade date (one working day for option transactions), commonly known simply as a cash account. See **regular way; Regulation T; settlement date; trade date.**

special commission   a fee paid by the seller in an exchange distribution. It is paid to participating member firms for their determination that an offering will or will not generate interest among buyers sufficient to justify its marketing. See **block; commission; exchange distribution.**

special convertible security account   a margin account set up expressly to transact in bonds that are either convertible to margin qualified stock, or include warrant or rights features for the purchase of margin stock. See **convertible security; margin account; rights; warrant.**

special miscellaneous account (SMA)   the amount of buying power represented in a customer's margin account, known as excess margin. Under Regulation T, the broker-dealer may limit use of the SMA. See **buying power; excess margin; margin account; Reg T excess; Regulation T.**

special offering   a form of offering used by institutional investors, in which the potential seller pays a special commission to the broker handling the offering. The buyer will not be assessed a commission and the offering must be made at a fixed price. It is used to transact large blocks. See **block; commission; institutional investor; offering; round lot; special bid.**

special omnibus account   a type of account in which one broker-dealer provides clearing services for the customers of another broker-dealer. Customer names are not disclosed, with all trades done in the name of the transaction-generating firm. See **broker-dealer; customer; Regulation T.**

special option an unexpired option offered for resale in the over-the-counter market, by an options broker. See **option; over-the-counter (OTC); secondary market.**

special situation description of a security that offers an unusual opportunity for investors, in the opinion of an analyst, firm or market advisory service. The opinion may be based on financial or technical information, and commonly indicates that the security currently is undervalued. See **fundamental analysis; investment advisor; technical analysis.**

special subscription account a margin account in which favorable credit terms are granted for the purchase of new issues and other margin securities. See **margin account; new issue; Regulation T.**

special tax bond a bond issue designed to repay principal and interest from a tax imposed for that sole purpose, also called a special assessment bond. See **bond; debt service; municipal bond; revenue bond.**

specialist an exchange member who acts as a broker in the execution of orders, and as a dealer by transacting for his own account. He maintains an orderly market in the limited securities with which he is involved, facilitating execution of odd-lot transactions. See **associate specialist; broker; dealer; odd lot; regular specialist.**

specialist block transaction the purchase of a block of stock by a specialist, for his own account or in behalf of an institutional investor. See **block; institutional investor; over-the-counter (OTC).**

specialist's book the record kept by specialists of orders placed with him for execution. The book may be in looseleaf or ledger form or consist of order ticket copies, or be kept on an automated system. See **book; order ticket.**

specialized company a mutual fund that specializes in investments of specific industries or groups of companies or products. See **investment company; mutual fund.**

speculation the taking of risks in an attempt to realize large short-term gains. As a rule, the greater the risk, the higher the chance for large gains or losses. Speculators are willing to risk a complete loss of capital in order to achieve gains, and the more rapidly profits are expected, the higher the risk level. See **investment objective; naked option; risk factor; short sale.**

spin-off an independent corporation, formed when a parent company distributes stock to the stockholders of a subsidiary. See **corporation; shareholder.**

split a change in the number of authorized shares in a corporation, undertaken upon stockholder approval and requiring an amendment to the corporate charter. The value of total outstanding stock does not change, but the number of such shares increases (in a split up) or decreases (in a split down). See **authorized shares; corporation; outstanding stock; par value; stockholder.**

split down a decrease in the number of authorized shares of a corporation. While outstanding shares are replaced with a fewer number, actual value remains the same. Stockholders surrender their certificates and receive fewer shares of higher value in return. See **authorized shares; outstanding stock; par value; reverse split; stockholder.**

split down		
	number of shares	
split	before split	after split
1 for 2	1,500	750
2 for 3	1,500	1,000
2 for 5	1,500	600

split offering (1) an offering that is simultaneously made as both a primary distribution and a secondary distribution.

(2) a bond issue with two parts: one established as a term bond and the other as a serial bond. See **bond; debt security; maturity date; municipal bond; offering; primary distribution; secondary distribution; serial bond; term bond.**

split rating descriptive of the quality rating given to corporations or to their securities, when two different rating services disagree on quality levels. See **corporation; rating systems.**

split up an increase in authorized shares of a corporation. While the number of outstanding shares is greater as the result of a split up, the actual dollar value remains the same. Stockholders surrender their certificates and receive more shares of lower value in return. See **authorized shares; outstanding stock; par value; stockholder.**

split up		
	number of shares	
split	before split	after split
2 for 1	1,200	2,400
3 for 1	1,200	3,600
3 for 2	1,200	1,800

Spokane Stock Exchange (SSE) 225 Peyton Building, Spokane WA 99201; one of the smaller of the regional stock exchanges, serving the Pacific Northwest. See **regional exchanges; stock exchange.**

sponsor an individual or firm, also called an underwriter and a wholesaler, depending upon the level of direct activity in relation to the marketing of an offering. The sponsor is responsible for the management of an investment program. See **direct participation program; mutual fund; underwriter; wholesaler.**

spot commodity commodity transaction resulting in payment and delivery of contracts, as opposed to a futures contract. In a futures investment, purchases and sales are made in the belief of a direction that values will change. A spot commodity results in actual delivery and payment of the commodity itself. See **cash contract; futures contract.**

spot secondary distribution a secondary distribution intended for immediate sale, that does not require a separate registration statement be filed with the Securities and Exchange Commission. See **registration statement; secondary distribution; Securities and Exchange Commission (SEC).**

spread (1) the bid less the offering price of a security.

(2) the amount of profit to the underwriter when selling securities to the public. The offering price is marked up from the amount paid by the issuer, creating the spread.

(3) a strategy involving the purchase and sale of options of the same underlying security, with the expectation of profits from changes in premium in either or both options.

(4) any strategy in which a purchase is offset by a sale, either in the same security or in securities that have related price movements or market reactions. See **bid; new issue; offering price; option; underwriter.**

spread load the fee structure of some contractual plan mutual funds, involving payment of sales charges over a period of years. The amount of sales charge that can be assessed in any one year is controlled, tied to a percentage of annual and cumulative contributions in the program. See **contractual plan; load; mutual fund; sales charge.**

spread option a combination strategy involving long positions in out-of-the-money calls and puts. Both sides of the transaction have the identical expiration date. The spread option investor will profit if movement in the underlying security is substantial enough to result in a profit in either the call or the put. See **combination; current market value (CMV); expiration date; option; out-of-the-money; underlying security.**

spread order a form of limit order used for option transactions. The investor specifies the difference in price (spread) between a long and short position, with a desire for execution at that spread, no matter at what premium the options are trading. See **limit order; option; underlying security.**

spread position reference to open positions in a customer's account when long and short options are held in the same underlying security. See **long; open; option; short; underlying security.**

stabilization the maintenance of a competitive bid price lower than current market value for a security. It is a legal form of manipulation allowed to syndicators to maintain interest in the aftermarket, so that members of the selling group will be able to place their allotted shares with investors. See **aftermarket; selling group; syndicate.**

staged payment a form of investing in a direct participation program in two or more installments. Each payment will be due on a specified date, commonly a year apart. The use of staged payments helps attract investors who may be unable or

spread option

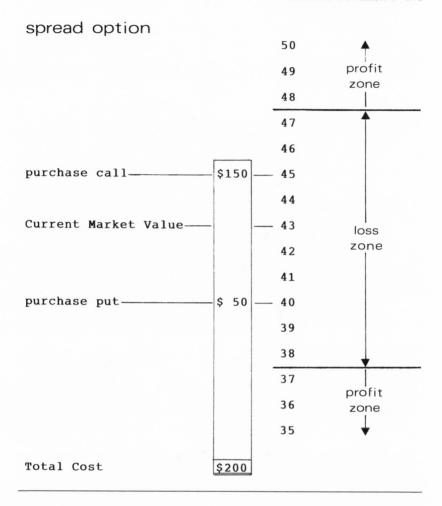

purchase call	$150
Current Market Value	
purchase put	$ 50
Total Cost	$200

unwilling to place a large sum of capital at one time. See **direct participation program; limited partnership; private placement; public offering.**

Standard and Poor's Corporation a registered investment advisory service that publishes ratings of corporate bonds, common stocks and preferred stocks, the blue list, and other investment and research services. See **blue list; corporate bond; rating systems.**

Standard and Poor's Index a popular index of market performance, watched by investors as an indicator of trends. The index includes the price movements of 500 widely traded industrial, transportation, financial and public utility stocks. See **averages; index; technical analysis.**

standard deviation a measurement of the price movement of a stock that establishes a norm for comparison to the rest of the market. See **BETA; technical analysis; volatility.**

statutory vote	cumulative vote
number of shares = number of notes for each candidate	number of shares x number of board candidates = total number of votes
number of votes applied for approval or rejection of each candidate	number of votes may be applied in any combination the share-holder desires

statutory vote

Standard and Poor's Corporation

highest quality	AAA	AA	A
medium quality	BBB	BB	B
lowest quality	CCC	CC	C
questionable value	DDD	DD	D

standby underwriter   an investment banker who agrees to purchase all shares of an offering that are not otherwise subscribed. The agreement specifies a price below subscription level, and will be executed following an offer to shareholders or rights holders. See **investment banker; rights offering; subscription privilege; underwriter.**

state securities agency   the regulatory department of a state government, responsible for the evaluation and approval of offerings and enforcement of state securities laws. See **blue-sky laws; compliance.**

statement of income   sometimes-used name for an income statement, a financial statement reporting a company's total sales, costs, expenses and net profits or losses. See **financial statement; fundamental analysis; income statement; profit and loss statement.**

statutory disqualification   suspension of an NASD member organization under terms of the agency's rules. See **member organization; National Association of Securities Dealers (NASD); self-regulatory organization (SRO).**

statutory underwriter   an individual or firm that involuntarily performs functions of an underwriter and, as a result, is subject to penalties under provisions of the Securities Act of 1933. See **due diligence; involuntary underwriter; Securities Act of 1933; underwriter.**

statutory vote   the most common form of voting privilege allowed to stockholders of a corporation, in which one vote per share is assigned in the selection of *each* board member. If five board members are being selected, each share is allowed to vote to accept or reject each of the five. See **corporation; cumulative vote; shareholder; voting privilege.**

stepped-up basis   the adjustment in basis of a limited partnership investment at the time of the owner's death, to be reflected in valuation of an estate, as provided in the Revenue Act of 1980. See **basis; estate tax; limited partnership; Revenue Act of 1980; tax basis.**

stock   the partial ownership of a corporation's equity resulting from contributed capital. Under the corporate form of organization, stock may be bought or sold without affecting the continuation of operations. See **common stock; corporation; issued and outstanding; preferred stock; treasury stock.**

stock split

	2 for 1 split up	original status	1 for 2 split down
number of shares	8 thousand	4 thousand	2 thousand
value per share	$10	$20	$40
total value	$80,000	$80,000	$80,000

stock ahead   the status of an unfilled order when other orders were executed at the same price. This occurs when others had priority over a particular broker, and a limited number of shares were available at the price. See **price; priority; round lot.**

stock certificate   a document identifying the registered owner, the security and the number of shares of stock owned. See **certificate; negotiability; street name.**

Stock Clearing Corporation (SCC)   an organization merged with the National Securities Clearing Corporation (NSCC) that is responsible for clearance of trades, handling of balance orders, and delivery and receipt of securities. See **balance order; clearance; National Securities Clearing Corporation (NSCC).**

stock dividend   a dividend paid in additional shares of stock rather than in cash. The dividend may be in the stock of the parent company or that of a subsidiary company. Stock dividends enable a corporation to provide a return on investment to its shareholders, without disbursing cash. There is no tax on a stock dividend until stock is sold. See **corporation; dividend; tax basis.**

stock exchange   the marketplace for the buying and selling of securities. Exchanges provide for the auction activities of daily trading and regulate their own members. See **auction marketplace; exchange; regional exchanges.**

stock power   a form used for assigning ownership of stock when it is inconvenient or impossible for owners to endorse the reverse of the stock certificate itself. The stock power transfers or assigns ownership, and the form is attached to the stock certificate. See **assignment; certificate.**

stock purchase warrant   a negotiable right to purchase shares of a corporation at a set price. These commonly are offered to existing shareholders when the same corporation issues additional shares, with the warrants given for a price lower than the public offering price. Warrants must be exercised prior to an expiration date. See **public offering price; rights; warrant.**

stock record   a brokerage's tracking system of all security positions, recording the beneficial owner of long positions and the location of all short positions. See **beneficial owner; brokerage house.**

stock record department   the back office department in a brokerage firm responsible for recording and tracking all security positions. See **back office; beneficial owner; brokerage house.**

stock split   a change in the number of shares of a corporation, without changing the actual dollar value of total shares. In a split up, the number of shares is increased. For example, four thousand shares valued at $20 per share can be split 2 for 1 (eight thousand shares valued at $10 per share). In a split down, the number of shares is reduced. Four thousand shares valued at $20 can be split 1 for 2, resulting in two thousand shares valued at $40 each. See **split down; split up.**

stockholder   the owner of a portion of net worth in a corporation, represented by ownership of shares of stock. A stockholder has certain rights: to vote, receive dividends and inspect corporate books. While the term "shareholder" is used to describe the same holder of stock, there is a subtle distinction. A shareholder does not always have the same rights, owning a share of equity rather than a specific

straddle

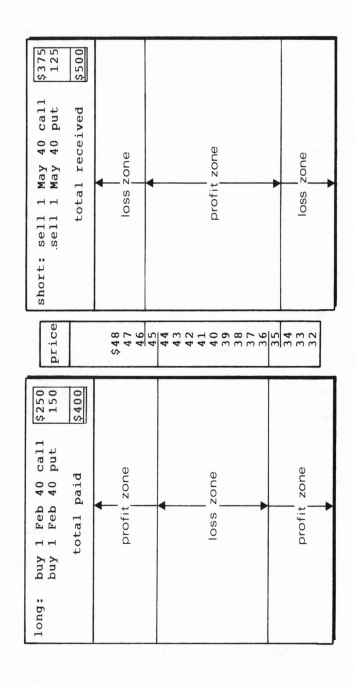

long:	buy 1 Feb 40 call	$250
	buy 1 Feb 40 put	150
	total paid	$400

short:	sell 1 May 40 call	$375
	.sell 1 May 40 put	125
	total received	$500

| price |
| $48 |
| 47 |
| 46 |
| 45 |
| 44 |
| 43 |
| 42 |
| 41 |
| 40 |
| 39 |
| 38 |
| 37 |
| 36 |
| 35 |
| 34 |
| 33 |
| 32 |

profit zone

loss zone

profit zone

loss zone

profit zone

loss zone

number of shares of stock (such as a limited partner or investor in a real estate investment trust). See **limited partner; shareholder.**

stockholder of record the registered owner of shares as shown on the books of the issuing corporation. This distinction is made for the purpose of paying dividends or requesting votes from stockholders. See **corporation; issuer; registrar.**

stockholders' equity a corporation's net value to its investors, consisting of total assets less total liabilities. See **assets; corporation; liabilities; shareholders' equity; net worth.**

stop-limit order a form of stop order that becomes a limit order once the specified "stop" has occurred. An example of such an order is "buy 100 XRX 43 stop 45 limit." This translates to a limit order to buy 100 shares at $45 per share, but only after the security has sold at or above $43 per share. A stop-limit order may be entered for sales as well. See **limit order; order ticket; stop order.**

stop-loss order an order to sell a security at the market once a specified price is reached or passed. It may be used by an investor showing a profit and desiring to sell only if the market begins to deteriorate for that security. It will cut losses if the price begins to decline, protecting paper profits. See **at the market; limit order; market order; order ticket; paper profit/loss.**

stop order an order to buy above (or sell below) a specified price, if reached. Upon the security's attaining or passing the "stop" level, this becomes a market order. See **market order; order ticket.**

stop-out price the lowest accepted price in a Treasury securities auction. To obtain a day's average price, the stop-out price and the highest price are used. See **auction marketplace; price.**

stopped stock the freezing of a price that will be paid for a security. Getting such a guarantee allows the seller to seek a better price without losing the commitment from a potential buyer who has stopped the price. See **market price; marketability; price.**

straddle an option strategy involving the purchase or sale of contracts with identical expiration prices and times. A long straddle is one in which calls and puts are purchased; a short straddle is the selling of call and put contracts. See **expiration date; long straddle; option; short straddle.**

straight-line depreciation a method of depreciation in which the asset is written off in equal amounts each year. Under rules of the Economic Recovery Tax Act of 1981 (ERTA), new depreciation periods were established, called the accelerated cost recovery system (ACRS). The straight-line options were amended under provisions of the Tax Reform Act of 1984, adjusting most real property from a 15-year class life to 18 years. Under ACRS rules, straight-line depreciation can be elected for all assets in a class life. See **accelerated cost recovery system (ACRS); accelerated depreciation; class life; depreciation; Economic Recovery Tax Act of 1981 (ERTA); Tax Reform Act of 1984.**

strap a bullish extension of a long straddle involving conventional options. Two calls and one put are bought on the same underlying security, with identical expiration dates and strike prices. The total premium is lower than it would be to

straight-line depreciation

Period	3 years	5 years	10 years
Asset Value	$ 6,000	$ 9,000	$ 15,000
Year 1	$ 2,000	$ 1,800	$ 1,500
Year 2	2,000	1,800	1,500
Year 3	2,000	1,800	1,500
Year 4	-0-	1,800	1,500
Year 5	-0-	1,800	1,500
Year 6	-0-	-0-	1,500
Year 7	-0-	-0-	1,500
Year 8	-0-	-0-	1,500
Year 9	-0-	-0-	1,500
Year 10	-0-	-0-	1,500

purchase each contract separately. A similar strategy involves buying two puts and one call (strip option). A strap is bullish because, with two calls, an upward price movement in the stock will produce more profits than a downward movement. See **conventional option; expiration date; long straddle; premium; strike price; strip option; underlying security.**

strap

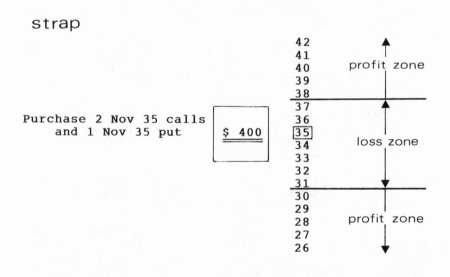

Purchase 2 Nov 35 calls and 1 Nov 35 put — $ 400

strategy a preplanned method of operation involving the timing and nature of investments, taking into account the level of risk one is willing to take, the desired return, and the investment objective. See **investment objective; return; risk.**

street   originally a reference to securities companies in the vicinity of Wall Street, the term applies today to the entire financial industry. See **securities.**

street book   a record kept by futures clearing members of each commodity trade. It includes identification of the trader, date, price, quantity and the commodity traded. See **clearing member; commodity; futures contract.**

street name   reference to the registration of securities in the name of an NASD member firm, in behalf of the beneficial owner.

Member firms with securities registered in street name are required to furnish information to owners as received from the issuing corporation, including financial statements; proxy materials; and annual reports.

Registration under street name allows investors to hold securities without needing to protect certificates, which are negotiable and may be lost. Protection for street name-registered securities is provided by SIPC insurance held by the member firm. See **beneficial owner; National Association of Securities Dealers (NASD); Securities Investors Protection Corporation (SIPC).**

strike price   the price of an underlying security upon which option contracts are issued. A "February 45" call is an option to buy 100 shares at the strike price of $45 per share, by the February expiration date. A "May 25" put option grants the right to sell 100 shares at the strike price of $25 per share, by the May expiration date. Every option includes a strike price, the measure of a contract's market value. See **expiration date; in the money; option; out of the money; premium; underlying security.**

strike price interval   the interval between available option contract strike prices. For stocks selling up to $100 per share, this interval commonly is five dollars. Above $100, the interval is expanded to $10. In cases of a split, there will be a temporary split-basis strike interval less than the usual spread. See **exercise price; option; premium; split; underlying security.**

strip option   a bearish extension of a long straddle involving conventional options. Two puts and one call are bought on the same underlying security, with identical expiration dates and strike prices. The total premium is lower than it would be to purchase each contract separately. A similar strategy involves the purchase of two calls and one put (a strap). The strip option is bearish because, with two puts, a downward movement in the stock will produce more profits than an upward movement. See **conventional option; expiration date; long straddle; premium; strap; strike price; underlying security.**

Student Loan Marketing Association (SLMA)   an organization that issues bonds to finance loans to students or universities. "Sallie Mae" bonds are backed by the full faith and credit of the U.S. Government. See **bond; Sallie Mae.**

Subchapter M   Internal Revenue Code section setting rules for the operation of mutual funds, real estate investment trusts (REITs), and other organizations passing through to investors all profits (the conduit theory), thus paying no income tax at the organization level. See **conduit theory; investment company; mutual fund; real estate investment trust (REIT).**

Subchapter S   Internal Revenue Code section governing S Corporations, those with a limited number of shareholders, electing to be taxed as a partnership (each shareholder is taxed for his or her share of profits each year), but legally conducting

strip option

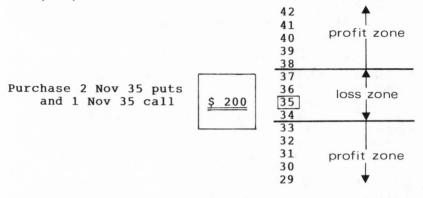

Purchase 2 Nov 35 puts and 1 Nov 35 call — $ 200

```
42
41
40    profit zone
39
38
37
36    loss zone
35
34
33
32
31    profit zone
30
29
```

business as a corporation, with limited liability and continuity of operations. See **corporation; partnership; S Corporation; small business corporation.**

Subchapter S Revision Act of 1982 legislation revising rules for S Corporations and their shareholders. The law moved the S Corporation closer to partnership rules and farther away from corporate rules for the computation and payment of taxes. See **corporation; S Corporation; small business corporation.**

subject market a quotation that cannot be accepted by a market maker or broker, pending acceptance by the customer being represented in the transaction. See **broker; market maker; quotation.**

subordination (1) condition of a debt that is to be repaid only after another, senior debt has been satisfied.
(2) interests of sponsors in direct participation programs, especially oil and gas ventures, that are not accrued or paid until limited partners have received a specified return, or until other conditions have been met. See **debt security; direct participation program; limited partner; oil and gas; priority; senior lien; sponsor.**

subscription privilege the right of common stockholders to purchase new issues of a company's stock. In some cases, preferred stock or convertible bonds may carry subscription privileges as well. The privilege must be exercised within a stated period of time, usually one or two months. See **common stock; rights; stock purchase warrant.**

subscription ratio the relationship between the number of shares existing prior to a new subscription, and the number of new shares offered. This ratio is used to determine the number of rights existing stockholders will accrue. See **common stock; new issue; stock.**

subscription right a stockholder's right to purchase shares of a new issue, in proportion to the number of shares they own. The right must be exercised in one or two months in most circumstances and extends to the purchase of common shares. See **common stock; rights; stockholder.**

subscription warrant   a form of security granted to investors, with features similar to both rights and options. See **option; rights; warrant.**

substantial net capital   a requirement placed upon members of the New York Stock Exchange (NYSE), that a healthy financial condition must be maintained. See **financial statement; New York Stock Exchange (NYSE).**

substantive interest   the actual controlling interests that determine the course of major decisions made by stockholders of a corporation. The individual or block of stockholders with this interest have a high degree of control over the decisions made by the entire body of stockholders or by directors. See **board of directors; corporation; stockholder; voting privilege.**

substitution   (1) replacement of one security with another in a margin account. The transaction has no major effect on the status of the margin.
(2) the appointment of one individual with another, to act in the same capacity. In securities transactions, a broker, attorney or other person acting as agent may be allowed a power of substitution for some actions. See **margin account; proceeds sale.**

suitability   the determination that an investor possesses the minimum qualifications to participate in an investment program. The question applies to all investments but is of particular concern in direct participation programs, especially private programs; option or commodity trading; short selling; margin trading; and highly speculative, risky or complicated strategies. Suitability may involve knowledge and experience, available cash balances, total net worth or the individual's tax bracket. See **commodity; direct participation program; net worth; option; private placement; risk; speculation; tax bracket.**

summary complaint proceedings   a procedure allowed by the National Association of Securities Dealers (NASD) under provisions of the Code of Procedure. The Business Conduct Committee of the NASD may allow a member who is in violation of the rules of fair practice to admit guilt to a minor infraction. By doing so, he or she waives all rights to appeal, and agrees to a maximum fine of $1,000 and censure. See **Business Conduct Committee; Code of Procedure; National Association of Securities Dealers (NASD); rules of fair practice.**

super-restricted rule   a provision applied to margin accounts when there is a substantial disparity between equity and collateral (primarily when equity is 30 percent or less than total collateral). See **collateral; equity; margin account.**

supervision   the responsibility of a broker-dealer to oversee the actions of its registered representatives. Supervision is required to the extent that the broker-dealer is liable for all infractions committed, even those by a remote branch office, of which it should have been aware. The broker-dealer is required to conduct periodic audits, notify branch offices of policies and procedures, enforce all regulations and rules that apply to operations, and produce a compliance manual, all as part of its supervisory duties. See **branch office audit; broker-dealer; compliance manual; registered representative; rules of fair practice.**

support level   the price of a security that represents the lowest range that the market will allow it to reach. A technical analyst assumes that at the support level, buyers will perceive the security to be a bargain. Subsequent interest will then

support level

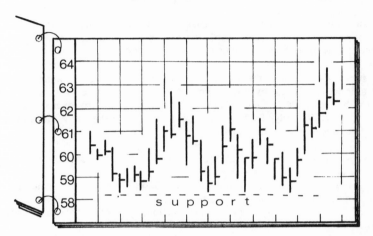

maintain or increase the security's market price. See **chartist; market price; resistance level; technical analysis.**

suspense account (1) on a broker-dealer's books, a record used to record unreconciled balances temporarily, pending resolution and reassignment.

(2) an accounting term for the recording of a transaction that will be reversed and recorded within a short period of time. See **broker-dealer; customer.**

swap fund (1) a closed-end mutual fund allowing investors to exchange securities for their shares, without having to recognize a capital gain or pay a tax. As of 1967, no new swap funds have been allowed to form.

(2) partnerships that allow investors to purchase units with other securities in place of cash. Under current tax laws, the investor is not allowed to defer capital gains in such a swap. The exchange of one security and purchase of units in the partnership are considered as two separate transactions. See **closed-end; direct participation program; limited partnership; mutual fund; tax deferral.**

swap order type of order to purchase one security and sell another at the same time. For some types of securities, the single order must be executed completely or not at all. For other securities and under the policies of some broker-dealers, the swap order must be treated as two separate orders. See **contingent order; proceeds sale; switch order.**

sweetener the addition of a privilege or other feature that makes the purchase of a security especially attractive, such as a conversion privilege, stock purchase warrants, or other subscription rights. See **conversion; stock purchase warrant; subscription right.**

switch order type of order that includes a buy and a sale of different securities at the same time, also called a contingent order, swap order or proceeds sale. See **contingent order; proceeds sale; substitution; swap order.**

switching (1) a mutual fund strategy involving the exchange of holdings in one fund for another, often within one family of funds. Proponents of the strategy claim that higher yields can be achieved if switching is executed with an understanding of current economic conditions.

(2) reference to the exchange of holdings in a portfolio for other securities of similar value. See **family of funds; mutual fund; portfolio; strategy.**

syndicate investment bankers who agree to raise capital to purchase the securities of an issuer. Also referred to as an underwriter, the syndicate works with the selling group to market shares or units of the issue at a fixed price. See **investment banker; issuer; selling group; underwriter.**

Syndicate

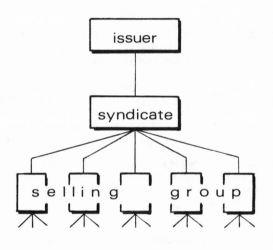

investors

syndicate management the range of responsibilities that are to be performed while an offering is being marketed by a syndicate. These duties include organization of a selling group, allocation of the issue, and financial reporting. See **issuer; selling group; underwriter.**

syndication fee a cost of selling a syndicated offering. Such costs must be treated as capital costs, and may not be deducted by the limited partners in the year spent. Fees include concessions paid to sell units and other selling costs. See **capital expenditure; concession; limited partner; tax basis.**

synthetic put a form of unlisted security. A broker-dealer sells short a security and, at the same time purchases one call for every 100 shares. This combined transaction creates a position that is then held by the customer as a synthetic put. See **broker-dealer; short sale; unlisted security.**

synthetic stock   an option position that places the investor in a situation that is viewed as equivalent to taking a position in the stock itself. If the investor is long a call and short a put, the position is synthetic long stock. Being short a call and long a put is synthetic short stock. See **long; option; short.**

T

take-out   (1) the commitment made by a lender to finance a GNMA short-term loan and issue long-term loans in its place.

(2) the amount by which a customer's portfolio is reduced when sales exceed purchases in a series of transactions.

(3) a trader's purchase of a portion of a customer's holdings or the holdings of another seller. See **Government National Mortgage Association (GNMA); long-term debt; short-term debt; trader.**

take-over   the purchase of one company by another. The price offered for shares or equity may exceed current market value to make the offer attractive to current shareholders. See **market value; merger; proxy fight.**

tandem plan   the Government National Mortgage Association's practice of buying mortgages for a price above market value and then selling them through the Federal National Mortgage Association. The practice accepts a limited loss in order to subsidize selected regions or projects. See **Federal National Mortgage Association (FNMA); Government National Mortgage Association (GNMA); mortgage pool.**

tangible drilling costs   costs in an oil and gas program that are treated as capital expenditures and must be depreciated rather than taken as deductions in the year that funds are expended. Included are property and equipment used to complete wells. See **capital expenditure; oil and gas.**

tangible value   the value of assets that is limited to physical worth, without regard for market value. For example, a company's book value represents the total amount of tangible assets, less liabilities. An offer may be made to purchase a company for an amount above book value, with the difference representing the desirability, market value, or goodwill of the company—intangibles. See **assets; book value; fundamental analysis; liabilities; market value.**

target benefit pension plan   a type of plan that is a hybrid between money purchase and defined benefit plans. See **defined benefit pension plan; money purchase plan; retirement plans.**

target company   a company that is the subject of take-over interest by another company. Upon acquiring five percent or more of the subject company's stock, the acquiring company is required to file notification of its intentions with the Securities and Exchange Commission (SEC). See **corporation; merger; Securities and Exchange Commission (SEC); take-over.**

tax-advantaged investment   a term used to describe tax shelters, programs offering investors favorable tax treatment. This may include unusually high deductions relative to the amount invested, exemption of income from tax, or substantial tax credits. See **direct participation program; limited partnership; private placement; public offering.**

tax anticipation bill (TAB) a short-term security issued by the United States with maturities occurring within a few days to one week after the due date of a large tax receipt (such as the filing deadline for corporate returns). Corporations with taxes due may purchase the bills at a discount and tender them at face value, with full credit. The result is equivalent to receiving several days of free interest on funds. See **debt security; short-term debt.**

tax anticipation note (TAN) a note sold to equalize revenues of municipalities, to be repaid from known tax receipts due on a specific date. Maturity may either be an exact date, or tied to the indefinite time of receipt of tax revenues. TAN's usually hold first claim against these receipts and commonly are issued at a discount. See **municipal note; note; short-term debt.**

tax basis (1) the basis in real estate, represented by the adjusted purchase price plus cost adjustments and less subsequent depreciation.
    (2) the cost of securities, including commissions paid. For computation of capital gains, the basis is subtracted from the net sales price.
    (3) the value of an asset for tax purposes. It may be different than actual market value if costs or expenses are included that cannot be taken into account when computing the amount of gain or loss. See **adjusted basis; capital gain; depreciation; real estate.**

tax basis

Purchase Price	$85,000
Plus: Closing Costs	4,200
Original Basis	$89,200
Plus: Additions	25,000
Less: Depreciation	(56,800)
Tax Basis	$57,400

tax bracket the rate at which the last dollars of income in a year are taxed. Not all income is taxed at the bracket rate (also called the "marginal tax rate"). Once a plateau of taxable income is reached, all additional dollars earned are subject to the bracket rate, up to the next bracket plateau. See **income; net income.**

tax deferral the postponement of tax on income. Tax shelters provide heavy deductions in the early years of a program, but taxable income in later years. Income is deferred through contributions to a qualified plan, so that upon retirement income will be taxed at a lower bracket rate. For cash-basis businesses, receiving income in a future period or paying expenses early are forms of deferral. See **cash basis; deferral; qualified plan; phantom income.**

tax district bond   a bond issued for a specific purpose served by a municipality, but not necessarily restricted to one city or county. School bonds are one example. The tax district may extend beyond the borders of an issuing city or county. See **general obligation bond (GO); municipal bond.**

Tax Equity and Fiscal Responsibility Act of 1982 (TEFRA)   legislation including several rules affecting investors, attempting to restrict the growth of abusive tax shelters. The sponsor of a shelter is subject to penalties for making false statements about the tax advantages of a program, or over-valuing property bought and sold by the program. The penalty is set at the lesser of $1,000 or 10 percent of the gross income generated through the program. See **direct participation program; limited partnership; private placement; public offering.**

tax-exempt fund   a mutual fund that invests solely in municipal bonds. Income from such a fund is free of income tax on the federal level and, in many cases, from state and local taxes as well. See **bond fund; investment company; mutual fund.**

Tax-Exempt Investor Program (TEIP)   a direct participation program designed especially for investors seeking high current income that will not be taxed in the current year. This category includes IRA, Keogh and other qualified plans. See **direct participation program; individual retirement account (IRA); Keogh plan; qualified plan.**

tax-exempt security   municipal securities that are not taxed at the federal level. Some municipal securities are exempt from local and state taxes as well. See **municipal bond; municipal note.**

tax-free rollover   the transfer of funds in a qualified pension or profit-sharing plan, into an IRA rollover account. If the transfer is completed within 60 days from the distribution, there is no tax on the proceeds. It is deferred until eventual withdrawal upon retirement. See **IRA rollover; pension plan; profit-sharing plan; qualified plan.**

tax loss carry-forward   a provision allowing losses to be claimed in years following the occurrence of loss. It comes up in two ways. First, when a limit applies to deductions in one year (capital loss limits for individuals, for example). Second, when a loss or credit has been applied to previous years (carried back), and remaining losses are then carried forward to future periods (operating business losses, for example). See **capital loss; carry-over; losses.**

tax loss to investment ratio   the "write-off" or ratio used by promoters of tax shelters, to explain the tax advantages of a program. In theory, the amount invested costs nothing if the ratio is 2 to 1 or better and the investor is in the 50% bracket. For every $100 invested, $200 of tax write-offs are estimated (in the 50% bracket, $200 of tax deduction produces $100 of liability reduction). See **direct participation program; phantom income; tax shelter.**

tax-managed trust   a mutual fund that has elected to be taxed as a corporation. Under this mode 85 percent of dividends received would be exempt from federal income tax (for domestic dividends). There is no distribution to shareholders, and

ratio	tax loss per $100	50% bracket tax savings per $100
1 to 1	$100	$ 50
1.2 to 1	$120	60
1.4 to 1	$140	70
1.6 to 1	$160	80
1.8 to 1	$180	90
2 to 1	$200	100
3 to 1	$300	150

tax loss to investment ratio

dividends are thus converted to long-term capital gains. A tax-managed trust may be penalized by the accumulated earnings tax. See **accumulated earnings tax; capital gain; dividend.**

tax preference a type of deduction that, when claimed, gives the investor special benefits. As a result, a tax is applied beyond the usual tax rate. Such items include the amount of depreciation above straight-line rates, capital gains on certain types of property, intangible drilling costs, and the investment tax credit (ITC). See **accumulated depreciation; capital gain; depletion; intangible drilling costs; investment tax credit (ITC); preference income.**

tax put a strategy used by investors holding stock currently valued below its purchase price. Stock is sold and a loss claimed in the current year. At the same time, a put is sold, so that the loss on stock is recaptured by the premium. The strategy produces one of three results: (a) the value of the stock rises above strike price before expiration and the option expires worthless; (b) the value of stock rises and the investor buys the put to close the position at a profit; or (c) the value of stock remains below exercise and the investor must perform on the contract, buying back the stock. In all three cases, the investor keeps the premium from selling the option, recapturing all or part of the loss on stock. See **in the money; option; strike price; tax basis.**

Tax Reform Act of 1969 tax legislation that eliminated many advantages to investors in certain types of programs. Major provisions included establishment of minimum tax limits and depreciation recapture rules. See **alternative minimum tax; depreciation; minimum tax; recapture.**

Tax Reform Act of 1976 legislation making significant changes in tax shelter rules. Under provisions of this act, an investor may claim deductions only to the extent "at risk" — money actually paid or pledged to the program. See **at risk; direct participation program; limited partnership; nonrecourse loan; recourse loan.**

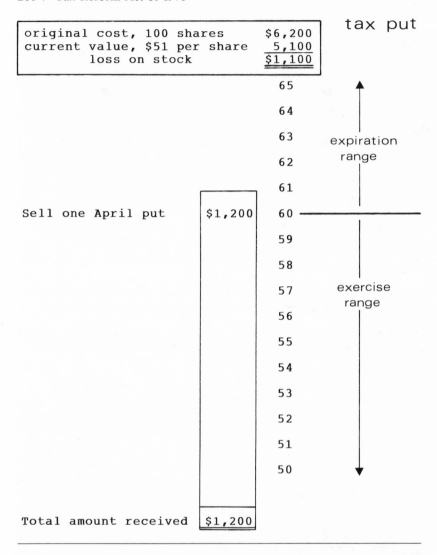

tax put

original cost, 100 shares	$6,200
current value, $51 per share	5,100
loss on stock	$1,100

Sell one April put $1,200

65
64
63   expiration range
62
61
60
59
58
57   exercise range
56
55
54
53
52
51
50

Total amount received $1,200

Tax Reform Act of 1978 tax law adjusting rules for investors in tax shelters. The act had the intention of restricting the benefit of making investments only for tax reasons. Real estate programs were exempted from many provisions of the act. See **at risk; direct participation program; limited partnership; real estate.**

Tax Reform Act of 1984 legislation bringing about major changes in rules for depreciation and capital gains, business use of automobiles, taxation of interest-free loans, and reporting rules for tax shelters. See **capital gain; depreciation; interest-free loan.**

tax shelter (1) a legitimate investment to defer income to a later period, such as a qualified retirement plan; or to produce income that is free of income tax, such as a tax-free municipal bond.

(2) a program designed to produce high deductions immediately, so that overall tax liability is reduced.

(3) an abusive program emphasizing tax benefits but containing little or no economic substance.

(4) term applied generally to all direct participation programs where some portion of income is offset by deductions. See **deferral; direct participation program; limited partnership; municipal bond; qualified plan; retirement plans.**

tax stop a provision included in a lease agreement for real property, under which property tax increases result in increased tenant payments. This protects the lessor from having to absorb the additional cost. See **real estate; tenant.**

tax straddle a transaction undertaken to cancel a current year's short-term capital gain, and create a long-term gain in the following year. It involved taking a loss in a commodity futures contract to offset another short-term profit, with the anticipation of a long-term gain in the following year. This strategy was eliminated by the requirement that the second part of the strategy is to be undertaken, under provisions of the Economic Recovery Tax Act of 1981. See **Economic Recovery Tax Act of 1981 (ERTA); futures contract; short-term capital gain; straddle.**

tax umbrella a reference to a corporation's ability to carry forward current losses to offset future profits. See **corporation; losses.**

teaser a clause in an adjustable rate mortgage (ARM) contract, offering an attractively low rate for the first one-to-two years, but which is reversed following the initial period. See **adjustable rate mortgage (ARM); real estate.**

technical analysis a method of forecasting price movements of securities and of the market, based upon factors such as investor mood, historical actions and reactions, trends, chart patterns, supply and demand, and volume. The method contrasts with fundamental analysis, the study of purely financial information. See **Dow Theory; fundamental analysis.**

technical indicator a measure of market activity used to determine and forecast near-term movement in individual issues, industry groups, or the market in general. See **advance-decline index; breadth of the market; new issue; short interest; volume.**

technical position status of the market. If securities are oversold, the technical position is strong. If an overbought condition prevails, it is a weak position. See **overbought/oversold.**

technical rally an increase in securities prices resulting from internal conditions rather than from true supply and demand. Such conditions may include factors such as chart trends and volume. See **rally; volume.**

technician one who practices technical analysis, depending upon trends in volume and price movement, economic and political factors, and investor sentiment to forecast the near-term future. See **chartist; technical analysis.**

ten percent guideline a general standard for comparing issues of municipal securities. It presumes that the total of bond issues outstanding should not be greater than ten percent of the value of real estate in the area. See **market value; municipal bond; real estate.**

ten-year averaging   provision of the tax law allowing special treatment of distributions from qualified retirement plans. A tax is computed and paid as though the distribution was received over a ten-year period, thus subject to a lower overall rate of tax. See **lump-sum distribution; qualified plan; retirement plans; tax basis.**

ten-year property   a class life under the accelerated cost recovery system (ACRS) that dictates a 10-year recovery period for railroad tank cars, residential mobile homes, and other assets. The class life includes straight-line recovery options of 10, 25 and 35 years. See **accelerated cost recovery system (ACRS); class life; depreciation.**

tenant   (1) physical occupant of a unit in a rental property.
(2) part owner in a security account or of an individual security. See **joint tenancy; joint tenants with rights of survivorship (JTWROS); real estate.**

tenants by the entireties   used in some states as another term for the status of accounts known more commonly as joint tenants with rights of survivorship (JTWROS). See **joint tenants with rights of survivorship (JTWROS).**

tenants in common   a form of ownership involving two or more individuals. Each holds title separately and may sell his portion of assets. Upon death, the owned portion passes to the individual's estate rather than to other tenants. See **joint tenancy; unity of possession.**

tender offer   a public notification of intention to purchase shares in another company. A tender offer is made at a fixed price that may be higher than current market value. See **market value; merger; SEC Rule 10b-6; take-over.**

Tennessee Valley Authority (TVA)   an agency sponsored by the U.S. Government, formed in 1933. It issues bonds to fund power projects in the Tennessee River area. See **agency bond; government bond.**

term bond   long-term bond with a single maturity date, as opposed to serial maturities. See **long-term debt; maturity date; serial bond.**

term certificate   a certificate of deposit with a maturity of five years or less, paying interest twice per year. See **certificate of deposit (CD); money market instrument.**

term loan   a commercial bank loan that is granted for a defined period of time, and with a specified repayment date. See **commercial bank.**

term repo   a repurchase agreement that is granted for a period of time greater than the standard overnight arrangement. See **repurchase agreement.**

terms   the specific contractual arrangements for a securities transaction, including price and size of the transaction. For option trading, terms also include the strike price and expiration date. See **expiration date; option; premium; price; strike price.**

testamentary trust   a form of trust that becomes effective upon the death of its creator. It appoints an institution or a person to administer a specified sum and in a specified manner, for the benefit of heirs. See **fiduciary; living trust; trust.**

theoretical value

$$\frac{\text{Market Price of Existing Stock} \quad \text{Less} \quad \text{Subscription Price of New Stock}}{1 + \text{Rights required to subscribe one share}} = \text{Theoritical Value}$$

theoretical value a value developed from a computed model, when no exact or tangible value can be determined otherwise. The term applies to options and spreads, and especially to rights. See **cum rights; new issue; option; rights; spread; subscription right.**

thin market a condition in a single issue, industry group or the entire market which lacks liquidity. This may be due to a small number of available shares, or a lack of buyer interest. See **liquidity.**

third market a term describing trading activity in listed securities, transacted by brokers and dealers in the over-the-counter (OTC) market. See **broker; dealer; listed company; over-the-counter (OTC).**

third party account a customer account that is held in the name of someone other than the actual owner. This arrangement is not a power of attorney, and is prohibited in the securities industry. See **customer; power of attorney.**

three-year property a class life of property under the accelerated cost recovery system (ACRS), specifying a three-year recovery period for autos and trucks, machinery and equipment. The class includes optional straight-line recovery periods of three, five or 12 years. See **accelerated cost recovery system (ACRS); class life; depreciation; recovery period.**

thrift institution an institution offering interest-bearing accounts to customers, including savings and loans and savings banks. See **institution; savings and loan association; savings bank.**

ticker symbol an abbreviation for a security's full name, used to transact buy and sell orders and developed for the convenience of all involved in recording trades. See **issue; securities.**

ticker tape the report of volume and prices of securities on a particular exchange, displayed shortly after each trade is executed. Few of today's displays are actually tape. Most are automated and are reported by way of a digital read-out. See **price; securities; volume.**

time deposit a type of bank deposit in which a minimum amount is left with the institution for a fixed term. In exchange, a fixed rate of interest is promised and paid that is higher than the prevailing rate for a conventional savings account. See **bank; commercial bank; interest; savings bank.**

time draft   a draft that cannot be converted to cash until the date on the draft, which may be issued in a post-dated form. See **draft.**

time order   a type of security that is to be executed at a specified time during the trading day. At the point specified, it becomes a market or a limit order. See **limit order; market order; order ticket.**

time spread   a synonym for calendar spread, a strategy involving transactions in options of the same underlying security, but with different expiration dates. See **calendar spread; diagonal spread; expiration date; horizontal spread; option; spread; underlying security.**

time value   that portion of an option's current premium above intrinsic (tangible) value. It is either the entire premium (when out of the money) or the amount of premium greater than the amount equal to the in-the-money value. As the expiration date draws near, time value evaporates from the option. See **expiration date; in the money; intrinsic value; option; out of the money; premium; tangible value.**

time value

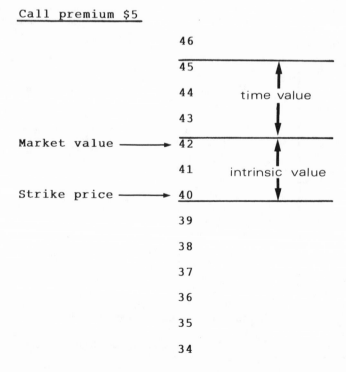

Call premium $5

46

45

44   time value

43

Market value ——▶ 42

41   intrinsic value

Strike price ——▶ 40

39

38

37

36

35

34

time value of money   one of two factors affecting the actual rate of return that an investor may earn. The other factor, interest, will compound over time to increase the overall rate earned. See **interest; present value; rate of return.**

time value of money

$2,000 at 8%	interest	base earned rate	time value rate
one year	$160.00	8.00%	8.00%
two years	172.80	8.64	8.32
three years	186.62	9.33	8.66
four years	201.55	10.08	9.01
five years	217.68	10.88	9.39

time value premium   that portion of an option's premium above intrinsic value. The premium is broken down into two parts: intrinsic value, if any, is the point-for-point value that an option is in the money with the underlying security. The balance is time value premium. See **intrinsic value; option; time value.**

tip   advice given to an investor or speculator to enter into a transaction. The information is based upon information not available to the general public, or upon rumors supposedly coming from an insider, someone in the position to have information that will affect the market value of a security. See **inside information.**

tombstone ad   an advertisement announcing the particulars of a new issue, including name, underwriter, total dollar amount, and a reference to the prospectus or offering circular. See **advertising; new issue; offering circular; prospectus; underwriter.**

top-heavy plan   a pension or profit-sharing plan in which a majority of the contributions are made for, or benefits are paid to, key employees. This category includes officers, stockholder-employees with five percent or more of total stock (including their family members), and the most highly compensated employees of the organization. See **pension plan; profit-sharing plan; retirement plans.**

total capitalization   total long-term debt, par value of common and preferred stock, and retained earnings of a corporation. "Total" capitalization refers to funding from both debt and equity sources. See **capitalization; common stock; funded debt; par value; preferred stock.**

total return   (1) the computed yield on an investment that takes into consideration both the current earnings and capital gains. It may also involve an additional factor, the tax savings from sheltered income and long-term gain rates.

(2) a comparative computation for writers of covered calls, that includes income from premiums received from the write, dividends on the underlying security, and capital gains on the total transaction. See **capital gain; covered option; option; premium; rate of return; underlying security; yield to maturity.**

---

total return

Sale of stock (100 shares, $40 per share)	$4,000
Basis (100 shares, $34 per share)	(3,400)
Capital Gain (15.0%)	$ 600
Premium for Oct 40 call (10.0%)	400
Dividend received (1.5%)	60
Total return (26.5%)	$1,060

---

track record the historical record of a sponsor's performance in the past, included in the prospectus or offering circular of a direct participation program. See **direct participation program; offering circular; prospectus; sponsor.**

trade a buy or sell of a security, either to establish a position that is long or short (open), or to offset an existing position (close) in a customer's account. See **close; long; open; position; short.**

trade date the date a trade order is executed, which precedes payment and delivery (settlement) by five working days for most stock transactions, or by one day for option transactions. See **delivery; payment date; regular way; settlement date.**

trader one who enters into securities transactions for his own account (a dealer) or for the account of a customer (a broker), or as an employee of a company engaged in the business of buying and selling securities. See **broker; dealer; SEC Rule 11a.**

trading at discount the purchase of bonds at a value lower than face value. If held to maturity date, the total yield includes the difference between face value and discounted price, as well as interest income received. See **bond; discount bond; face value; maturity date.**

trading authorization permission that is given by a customer to a broker-dealer to enter into transactions in an account. The authorization gives the power of attorney to act in the customer's behalf. See **broker-dealer; customer; fiduciary; power of attorney.**

trading on equity the act of raising capital by issuing bonds. This form of leverage may be undertaken to increase working capital, but also raises debt service and interest expense. It is profitable only when the influx of capital increases net profits above the cost of repaying the bonds that have been issued. See **capitalization; funded debt; leverage; return on equity.**

transfer (1) the act of moving securities from one owner to another and, in the process, recording on the corporation's records the new owner's registration.

(2) replacement of one limited partner with another in a direct participation program, when units are sold. This action requires an amendment to the certificate of limited partnership. See **certificate of limited partnership; direct participation program; limited partner; registrar; street name.**

transfer agent the appointed individual or firm (often a commercial bank) responsible for recording registered ownership of securities, as well as completion of documents for changes in ownership, cancellation and reissuance of certificates. See **certificate; commercial bank; corporation; issuer; registrar; shareholder.**

Treasury bill a U.S. Government security issued with a maturity between 90 days and one year. They are issued at a discount, yielding a return based upon the holding period rather than a stated amount of interest. See **debt security; short-term debt; tax anticipation bill (TAB).**

Treasury bond a U.S. Government security issued with a maturity between five and 35 years. They pay a fixed rate of interest and may trade above or below face value. See **debt security; discount; face value; interest; long-term debt; premium.**

Treasury certificate a U.S. Government security no longer available to the public, issued with maturity between six and 12 months. They are used today for the temporary investment of funds being moved between the Federal Reserve and member banks. See **certificate of indebtedness; commercial bank; Federal Reserve Board (FRB); short-term debt.**

Treasury note a U.S. Government security issued with maturity between one and 10 years. They pay a fixed rate of interest and may trade above or below face value. See **debt security; discount; face value; interest; long-term debt; premium.**

treasury stock stock that is authorized and issued and, subsequently, reacquired by the issuing corporation. While held as treasury stock, no dividends are earned and no voting privilege is allowed. The stock may be reissued, retired, or held indefinitely by the corporation. A company profits from buying back its own stock in two ways: reduction of dividend payments, and appreciation in cases where the market price rises while stock is held. See **authorized shares; dividend; issued and outstanding; market price; outstanding stock; voting privilege.**

triangle description of price movements of securities, used by chartists to explain price levels at certain points, and to predict as a technical point the timing and likelihood of future price movement patterns. See **chartist; technical analysis.**

triple exemption the status of a municipal bond allowing its holder tax-free status from federal, state and local taxes. Most municipal issues are exempt in the state where issued, and would thus provide triple exemption to buyers in that state. See **municipal bond; tax basis.**

true investment yield ratio a financial ratio comparing net income to net worth rather than to gross sales. It is based on the premise that the real return should be based on total equity placed into the corporation, rather than upon the volume of

triangle

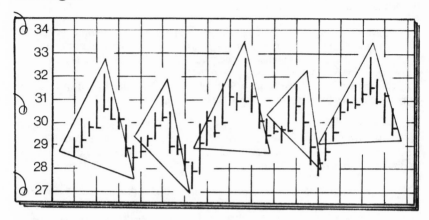

sales with varying markups and market conditions in effect. See **combined ratios; fundamental analysis; ratios.**

$$\frac{Net\ Income}{Net\ Worth} = Ratio$$

$$\frac{\$426,800}{\$8,206,300} = 5.2\%$$

true investment yield ratio

trust   an entity established for the caretaking of assets. The trust's creator appoints a trustee to manage assets for the benefit of another person or group of people. Trusts may be created and operated during the creator's lifetime (living trusts) or to take effect upon the creator's death (testamentary trusts). See **Clifford trust; fiduciary; living trust; revocable trust; testamentary trust.**

Trust Indenture Act of 1939   a federal law establishing standards for the issuance of corporate bonds. It specifies that issues exceeding $1 million must be made under an indenture, and that the indenture must include pertinent information: maturity date, total amount being issued, rate of interest and method of repayment. See **corporate bond; debt security; indenture.**

trustee   an individual or firm (such as a commercial bank) appointed to carry out the terms of a trust, including investing in securities specified or limited by the trust's terms, and to disburse the trust's proceeds at the proper time. See **commercial bank; fiduciary.**

turnaround (1) the improvement of cash flow, yield, market value or profits in a limited partnership. The term is used in real estate programs to describe an improvement in management of a property.

(2) a change in strategy. A day trade turnaround is the buying and selling of securities that change positions in a short period of time.

(3) a complete change in an individual's investment objective, accompanied by a repositioning of assets in a portfolio.

(4) the reversal from a loss posture to a profitable one. In analysis of corporate performance, a profitable period that follows one or more loss periods is called a turnaround. See **day trade; investment objective; limited partnership; real estate; strategy.**

turnover (1) the frequency with which inventory is replaced, on average, involving one of two computations: the comparison of costs of goods sold to average inventory (real turnover) or to sales (traditional turnover).

(2) usage of assets in operations, to determine trends and effective utilization.

(3) of working capital (current assets less current liabilities), used as a test of the effective application of available cash and of the use of short-term financing. See **fundamental analysis; inventory turnover; short-term debt; working capital.**

$$\frac{\text{Cost of Goods Sold}}{\text{Average Inventory}} = \text{Turnover}$$

$$\frac{\$6,420,100}{\$1,949,600} = 3.29 \text{ to } 1$$

turnover

turnover rate (1) a measure of volume in a security, industry group, or stock exchange, or the holdings of an institutional investor. Total traded shares are compared to the total shares available to develop the rate.

(2) the frequency with which inventory or other assets are replaced or utilized by the organization. See **institutional investor; inventory turnover; volume.**

20-day period the time between a registration's filing with the Securities and Exchange Commission (SEC) and the effective date of the offering. During this time (called the cooling-off period), the SEC examines the registration statement, then approves, rejects, or extends the time until effective date, if needed. See **cooling-off period; effective date; registration statement; Securities and Exchange Commission (SEC).**

$$\frac{\text{Shares Traded}}{\text{Total Listed Shares}} = \text{Turnover Rate}$$

$$\frac{2,350,000}{162,400,000} = 1.45\%$$

turnover rate

25 percent rule a general standard used in comparing and rating municipal bonds. Under this standard, the total of bonds outstanding should not be greater than 25 percent of the municipality's yearly budget. See **debt security; municipal bond.**

20 percent cushion rule a general standard used in comparing and rating municipal revenue bonds. Under this standard, anticipated revenues should be 20 percent or more above the combined costs and expenses of the facility and debt service of the bond. See **debt security; municipal bond; revenue bond.**

two-dollar broker a broker who will complete orders for other brokers in their absence or at times of heavy volume and workload. See **broker; New York Stock Exchange (NYSE).**

200-day moving average a method used by some technical analysts to chart the movement of a security's price over a 200-day period. Each day's movement reflects an average for the last 200 days. The belief is that use of this larger base gives a more dependable trend than shorter periods or daily charting. See **chartist; technical analysis.**

U

U-4 an application that must be completed by all individuals desiring to operate as registered representatives in affiliation with a broker-dealer. The form must be completed prior to taking a securities examination for the first time, and again upon affiliation with a new broker-dealer. It asks for compliance and legal history and previous affiliations. The U-4 is filled out and signed by the applicant and submitted to the broker-dealer. Upon review, the broker-dealer forwards the U-4 to the National Association of Securities Dealers (NASD) and the state securities agencies in which the person seeks registration. See **broker-dealer; National Association of Securities Dealers (NASD); registered representative; state securities agency.**

200-day moving average

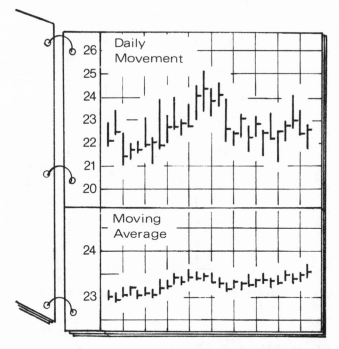

U-5 an application that must be completed by a broker-dealer when a registered representative is terminated. It is sent to the National Association of Securities Dealers (NASD) and applicable state securities agencies. See **broker-dealer; National Association of Securities Dealers (NASD); registered representative; state securities agency.**

uncovered option (1) an open short position in one or more call option contracts, when shares of the underlying security are not held. As each call option represents 100 shares of stock, an option is considered uncovered whenever it is sold to open a position, and the seller owns less than 100 shares per contract. An uncovered option is said to have an unlimited liability or loss potential, as the market price of the underlying security may rise indefinitely.

(2) the opening sale of a put option contract, regardless of the seller's holdings in the underlying security. An uncovered put has a limited loss potential, because the maximum downward movement of the stock can go only to zero. See **covered option; naked option; open; option; short; underlying security; write.**

underlying commodity the commodity against which a futures contract is written. See **commodity; futures contract.**

underlying security the security that is subject to purchase or sale under the terms of an option contract. A call option grants its buyer the right to purchase 100 shares of the underlying security, at the specified strike price. A put option grants its buyer the right to sell 100 shares of the underlying security at the specified strike price. Option writers (sellers) give these rights to other investors in exchange for the premium they receive. See **call; option; premium; put; strike price.**

uncovered option

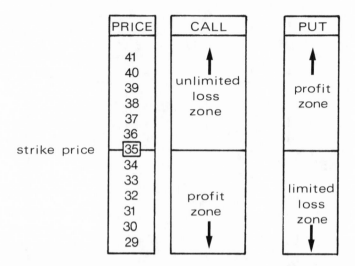

undervalued security   description of a security that is believed to be selling at a price below its current fair value. This opinion may be based on earnings history, the movement of an industry group, the price-earnings ratio (P/E), recent or historical movement of the security itself, or the opinion of the analyst. See **auction marketplace; fair value; market value; price-earnings ratio (P/E).**

underwriter   generally, any person or company who purchases an issuer's securities for the purpose of resale. An underwriter — also called an investment banker — may form a selling group to sell shares or units to investors. In some types of programs, the underwriter is also called the wholesaler or sponsor. See **investment banker; issuer; SEC Rule 10b-6; selling group; sponsor; wholesaler.**

underwriting spread   the profit an underwriter realizes through mark-up of an issue; the public offering price, less the price paid by the underwriter to the issuer. See **gross profit; issuer; public offering price.**

undivided interest   description of an ownership share in property in which investors hold a portion of the total, but not an identified section or part of the property itself. A form of "tenants in common" registration, it is common to direct participation limited partnerships. See **direct participation program; limited partnership; tenants in common.**

Uniform Gift to Minors Act (UGMA)   a law in effect in all states, which simplifies the procedure under which a minor may own property. A UGMA account has features similar to a trust, without the need for formal trust arrangements or legal documents. See **beneficial owner; custodian; minor; trust.**

Uniform Limited Partnership Act (ULPA)   the law that standardizes the rules for formation and operation of a limited partnership. See **certificate of limited partnership; direct participation program; limited partnership; partnership.**

Uniform Partnership Act (UPA) a law regulating general partnership and joint venture operations, and defining business organizations that qualify as partnerships. See **general partnership; joint venture; partnership.**

Uniform Practice Code (UPC) a series of rules set forth by the National Association of Securities Dealers (NASD) for securities transactions, settlement and delivery. Provisions are enforced and disputes settled by a committee in each NASD district. See **board of governors; clearance; delivery; execution; good delivery; National Association of Securities Dealers (NASD); settlement date.**

uniform practice committee a committee of an NASD District that enforces and interprets the Uniform Practice Code (UPC). See **board of governors; National Association of Securities Dealers (NASD).**

uniform securities agent state law examination (USASLE) a securities examination that qualifies a registered representative to meet a state's criteria to transact securities business. It is applicable in those states that do not recognize the general securities registered representative exam in and of itself to qualify for registration. See **registered representative; Series 63.**

unincorporated association an organization operating with two or more members that are not formed as a corporation. Included are some charitable or tax-exempt organizations, and partnerships. See **corporation; partnership.**

unissued stock authorized stock of a corporation that has never been issued (as opposed to treasury stock, which has been issued and repurchased). Unissued stock must be kept on hand to honor rights or warrants that are outstanding and may be exercised. See **authorized shares; rights; stock; treasury stock; warrant.**

unit (1) ownership in a direct participation program. The partnership offers a specific number of units, each with an initial dollar value. Holdings of units represent the investor's equity in the program.
(2) a combination sale involving two or more types of securities, such as shares with warrants or rights, or bonds with warrants.
(3) descriptive of exchange specialists who, collectively, are responsible for a fair and orderly market in an individual security, industry grouping, or other grouping of securities. See **direct participation program; partnership; rights; specialist; warrant.**

unit investment trust (1) a fixed trust that purchases a portfolio of securities identified before investors place their money. Earnings are distributed periodically, and proceeds returned as each bond matures. A common form is the tax-free trust, investing only in municipal bonds.
(2) a contractual plan mutual fund, also known as a participating trust. See **contractual plan; fixed trust; municipal bond; mutual fund; Investment Company Act of 1940; participating trust; trust.**

unit of trade the minimum acceptable trading quantity of a security transaction, also known as a round lot. Investors transacting less than an acceptable unit (an odd lot) are penalized a differential in the price paid. See **differential; odd lot; round lot.**

unit refund annuity a form of annuity contract under which periodic payments are made to the annuitant while still living. It has some of the same characteristics as a joint and survivor annuity, in which payments are made as long as the survivor lives. But a unit refund annuity includes the provision that if, upon the death of the annuitant, the total of payments made is less than the amount of original purchase, the balance will be paid in one lump sum to the beneficiary. See **annuity; beneficiary; joint and survivor annuity; life annuity.**

united account also called an eastern account, a syndicate arrangement for municipal bonds and other offerings, in which all participants in the underwriting have equal liability for unsold portions of the total. Even when individual members fulfill their commitment to place a portion, they are severally and jointly responsible with the other members for all unsold portions. The less common western account holds each member responsible only for the allocated share of the total underwriting. See **eastern account; municipal bond; severally and jointly; underwriter; western account.**

United States Government Securities Treasury bills, bonds and notes, and series bonds issued by the federal government and its agencies. See **government bond; Series E bond; Series EE bond; Series H bond; Series HH bond; Treasury bill; Treasury bond; Treasury note.**

unity of ownership descriptive of the status of two or more owners in a joint tenancy account, each having equal rights to the property held. See **joint tenancy; tenants in common.**

unity of possession descriptive of the rights to properties held by two or more owners, to take possession of or to occupy an entire property held in joint tenancy. See **joint tenancy; tenancy in common.**

unlisted security a security that is not listed on an exchange, either because the company's financial strength, profits, or number of shareholders do not qualify for a listing, or because a listing has not been sought. See **exchange; over-the-counter (OTC).**

unlisted trading privileges privileges granted to trade a security on an exchange that is not listed. The New York Stock Exchange does not trade any unlisted securities. For other exchanges, permission must be granted by the Securities and Exchange Commission (SEC), and disclosure made to the public. See **listed stock; New York Stock Exchange (NYSE); over-the-counter (OTC); Securities and Exchange Commission (SEC).**

unsecured debt a debt that is not backed by any collateral, based only upon the credit and reputation of the issuer. See **collateral; commercial paper; debenture; debt security; note; secured debt.**

up-and-out option a grouping of 10 or more puts, sold in the over-the-counter (OTC) market. They have the same features as a standard put contract, with one exception: if the price of the underlying security rises above a specified level prior to expiration, the contract is cancelled immediately (out). See **expiration; option; over-the-counter (OTC); put; underlying security.**

uptick a price higher than the preceding round lot price for the same security. See **downtick; plus tick; short sale.**

user leaseback   a transaction in which an owner sells real property and subsequently leases the same property from the buyer for a business purpose. See **equipment leasing; real property.**

U.S. savings bond   a form of debt security issued by the U.S. Government. First seen in 1935 to counteract federal deficits, they were used later to provide funding for wartime production. See **debt security; Series E bond; Series H bond.**

V

value   a determination of an investment's potential for future growth and income (measured by the price-earnings ratio, for example), versus the risks involved. The more risk, the greater the potential for future profits. Value is distinguished from price by the addition of the risk-reward factor. See **price; price-earnings ratio (P/E); risk.**

Value Line   abbreviated title of Value Line Investment Survey, the most widely distributed independent investment service for serious investors. The service provides a thorough fundamental and technical analysis of 1,700 common stocks. Offered since 1935, it provides rankings for timeliness and for safety, a history of earnings and dividends, other financial information, narratives about prospects for future price movement, projections, and price charts. The service also ranks industries and individual stocks by several classifications, and offers a separate service for options and convertible securities. See **convertible security; fundamental analysis; option; rating systems; technical analysis.**

variable annuity   a contract issued by a life insurance company that will pay the annuitant a periodic benefit that is not fixed. It is based upon the investment experience in a portfolio rather than upon a fixed and guaranteed level of payment. See **annuity; fixed annuity.**

variable hedge   a strategy involving loaded offsetting positions (other than one to one), used commonly in option trading. Positions may be long or short. Example: buy three May 65 calls and sell one May 60 call. See **hedge; long hedge; option; short hedge.**

variable limit margin   a performance deposit required when commodity trading limits are increased. See **commodity.**

variable rate mortgage   also called an adjustable rate mortgage (ARM) or flexible rate mortgage, a contract in which the interest rate is modified periodically, based upon an independent index of rates (such as the CPI or a rate for Treasury securities). See **adjustable rate mortgage (ARM); flexible rate mortgage; mortgage; real estate.**

venture capital   money invested in risky or unproven businesses, often in return for partial ownership in the organization that is financed. The high risk venture capitalists take also offers the potential for substantial profits. See **capitalization; risk.**

variable hedge

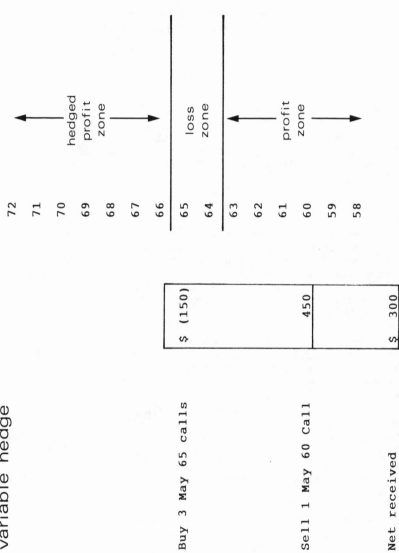

Buy 3 May 65 calls	$ (150)	
Sell 1 May 60 Call	450	
Net received	$ 300	

72
71
70 ← hedged profit zone →
69
68
67
66
─────
65 loss zone
64
─────
63 ← profit zone →
62
61
60
59
58

vertical line chart   a popular method of reporting a security's price movements. A vertical line reports the day's trading range from high to low, and a horizontal line shows the day's closing price. See **chartist; technical analysis.**

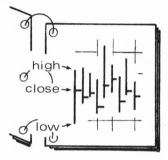

vertical line chart

vertical spread   an option strategy that includes the purchase and sale of options in the same security, and with identical expiration dates, but with different strike prices. See **bear spread; bull spread; horizontal spread.**

vesting methods   the specific methods under which participants in a profit sharing or pension plan achieve vestation. Contributions are made in behalf of each employee and accumulate to their benefit. However, ownership of the accumulated asset is achieved over time, as an incentive to remain with the employer for many years. (Note: voluntary contributions are treated separately, and are 100% vested.)

Under provisions of the Employee Retirement Income Security Act (ERISA), all qualified employees must be at least 50% vested after the tenth year of service, and 100% vested after the 15th year.

Full vesting recognizes the entire accumulation after the tenth year, with no partial vestation until that time.

Graded vesting starts at a given percentage after a number of years, and an additional percentage thereafter. Example: 25% after the fifth year; an additional five percent for the next five years; and an additional ten percent for the next five years.

The Rule of 45 is a method that begins to vest when the employee's age, plus years of service add up to the number 45. Example: 50% when the number 45 is reached, followed by an additional ten percent vesting each year following. See **Employee Retirement Income Security Act (ERISA); full vesting; graded vesting; pension plan; Pension Reform Act of 1974; profit-sharing plan; retirement plans; rule of 45.**

visible supply   the total amount of new issues of municipal bonds that will be available to investors within the next 30 days, used as a measurement of available investments versus the market interest in such securities. See **municipal bond.**

volatility   a measure of price movement in a security, industry group, or the entire market. The standard deviation of a security is the most common measurement of volatility, while BETA is a relative guideline of a security's reaction to the price movements of the market in general. See **BETA; standard deviation.**

volume   the number of shares traded during a period of time. Daily volume of the entire market indicates investor interest, and periodic comparisons point to trends

vertical spread

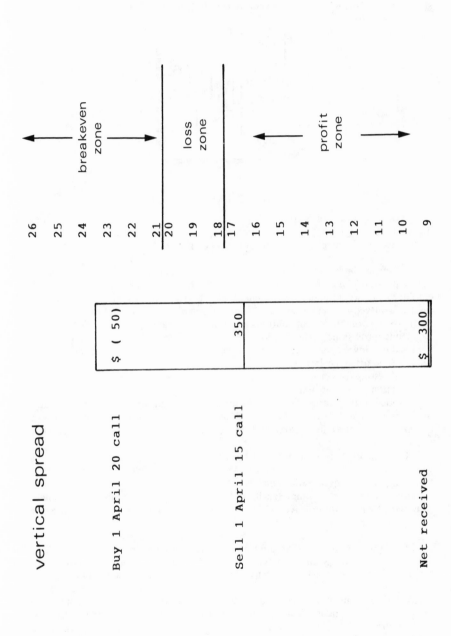

Buy 1 April 20 call	$ (50)
Sell 1 April 15 call	350
Net received	$ 300

breakeven zone

loss zone

profit zone

26
25
24
23
22
21
20
19
18
17
16
15
14
13
12
11
10
9

vesting methods

Employee Age	Years of Service	Accumulated Contributions ($5,000 per year)	Base vested amount		
			Full Vesting	Graded Vesting	Rule of 45
34	1	$ 5,000	$ -0-	$ -0-	$ -0-
35	2	10,000	-0-	-0-	-0-
36	3	15,000	-0-	-0-	-0-
37	4	20,000	-0-	-0-	-0-
38	5	25,000	-0-	6,250	15,000
39	6	30,000	-0-	9,000	21,000
40	7	35,000	-0-	12,250	28,000
41	8	40,000	-0-	16,000	36,000
42	9	45,000	-0-	20,250	45,000
43	10	50,000	50,000	25,000	55,000
44	11	55,000	55,000	33,000	60,000
45	12	60,000	60,000	42,000	65,000
46	13	65,000	65,000	52,000	70,000
47	14	70,000	70,000	63,000	70,000
48	15	75,000	75,000	75,000	75,000

$$\frac{\text{annual high} - \text{annual low}}{\text{annual low}} = \text{volatility}$$

high	low	volatility
44	37	18.9%
61	58	5.2
26	14	85.7%

volatility

that are used by technical analysts to forecast near-future movements. Market-wide volume is measured in millions of shares. Volume in individual securities — measured in thousands or hundreds — is watched for similar trends or to anticipate price movements. See **technical analysis.**

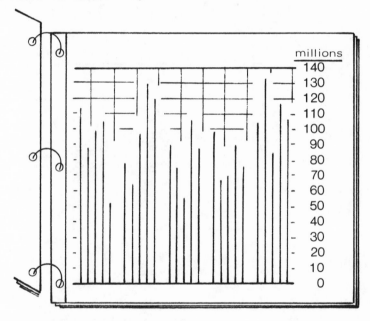

volume

voluntary accumulation program   investment in a mutual fund where the investor can deposit funds at varying times and in varying amounts, without any variation in the percentage of sales load. See **load mutual fund; mutual fund; no-load (NL).**

voluntary association   an unincorporated business that has features of corporations and of partnerships. Like a corporation, it has a continuity of operations even when members leave and are replaced. And like a partnership, there is an unlimited liability to the members. See **corporation; partnership.**

voluntary employee's beneficiary association (VEBA) a trust established to fund benefits to employees, such as life and health insurance. Contributions to the trust, if qualified as necessary business expenses, are deductible to the employer. See **tax basis; trust.**

voluntary underwriter a person or company who purchases securities from an issuer and resells them to the public, when those securities are registered and have been assigned an effective date; the opposite of a statutory, or involuntary underwriter. See **effective date; involuntary underwriter; registration statement; statutory underwriter; underwriter.**

voting privilege the privilege of shareholders with voting classes of stock to participate in decisions of the corporation, including election of a board of directors, and questions of mergers, acquisitions, and major capitalization decisions. See **corporation; proxy; shareholder.**

voting rights the distinction of voting privileges of shareholders, the common forms being statutory (one vote for each share) and cumulative (one vote for each share, multiplied by the number of directors to be selected). See **cumulative vote; statutory vote.**

voting trust a trust established (usually with a commercial bank) to hold shares, formed by a group of shareholders desiring to take control of a corporation. The trust results from a successful proxy contest, in response to poor operating results or management practices. See **proxy contest.**

voting trust certificate (VTC) a receipt given to shareholders who deposit their shares with a voting trust. They retain all rights and privileges except their voting rights. These are surrendered for the life of the trust. See **shareholder.**

W

warehousing the illegal sale of a security under an agreement to repurchase it at a later date and for a specified price. See **manipulation.**

warrant a security issued directly by a corporation to induce investors to purchase, offering the privilege of subscribing to additional shares at a specified price. Warrants may or may not have an expiration date, and rise in value as the price of the underlying security rises. See **option; subscription right; subscription warrant; underlying security.**

wash sale the sale and repurchase of the same security within 30 days. Losses resulting from a transaction that is reversed within the 30-day period are disallowed for tax purposes. See **short-term capital loss; tax basis.**

wash trading activity in the market that creates the appearance of buying and selling when, in fact, the trader's positions are not changed. The practice is forbidden under terms of the Securities Exchange Act of 1934. See **manipulation; Securities Exchange Act of 1934; trade.**

wasting assets assets that are depleted by extraction; a natural resource. See **depletion; oil and gas.**

watered stock the condition of stock in a corporation when additional stock is issued without a corresponding capital contribution. It has the effect of reducing the value of existing shares of the company. See **dilution; issued and outstanding; outstanding stock; stockholders' equity.**

week order an order that will expire automatically at the close of business on the last working day of the week in which the order is placed, unless the order is executed or cancelled prior to that time. See **contingent order; good til cancelled (GTC); order ticket.**

western account an agreement in which the underwriters in a syndicate agree to be held liable only to the extent of an offering that they agree to place. The opposite, an eastern account, is one in which all members agree to be held liable proportionately for all unsold shares or units, even if they place their own alloted portions. See **eastern account; severally but not jointly; syndicate; underwriter.**

when issued/distributed transactions made on a contingent basis, when the security is pending issue and distribution, and made on the assumption that issue/distribution will occur in the near future. The term is an abbreviation of "when, as and if" issued and distributed. See **delivery; issue; payment date.**

whipsaw the consequence of a rapid price movement in a security, first in one direction and then in the other, when an investor has potential losses from both price movements. Writers of short straddles, for example, could lose on both sides of the transaction. See **risk; short straddle; straddle.**

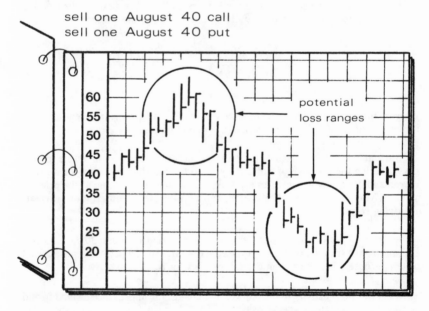

whipsaw

white knight   a corporation that offers to purchase the stock of another corporation in reaction to an unfriendly take-over attempt by another organization. See **merger; take-over.**

white sheets   daily publication of the National Quotation Bureau (NQB), summarizing over-the-counter trading in San Francisco, Chicago and Los Angeles. See **market maker; National Quotation Bureau (NQB); over-the-counter (OTC); pink sheets; yellow sheets.**

White's Rating   a rating system offered by subscription for municipal bond trading markets. It is offered by White's Tax-Exempt Bond Rating Service. See **municipal bond; rating systems; tax-exempt security.**

whole life insurance   a form of life insurance combining savings with insurance protection. As cash values build, the amount of insurance drops, to the point that the entire face amount of the policy is represented by savings. Premiums are frozen for the entire duration of the policy, and the entire face amount is payable upon the death of the insured. See **life insurance.**

whole life insurance

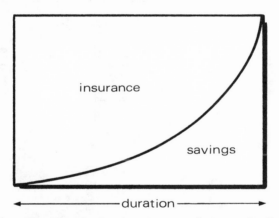

wholesaler   (1) an organization that represents the issuer of a direct participation program by selling units to investors.

(2) the underwriter of a mutual fund.

(3) a broker-dealer who trades securities with other broker-dealers for prices below market value or for a selling concession. See **broker-dealer; concession; direct participation program; mutual fund; offering; sponsor; underwriter.**

will   a document prepared for the purpose of providing instructions following death. A will appoints an executor to distribute assets to heirs, and a trustee when one is required, and names the recipients of all assets. See **custodian; estate planning; fiduciary; trustee.**

windfall profit tax   legislation enacted in 1980 (the Crude Oil Windfall Profit Tax of 1980) to tax domestic crude oil production profits. The legislation identified three levels of oil and gas income and tax rates. Partners in oil and gas direct participation programs were subjected to a tax on their proportionate share of income. See **direct participation program; oil and gas; tax basis.**

working capital

BALANCE SHEET

Cash	$	83,400
Accounts Receivable		465,100
Marketable Securities		230,000
Inventory		118,600
Total Current Assets	$	897,100
Long-Term Assets	$	881,400
Less: Reserve for Depreciation		(318,000)
Net Long-Term Assets	$	563,400
Total Assets		$1,460,500
Accounts Payable	$	248,000
Taxes Payable		16,300
Current Notes Payable		160,600
Total Current Liabilities	$	424,900
Long-Term Notes Payable	$	750,000
Total Liabilities		$1,174,900
Common Stock	$	50,000
Retained Earnings		235,600
Total Net Worth	$	285,600
Total Liabilities and Net Worth		$1,460,500

working capital

$897,100
(424,900)

$472,200

window settlement   the delivery of securities with payment made physically and at the same time, derived from the traditional window at which transactions were settled in a brokerage's office. Today, the majority of transactions are cleared through a national depository, a process called continuous net settlement. See **continuous net settlement (CNS); delivery versus payment (DVP).**

wire house   (1) general term describing the large brokerage firms that are members of an exchange.
(2) a member organization that links its branch offices and/or the branches of nonclearing members, via an electronic communications network. See **brokerage house; member organization; nonclearing member.**

wire room   a department of a broker-dealer that receives orders for security transactions and forwards them for execution on the floor of the exchange. See **back office; broker-dealer.**

withholding   the practice of selling shares of an issue to employees. This is forbidden by the rules of fair practice of the National Association of Securities Dealers (NASD) if the security is classified as a hot issue. See **hot issue; National Association of Securities Dealers (NASD); rules of fair practice.**

working capital   also called net working capital, the difference between current assets and current liabilities of an organization. The calculation is used to judge the strength of cash flow and management of financial resources. See **current assets; current liabilities; financial statement; net current assets.**

working capital ratio   the ratio comparing current assets to current liabilities, also called the current ratio. For most industries, a working capital ratio of 2 to 1 or better is considered healthy. See **current ratio; fundamental analysis.**

$$\frac{current\ assets}{current\ liabilities} = ratio$$

$$\frac{897,100}{424,900} = 2.1\ to\ 1$$

working capital ratio

working control   the capability of an owner or owners of stock in a company to control corporate policy. To have working control, one individual or group must own a majority of voting stock, or a large-enough block when other shares are distributed too widely to hold collective control. See **corporation; voting rights.**

working interest   a portion of the rights in an oil and gas venture, belonging to the lessee, with royalty and mineral rights going to the owner. See **oil and gas.**

World Bank an abbreviated title of the International Bank of Reconstruction and Development (IB). See **bank; capital market; International Bank of Reconstruction and Development (IB).**

wraparound annuity an annuity contract in which the purchaser is allowed to select specific investments, but has the privilege of deferral on resulting income. See **annuity; tax deferral.**

wraparound mortgage a type of financing arrangement in which the seller keeps an original, low-interest rate mortgage. The buyer makes payments to the seller, who forwards a portion to the lender holding the original note. See **mortgage; real estate.**

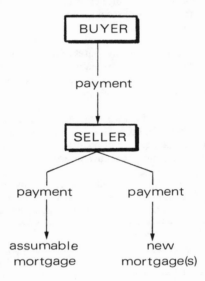

wraparound mortgage

write the act of selling an option with an opening transaction, the position to be closed by one of three events: (a) a purchasing transaction that closes the write; (b) exercise by the buyer; or (c) expiration of the contract.

A write may be covered (when 100 shares of the underlying security are owned for each call option contract written), or uncovered (naked). This condition exists when a call is sold without ownership of 100 shares of stock, or when a put is sold in an opening transaction under any circumstances. See **covered option; naked option; option; short; uncovered option; underlying security.**

writer an investor who sells an option contract in an opening transaction. Taking this action obligates the writer to perform in the event the buyer exercises the contract. With a call, the writer must sell 100 shares of the underlying security at the strike price. If a put, the writer agrees that, if the contract is exercised, he will purchase 100 shares at the strike price. See **exercise; open; option; short; strike price; underlying security.**

X

XD   an abbreviation of exdividend date, the date after which dividends will not be paid for the current period, to purchasers of a security. See **exdividend date.**

Y

Yankee bond   a bond issued outside the United States but registered for sale in the U.S. and traded in dollars. See **bond; issue.**

yellow sheets   a daily publication of the National Quotation Bureau (NQB), showing prices and market makers in the corporate bond market. See **bond; corporate bond; National Quotation Bureau (NQB); pink sheets; white sheets.**

yield   the percentage of return an investor receives, not considering capital gains or losses. It is based either upon original cost or current market value. See **profit; rate of return.**

yield equivalence   the comparison of different investments, with adjustments in price made to produce identical yields. The term is applied to securities of the Government National Mortgage Association when delivery is made with different mortgage pools. See **equivalent positions; Government National Mortgage Association (GNMA); mortgage pool.**

yield on common stock   a ratio comparing the dividend rate to market price per share of common stock. This ratio shows the potential for growth of a company as well as return to the investor. See **dividend yield; fundamental analysis; market price; ratios.**

$$\frac{annual\ dividend}{market\ price} = ratio$$

$$\frac{\$3.15}{\$85} = 3.7\%$$

yield on common stock

yield to average life (1) estimated compound earnings in a GNMA security, assuming reinvestment of all income.

(2) as applicable to bond mutual funds, the estimate of yield an investor would receive, assuming the portfolio of securities will not change and all income is reinvested. The calculation is based upon the average length of time until maturity of debt securities. See **bond fund; debt security; Government National Mortgage Association (GNMA); reinvestment rate.**

yield to maturity the expected rate of return that will be earned on a bond if it is held until maturity. The calculation assumes that all income will be reinvested at the same yield currently being paid on the bond, and adjusts for any premium or discount involved. See **bond; discount; premium; rate of return.**

Z

zero coupon bond a form of bond that pays no interest during its holding period. It is issued at a discount and will mature in one year or more. For investors other than those in a tax-deferred plan such as an IRA, the amount of discount is treated as taxable interest income over the holding period. See **bond; discount bond; interest; tax deferral.**

zero-minus tick a price that is equal to the last round lot price for the same security, but lower than the last different price. See **minus tick; round lot.**

zero-plus tick a price that is equal to the last round lot price for the same security, but higher than the last different price. See **minus tick; round lot; SEC Rule 10a-1; short sale.**

zero rate mortgage a type of home mortgage in which a large downpayment is made, along with a one-time interest payment. Subsequently, the principal balance is repaid in fixed monthly installments. See **interest; mortgage; real estate.**

Abbreviations

ACE	American Commodity Exchange
ACRS	accelerated cost recovery system
ACV	actual cash value
ADR	American depository receipt
ADR	asset depreciation range
AEP	aggregate exercise price
AMBAC	American Municipal Bond Assurance Corporation
AMEX	American Stock Exchange
AMFOD	Association of Member Firm Option Department
AMOS	AMEX Options Switching System
AON	all or none
APR	annual percentage rate
ARM	adjustable rate mortgage
ASECC	American Stock Exchange Clearing Corporation
BAN	bond anticipation note
BSE	Boston Stock Exchange
BW	bid wanted
CA	callable bond
CBOE	Chicago Board Options Exchange
CBT	Chicago Board of Trade
CCC	Commodity Credit Corporation
CCF	Committee of Corporate Finance
CCS	Central Certificate Service
CD	certificate of deposit
CFP	Certified Financial Planner
CFTC	Commodity Futures Trading Commission
CME	Chicago Mercantile Exchange
CMV	current market value
CNS	continuous net settlement
COMEX	Commodity Exchange of New York
CO-OP	Bank For Cooperatives
CPI	Consumer Price Index
CRD	Central Registration Depository
CSD	Corporate Services Department
CSE	Cincinnati Stock Exchange
CTS	Consolidated Tape System
CUSIP	Committee on Uniform Securities Identification Procedures
DBCC	District Business Conduct Committee
DEFRA	Deficit Reduction Act of 1984
DJIA	Dow Jones Industrial Average
DK	don't know
DNR	do not reduce

DOT	designated order turnaround
DTC	Depository Trust Company
DVP	delivery versus payment
ERISA	Employee Retirement Income Security Act
ERTA	Economic Recovery Tax Act of 1981
FASB	Financial Accounting Standards Board
FCA	Farm Credit Administration
FDIC	Federal Deposit Insurance Corporation
FFB	Federal Financing Bank
FFMC	Federal Farm Mortgage Corporation
FHLB	Federal Home Loan Bank
FHLMC	Federal Home Loan Mortgage Corporation
FICB	Federal Intermediate Credit Bank
FIFO	first in, first out
FLB	Federal Land Bank
FMAN	February/May/August/November
FmHA	Farmers Home Administration
FMV	fair market value
FNMA	Federal National Mortgage Association
FOCUS	financial and operations combined uniform single report
FOK	fill or kill
FOMC	Federal Open Market Committee
FRB	Federal Reserve Board
FRN	floating rate note
FSLIC	Federal Savings and Loan Insurance Corporation
GAAP	generally accepted accounting principles
GNMA	Government National Mortgage Association
GNP	Gross National Product
GO	general obligation bond
GTC	good til cancelled
HLC	Homeowner's Land Corporation
HSE	Honolulu Stock Exchange
IADB	Inter-American Development Bank
IAFP	International Association of Financial Planners
IB	International Bank For Reconstruction and Development
ICC	Interstate Commerce Commission
IMM	International Monetary Market
IOC	immediate-or-cancel
IRA	individual retirement account
ISE	Intermountain Stock Exchange
ITC	investment tax credit
JAJO	January/April/July/October
JTWROS	joint tenants with rights of survivorship
KCBT	Kansas City Board of Trade
LAC	Legal Advisory Committee
LCAC	Listed Company Advisory Committee
LIBOR	London interbank offered rate
LIFO	last in, first out
LMV	long market value
MACE	Mid-America Commodity Exchange
MBIA	Municipal Bond Insurance Association
MDS	Market Data System
MGE	Minneapolis Grain Exchange
MIT	municipal investment trust

MJSD	March/June/September/December
MOSS	Market Oversight Surveillance System
MP	mortgage-participation certificate
MPC	Market Performance Committee
MSE	Midwest Stock Exchange
MSRB	Municipal Securities Rulemaking Board
NAIC	National Association of Investors Corporation
NAREIT	National Association of Real Estate Investment Trusts
NARS	National Annual Report Service
NASAA	North American Securities Administrators' Association
NASD	National Association of Securities Dealers
NASDAQ	National Association of Securities Dealers Automated Quotations
NAV	net asset value per share
NBER	National Bureau of Economic Research
NBV	net book value per share
NCC	National Clearing Corporation
NFA	National Futures Association
NH	not held
NIC	net interest cost
NMAB	National Market Advisory Board
NMS	National Market System
NOW	negotiable-order-of-withdrawal
NQB	National Quotations Bureau
NQC	National Quotations Committee
NSCC	National Securities Clearing Committee
NSE	National Stock Exchange
NSTA	National Security Trading Association
NSTS	National Security Trading System
NYFCC	New York Futures Clearing Corporation
NYFE	New York Futures Exchange
NYMEX	New York Mercantile Exchange
NYSE	New York Stock Exchange
OARS	Opening Automated Report Service
OBO	order book official
OCC	Options Clearing Corporation
OID	original issue discount
OPG	at the opening
OPIC	Overseas Private Investment Corporation
OPRA	Options Price Reporting Authority
OSJ	Office of Supervisory Jurisdiction
OTC	over-the-counter
OW	offer wanted
P/E	price-earnings ratio
Phlx	Philadelphia Stock Exchange
PN	project note
PNI	participate but do not initiate
PPI	Producer Price Index
P-S	purchase and sales department
PSE	Pacific Stock Exchange
RAN	revenue anticipation note
REIT	real estate investment trust
RESSI	Real Estate Securities and Syndication Institution
RIA	registered investment advisor
ROP	registered options principal

SBA	Small Business Administration
SCC	Stock Clearing Corporation
SEC	Securities and Exchange Commission
SECO	Securities and Exchange Commission Organization
SEP	simplified employee pension plan
SIA	Securities Industry Association
SIAC	Securities Industry Association Corporation
SIPC	Securities Investors Protection Corporation
SLMA	Student Loan Marketing Association
SMA	special miscellaneous account
SMV	short market value
SRO	self-regulatory organization
SROP	senior registered options principal
SSE	Spokane Stock Exchange
SWIFT	Society For Worldwide Interbank Finance Telecommunications
TAB	tax anticipation bill
TAN	tax anticipation note
TEFRA	Tax Equity and Fiscal Responsibility Act of 1982
TEIP	tax-exempt investor program
TVA	Tennessee Valley Authority
UGMA	Uniform Gift to Minors Act
ULPA	Uniform Limited Partnership Act
UPA	Uniform Partnership Act
UPC	Uniform Practice Code
USASLE	uniform securities agent state law examination
VEBA	voluntary employees' beneficiary association
VTC	voting trust certificate
XD	exdividend date

Guide to Prospectus
and Offering Documents

In most forms of investment activity, the investor must be given a prospectus or other offering document. This document summarizes the important features and risks of a program.

But because it is a lengthy and confusing report, the prospectus usually is not read. Most of those entering an investment for the first time depend upon the assurances of an investment advisor or stockbroker for the program. Yet, in many cases, the advisor has not read the document either.

There are several forms this report takes:

1) mutual fund prospectus: a fairly standard summary of the fund, its board of trustees and investment managers, and the securities in which the fund invests. Included will be identification of the objective: for example, growth, taxable income, or preservation of capital.

2) variable annuity prospectus: standardized much like the mutual fund document, this provides the information and details of the contract: surrender charges and terms, annuitization, investment choices, beneficiaries, and information about the life insurance company itself.

3) public offering prospectus: for investors looking at publicly available limited partnerships. These are registered with the Securities and Exchange Commission (SEC), although the registration in itself is no guarantee that the program is legitimate or will meet an individual's objectives, nor that it will be profitable.

4) private offering circular: similar to the prospectus, this document is for a program that is offered to a limited number of investors (private) or is to be offered publicly, but in one state only.

5) new offering prospectus: given out when a new issue or subsequent issue of an existing corporation is made. This spells out the particulars of how the stock will be distributed, at what public offering price, and by whom.

6) activity prospectus: a prospectus that is given out for a form of investing generally, but not for a particular investment. An example is the option prospectus published by the Options Clearing Corporation (OCC), that is given to everyone desiring to trade in the options market.

The mutual fund prospectus is a very standardized report. In virtually all such documents, the information that is given is consistently reported in format and content. And the options prospectus is a one-of-a-kind specialized disclosure report, required due to the sophistication required of option traders.

But for the direct participation market — public and private limited partnerships — this is not the case. There are a wide variety of formats and content, and the public program's prospectus or private program's offering circular may be vastly different between investments.

Because the prospectus is a long and tedious series of disclosures, written largely in "legalese," few investors take the time to read through them. It isn't necessary to read the entire report, if the key sections are reviewed. From the prospectus, it is possible to gain enough information about a program to compare it to others, decide whether or not it meets one's individual objectives, and is managed by competent professionals.

Priorities

A prospectus should be reviewed with the priority of information in mind. What are the most important facts to discover about a program?

First, an investor needs to determine the purpose and objective of the program. Decide what type of investment activity will be undertaken and for what purpose. Example: if in a high tax bracket and interested in long-term capital gains, do not seek a program that will attempt to produce a high level of current income. Choose one that will hold a property for several years and then sell at a profit.

Many investors have problems identifying what they are looking for in an investment. As a result, the choices they make don't give them what they need. Establishing an objective is necessary in order to qualify a program.

The second area for review is suitability. Do you meet the standards as spelled out in the prospectus? These commonly relate to net worth and income level. But beyond that, also understand the nature of the investment to be truly suitable – the special risks, markets and competition in the industry.

Some advisors suggest a review of the literature that accompanies the prospectus. In some cases, this information does provide a good overview of the program's highlights. But as often as not, it will exclude the conflicts of interest, poor track record or unusual risks that can be determined only in the prospectus.

While other literature can be helpful, there is some information that will be found out only by reviewing the prospectus and, beyond that, asking questions of a financial advisor. Before investing, these should be answered to the investor's satisfaction.

Because the terminology used in the prospectus is different in each case, it isn't always easy to derive answers. For example, general partners may profit from organizing the partnership in several ways. They may be paid a management fee, and additional fees for other services they provide. These can include commissions or finder's fees for real estate transactions, property acquisition or management fees, and a number of other uses of cash.

The difficulty: some programs do not identify in the prospectus to whom these fees are paid. Others may identify a company that is, in reality, one formed by the general partners themselves. So a "loan acquisition fee" may be merely a transfer of cash from one pocket to the other, and the investor has no way to know that.

The solution: be sure you know exactly where all your dollars are going, and who really benefits. For every dollar invested, some portion goes out to others as part of the start-up cost of a program. Find out how many of those payments are made to general partners, before investing.

Sections of the Document

Information in a prospectus can be broken down into two types: the standard disclosures and statements found in all prospectuses, and the special information unique to each program. The secret is to determine what special points to review out of a large document.

Below is a summary of the major sections found in the prospectus, and what each contains. Note that the information is not always presented in this order.

Cover page. Provides the basic information about each program: name, total amount of the offering, minimum subscription, the period it will be offered, and selling commissions that will be paid. It also includes the required disclosure: "These securities have not been approved or disapproved by the Securities and Exchange Commission nor has the commission passed upon the accuracy or adequacy of this prospectus. Any representation to the contrary is a criminal offense."

Contents. A table of the major sections and their page in the document.

Summary of the program. A description of the activities and purpose of the program, including the type of properties that will be leased or purchased. This section should disclose whether the partnership has identified the properties it will purchase (a "specified" program) or will seek properties of a certain classification (a blind pool program). More details may be included on terms, subscriptions, and the partnership itself, and some prospectuses include the summary on the cover page.

Investor suitability. Identifies the minimum income and/or net worth of an investor. For programs sold in several states, a general statement of suitability may be amended by listings of the additional standards in each state. Also in this section: discussion of the minimum allowable purchase of units.

Investment objective. Critical section that identifies what a program's objective is. For each investor, a comparison of this with personal objectives will reveal how well suited the program may be. Some prospectuses never state an objective or investment policy very clearly, and it cannot be determined what activities will be undertaken. Others are so vague they say nothing, such as: "The objective of this program is to preserve the investor's capital, provide long-term capital gains from appreciated properties, and high current income." This objective sounds like it will work for everyone, but it isn't clear. A clear objective would give the priority: "This program seeks investment in properties producing positive cash flow, and with the greatest potential for substantial appreciation in value over three to five years, resulting in maximum long-term capital gains."

Definitions. Because the language of the prospectus is so complex, many of them contain a "definitions" section or a glossary. The more complete this is, the better. Most glossaries in prospectuses contain too little to provide substantial value.

Estimated use of proceeds. A key section, where the investment is broken down between payments to various people and organizations, and the amount that actually goes into the program. There commonly are two versions of proceeds applications: one assuming minimum subscription to the program, the other assuming maximum subscription.

The use of proceeds should be given in one place. If it's broken up into various sections throughout the document, it could be a sign that some facts are being cloaked. Determine what percentage of your investment will get invested. If the so-called front-end load is greater than 15 percent, look at the program carefully. That means only eight-five cents of every dollar will go to work in the project. Some programs exceed 30 percent front-end load, with a few even higher than that.

It is difficult in reviewing use of proceeds to tell what payments are for. A financial advisor can find out exactly what is included in vague payments, such as acquisition fees and expenses, loan acquisition fees and offering expenses. Those payments may be going to general partners, their subsidiaries, relatives, or business associates.

Financing. A section describing borrowings the partnership will undertake, unless it is an unleveraged program. The borrowing plan should be a sound one, in view of the purpose, cash flow, and investment policies described for the program, and general partners should not stand to benefit from a proposed lending arrangement. Check the relationship between the proposed lender and the general partners.

Plan of distribution. Describes the underwriting arrangements that have been made, and tells how the units or shares will be sold to the investors.

Cash distributions. Describes how payments will be made to the investors. It should cover several issues: periodic payments of income, capital gains, and final distribution. The investor should be able to tell how the general partners plan to liquidate the program, and how long that will take.

The final distribution and liquidation of interests should be one of the key concerns when entering an investment. But in many prospectuses, this is difficult if not impossible to find. How the general partners will share in final distributions is also a key point. Will they receive a larger portion of final profits than the limited partners earn? If so, calculate their total risk and potential return, versus the investor's risk and return. Some programs are weighted in favor of the general partners when properties finally are sold.

Management compensation. Explains how the managers, or general partners are to be paid. The best prospectus is one that breaks down the different forms of compensation in one place, as there may be several sources of income involved: underwriting commissions, acquisition fees, property management income, partnership management fees, and cash distributions.

Is the compensation of general partners reasonable in terms of the investor's potential income from the investment? Determine whether any of the payments from proceeds will go to general partners indirectly (other than those payments listed in this section), such as fees paid to the general partners under a different company name.

Conflicts of interest. In this section, many of the conflicts listed will be fairly standard. For example, many prospectuses will include mention of a general partner's involvement in properties of the same type the program will buy or lease; or conflicts due to their involvement in similar programs.

Look for mention of general partners in dual roles: investor and lender, recipient of payment for services from the program, and involvement of relatives in management of the program.

Risk factors. There are risks to all investments, but each individual program has special risks associated with it. This section summarizes and discloses all of these risks. If the section is unclear, request clarification through a financial advisor.

Risks can take several forms: liquidity (the length of time your money will be tied up); cash flow (distributions you may or may not receive); loss of capital; tax risks (the chance you'll be audited or lose deductions you thought you'd receive); faulty assumptions about the program; assessments (if the program is of the type that can request additional capital from you); leverage (if the general partners over-borrow); and economic conditions (from a changing marketplace).

Income tax consequences. A disclaimer section, stating that the program's projected tax benefits may or may not be allowed by the Internal Revenue Service, and denying any liability that arises from disallowed deductions or credits. This section also should point out any special risks associated with the program.

Legal opinion. Another disclaimer section, in which the general partners' attorney states the belief that all assumptions in the prospectus are reasonable.

Management. A listing of each manager's background and experience. This section should give enough information to determine whether the principals are qualified to manage an investor's money. More information than is provided can be requested. A reputable management will gladly supply more detailed information.

Prior programs. Select a program offered by general partners experienced in the type of activity being proposed. Thus, the prospectus should include a complete record of past performance. If this is lacking, request it and study it carefully. Did investors in those past programs make a profit? If programs are still active, will the current program have any financial dealings with them? If it does, you may be investing in a "bail-out" program; this could be a danger signal.

Competition and markets. A section discussing the competition and markets involved in the proposed activity. If it doesn't include this information, request it. Verify independently if possible what the market conditions really are.

Summary of partnership agreement. The actual agreement to be entered (normally included at the end of the prospectus) is highlighted here.

Accountant's report. A standard audit statement that always accompanies a certified statement.

Balance sheet. A summary of assets, liabilities and net worth of the general partnership.

Notes to financial statement. Notes should be read as carefully as the financial statement itself. Any problems will be mentioned in this section.

Partnership agreement. The entire text of the agreement itself.

Subscription form. An insert for completion upon deciding to go ahead and invest. Investors should not send money until all their questions have been answered.

The prospectus format is a complicated one, containing many components that aren't arranged for the most convenient review by a potential investor. And the majority of those choosing a product do not bother with a detailed analysis. However, there is information to be gained from such a review.

The key elements to be kept in mind while reviewing a prospectus are:

1) Is the objective of the program in line with the investor's own objective?

2) Are the general partners experienced in the type of program being offered?

3) Is the front-end load reasonably set so that at least 85% of dollars invested will go to the program, and not to fees?

4) Is the proposed risk level one the investor is willing and able to take?

5) Does the investor meet the suitability standards listed in the prospectus?

6) Are the details of the program comprehendable to the investor?

7) Is the investor willing to tie up capital for as long as it will take to realize final liquidation?

8) Are additional investments required later on in the program, and are these affordable to the investor?

9) Is the level of management compensation reasonable?

10) Are all conflicts of interest disclosed, and are any of them unusual enough to warrant further investigation?

Bond Classification List

Investments can be made in one of two broad forms: equity and debt. An equity security is one in which the investor has ownership. This occurs through positions in common or preferred stock, or shares of a fund investing in the stock of corporations.

Debt securities include notes, bills, bonds or money market instruments. In these instances, the investor is a creditor of the issuing corporation or agency, and earns a return in the form of interest. There are five major distinctions of debt securities:

1) A debt security investor is a creditor of the issuer, while an equity security investor owns a portion of the company.

2) Income is earned in the form of interest, while equity securities pay dividends or offer the chance for an increase in value (capital gains).

3) A debt security has a limited life and value, with a specific maturity date and face value. Equity securities may be held for an indefinite period of time.

4) Debt securities may be convertible in some cases to equity securities. Some corporations issue convertible bonds, and may exercise the right to exchange the debt for shares of common stock.

5) While equity securities are available for a current market value that may change from day to day, debt instruments adjust to changing demand through premiums (when the current price of a bond is higher than face value) or discounts (bonds sold below face value).

Classifications of Debt Securities

Corporate Bonds:
    a) secured bonds:
        1) Mortgage Bonds
        2) Collateral Trust Bonds
        3) Equipment Trust Bonds
    b) unsecured bond:
        1) Debentures

U.S. Government Securities:
    a) nonmarketable securities (offered only through the U.S. Treasury):
        1) Series EE Bonds
        2) Series HH Bonds
    b) marketable securities (freely bid and traded in the auction marketplace):
        1) Treasury Bills
        2) Treasury Notes
        3) Treasury Bonds

U.S. Government Agency Bonds:
    a) agricultural:
        1) Bank For Cooperatives
        2) Federal Intermediate Credit Banks
        3) Federal Land Banks
    b) home building and mortgage:
        1) Federal Home Loan bank
        2) Federal National Mortgage Association (Fannie Mae)
        3) Government National Mortgage Association (Ginnie Mae)
    c) student financing:
        1) Student Loan Marketing Association (Sallie Mae)

International Bonds:
    a) Export-Import Bank
    b) Inter-American Development Bank
    c) International Bank For Reconstruction and Development (World Bank)

Municipal Securities:
    a) General Obligation Bonds
    b) Revenue Bonds
    c) Municipal Notes
        1) Bond Anticipation Notes
        2) Revenue Anticipation Notes
        3) Tax Anticipation Notes

Money Market Debts:
    a) Banker's Acceptances
    b) Certificates of Deposit
    c) Commercial Paper